The Young Nixon
and His Rivals

Political cartoonist Paul Arlt captured the essence of the California Republican rivalry with his depiction of the four men preparing themselves backstage to play the role of President of the United States (Paul Arlt, California Politics, 1955, watercolor on paper mounted on board, gift of Ronay Menschel, Picker Art Gallery, Colgate University, 2008.3.18).

# The Young Nixon and His Rivals

*Four California Republicans Eye the White House, 1946–1958*

JAMES WORTHEN

McFarland & Company, Inc., Publishers
*Jefferson, North Carolina, and London*

ALSO BY JAMES WORTHEN

*Governor James Rolph and the
Great Depression in California* (McFarland, 2006)

LIBRARY OF CONGRESS CATALOGUING-IN-PUBLICATION DATA

Worthen, James.
　　The young Nixon and his rivals : four California Republicans eye the White House, 1946–1958 / James Worthen.
　　　p.　　cm.
　　Includes bibliographical references and index.

　　ISBN 978-0-7864-4171-6
　　softcover : 50# alkaline paper

　　1. Nixon, Richard M. (Richard Milhous), 1913–1994.
2. Warren, Earl, 1891–1974.　3. Knowland, William F. (William Fife), 1908–1974.　4. Knight, Goodwin, 1896–1970.
5. United States — Politics and government —1945–1953.
6. United States — Politics and government —1953–1961.
7. Presidential candidates — United States — History — 20th century.　8. Republican Party (U.S. : 1854– ) — History — 20th century.　9. California — Politics and government — 1951–　I. Title.
E856.W67　2010
973.92 — dc22　　　　　　　　　　　　　　　　　　　2010020186

British Library cataloguing data are available

©2010 James Worthen. All rights reserved

*No part of this book may be reproduced or transmitted in any form or by any means, electronic or mechanical, including photocopying or recording, or by any information storage and retrieval system, without permission in writing from the publisher.*

On the cover: The four rivals —*from left*, William Knowland, Goodwin Knight, Richard Nixon and Earl Warren — are all smiles as they campaign together for the Eisenhower-Nixon ticket in 1952 (Richard Nixon Presidential Library/National Archives and Records Administration)

Manufactured in the United States of America

*McFarland & Company, Inc., Publishers
　Box 611, Jefferson, North Carolina 28640
　　www.mcfarlandpub.com*

# Table of Contents

*Preface* 1 • *Introduction* 5

### PART ONE: THE RIVALS IN 1946
1: Earl Warren: Going His Own Way — 15
2: William Knowland: Smooth Ride to the Top — 23
3: Goodwin Knight: Charisma to Spare — 32
4: Richard Nixon: A New Kind of Politician — 38

### PART TWO: THE RIVALS IN WARREN'S SHADOW (1946–1952)
5: "Defending California from Goodie" — 50
6: The Rivals and the Nixon-Douglas Race — 60

### PART THREE: THE RIVALS COLLIDE
7: The 1952 Republican Convention — 78

### PART FOUR: THE RIVALS UNDER EISENHOWER (1953–1958)
8: Knowland, Nixon and the President, 1953–1955 — 118
9: The Rivals and the 1956 Convention — 136
10: The Big Switch of 1958 and the End of the Rivalry — 168

*Epilogue* 189 • *Notes* 205 • *Bibliography* 221 • *Index* 229

# *Preface*

Generally speaking, this book is a study of the influence of personality on political behavior. It is an extension of my professional interest during many years as an analyst and senior manager with the federal government. Since leaving Washington, D.C., I have sought to apply this approach to the assessment of former political leaders in California, my home state. My first book, *Governor James Rolph and the Great Depression in California*, explained how the politics of personality—so successfully deployed during Rolph's twenty years as mayor of San Francisco—failed to address the state's serious economic and social problems after his election as governor.

By the late 1940s, California was the fastest growing and most dynamic state in the union, and its leaders automatically were considered candidates for national leadership. The simultaneous rise of four Republican politicians—sometimes called the "four giants" by the media—during the immediate postwar period led to an intense personal rivalry that would affect presidential politics for over a decade. The complicated relationship among Richard Nixon, Earl Warren, William Knowland and Goodwin Knight seemed a natural subject for my second project.

Though the four rivals campaigned for public office with reference to the great issues of the day, this is not a book about policy. The role of ideological differences in their competition is explored, but readers seeking detailed information on such topics as Knight's position on water resource development or the evolution of Nixon's foreign policy views will be disappointed. The focus is on their relationships with each other and on the motivating force of their rivalry.

In writing what is in many ways a collection of interrelated political biographies, I have relied heavily on the main repositories of each man's political and personal papers. The Richard Nixon Library in Yorba Linda was a vital source of information. Archivist Gregory Cumming and his colleagues went out of their way to help locate relevant materials and bring them to my attention. In researching the careers of the two California governors in this story, I made extensive use of the Earl Warren papers at the California State Archives in Sacramento and the Goodwin Knight papers at Stanford University.

The Bancroft Library of the University of California at Berkeley is indispensable to any California historian. It is the home of the voluminous and still largely unorganized William Knowland papers, which nevertheless were of considerable value in writing this book.

The Bancroft also houses the Regional Oral History Office, which undertook years ago to interview every significant figure in the Earl Warren and Goodwin Knight administrations and to ask questions about, among other subjects, the interaction of the California rivals. The Warren and Knight oral history projects were the most important sources for this study.

As much as possible, I have allowed the rivals to speak for themselves. The colorful quotes in this book come from a variety of publications, including those listed above, but also from the memoirs and recollections of the four men and their closest associates as well as the journalists who covered national and state politics during the 1940s and 1950s.

I owe an enormous debt to the many biographers of Nixon and Warren who have already mined most of the primary sources of information on the two men and thus saved people like me considerable time. Among the books that focus on Nixon's early years in politics, two are worthy of particular note — Roger Morris' *The Rise of an American Politician*, a well-written and generally critical examination of Nixon's conduct during his 1946, 1950 and 1952 campaigns, and Irwin Gellman's *The Contender*, which attempts to refute many of Morris' arguments. Because it is the only biography of Knowland, *One Step from the White House*, by Gail B. Montgomery and James W. Johnson, contains much of what we know about this complex figure. Knight, another interesting and many-faceted character, still awaits a biographer.

The four rivals spent considerable time together and made many joint public appearances, so they were frequently photographed in each other's company. I have included several of these photos taken at critical career junctures. A political drawing by the noted artist Paul Arlt (see frontispiece), which appeared in *Collier's* magazine during the 1950s, aptly summarizes the main story line of this book. For the privilege of reproducing that drawing in these pages, I am indebted to Arlt's daughter, Ronay Menschel of New York City. The original drawing resides in the Picker Art Gallery at Colgate University, Arlt's alma mater.

All writers need additional pairs of eyes on their manuscripts to judge whether their ideas cohere and their writing flows. I want to thank two outstanding thinkers and students of the English language—David Overton, of Thetford Center, Vermont, and Walter Picker, of Cambria, California—for their perceptive comments and criticisms and their inspired suggestions for improvement. I also want to commend those closest to me, especially my wife, Claudia, for their patience in accommodating my deadlines and out-of-town trips to research libraries.

# *Introduction*

In the aftermath of World War II, four talented and ambitious men became the leading politicians in California. Each sought to harness the state's growing political clout in the service of his pursuit of national leadership. This concentration of ability in one state in one era was unusual enough, but, in addition, all four men were members of the same political party. Up until 1952, as Republican officeholders of national stature, they worked to end many years of Democratic rule in Washington by electing one of their number to the White House.

The rivalry among Richard Nixon, William Knowland, Earl Warren and Goodwin Knight helped to shape national politics for more than a decade. Publicly, they were committed to each other's electoral success, as they were to the success of all Republicans. But each rival considered himself a potential president. Given the political reality that only one Californian could expect to be on a presidential ticket, none of them would be able to achieve his personal goal except at the expense of the other three.

Theirs was a cautious and carefully managed rivalry. They knew each other well because their political obligations brought them into frequent contact. All of their families were well acquainted from encounters on the campaign trail, at party conventions, and at fund-raising events. The rivals exchanged notes of encouragement and consolation and commiserated over the shared difficulties of a life in politics. Knowland and Warren had even been boyhood friends, and they remained close well into adulthood.

None of the four could aspire to a particular position or plot a personal strategy without taking into account the plans of the others. They avoided running for the same office at the same time. When two of them, Knight and Knowland, finally did, the result was disastrous for both. Nixon, the youngest, and ultimately most successful of the four, went out of his way to be deferential to his more senior colleagues. Before deciding to run for the

Senate in 1950, he waited patiently until Knight and Warren finally ruled out running themselves. The competition of the four, though often bitter and emotional, was thus softened by personal bonds and shared party loyalty.

The rivalry among the "four giants" began in 1946. That year, they all ran for political office and won, beginning a twelve-year struggle for power and influence. Their success on the state level or in Congress persuaded them in time that California was too small a stage for their ambitions.

The rivals traveled very different roads before 1946. As a result of their unique early experiences and environments, they developed strikingly dissimilar personalities, styles, strengths and weaknesses. They attained public office by impressing voters with their formidable skills, while keeping their flaws and insecurities hidden from public view. The latter colored their mutual relations, producing often unwarranted feelings of resentment and suspicion.

Of the four, Earl Warren was by far the most prominent in 1946. He had already been governor of California for four years and was the state's attorney general for seven years before that. Despite his Republican roots, he believed state government was no place for partisanship. One measure of his immediate success as governor was that Thomas E. Dewey, the Republican candidate for president in 1944, asked Warren to join him on the ticket. Warren refused—he felt he owed California's voters a full four-year term. In 1946 he ran for reelection as governor and won easily. From then until the Republican convention of 1952, every other state politician labored in his shadow.

The second rival, William Knowland, was one of Warren's oldest friends and the son of long-time *Oakland Tribune* owner and publisher Joe Knowland. His father had discovered Warren in the 1920s and placed the *Tribune*'s considerable resources behind his political advancement. Thus, Warren came to owe the Knowland family a significant debt. Because Bill, Joe's son, was a political prodigy in his own right, Warren showed his gratitude by appointing the 37-year-old Army major to a vacant U.S. Senate seat in 1945. It was the first and last time Warren would make an appointment based on personal considerations. A year later, Bill Knowland ran on his own and won reelection.

Next in importance as the rivalry began was a flamboyant Los Angeles judge named Goodwin Knight. Known for his hearty manner, his public-speaking skills, and his endless supply of jokes and anecdotes, Knight had dreamed of being governor since childhood. During the 1930s, he was appointed a judge and became a public figure by hosting a radio show. For the next decade he appeared frequently around southern California in support of Republican causes. After considering a bid for the Senate in 1944, he decided to run for lieutenant governor on Warren's ticket in 1946 and won an impressive victory.

A fourth California Republican was just beginning his political career in 1946. Richard Nixon had recently left the U.S. Navy and joined a small law practice in the Whittier area when a committee of local businessmen offered him their support in a bid to unseat veteran liberal Congressman Jerry Voorhis. Jumping in with both feet, Nixon used the growing fear of Communism and his strong debating skills to unseat Voorhis in a campaign that would raise questions about his tactics and ethics.

By 1946, then, Warren, Knowland, Knight and Nixon were launched on a trajectory that would lead to White House dreams and — in Nixon's case — the vice presidency. Their competition would come to a sudden end amid the high drama of the so-called "big switch" of 1958, when Knowland and Knight sought each other's jobs. When the smoke cleared, only one of the four rivals still had a political future.

The personalities of these four Republicans were an incendiary mix. Governor Warren's genial exterior hid an aloofness, arrogance and indifference to the fortunes of his fellow Republicans that infuriated Nixon and Knight. Senator Knowland, though highly principled, was utterly lacking in subtlety, finesse, or people skills, and his stubbornness angered all who dealt with him. The gregarious and emotional Knight was a natural politician but also insecure, sensitive to slight, impulsive, and indecisive at crucial moments.

Then there was Nixon, one of the most reviled — and admired — men in American political life. Much has been written about his painfully difficult childhood and its effects on his development into a man who was at once shy and aggressive. His hard-hitting political style, with its use of innuendo, half-truths and cleverly misleading statements, was offensive to a great many of the country's political leaders, especially Democrats. Warren, Knowland and Knight, who had many differences, ended up united in their dislike of the young man from Whittier.

Even had Nixon's rivals liked and respected him, they would have viewed his rapid rise in California politics as a threat. Nixon was twenty years younger than Warren and considerably less experienced than Knowland, but he managed to eclipse them both in importance with his dramatic selection as Dwight Eisenhower's running mate in 1952. Even so, it was how he accomplished that feat, rather than the fact of it, that caused the breach in their future relations.

This book is largely about how Warren, Knight and Knowland reacted to the rise of a man they deeply distrusted. But it also explores the evolving attitudes of the rivals toward each other and examines how they managed the tension between advancing their careers and maintaining civil relations.

The era of the young Nixon and his California rivals divides naturally into two six-year periods. In the first —1946 to 1952 — Warren and Knowland are the dominant figures, and Nixon and Knight the strivers and supplicants. In the second —1952 to 1958 — Nixon becomes preeminent, Warren drops out of the rivalry because of his appointment to the Supreme Court, and the struggle among the remaining three men intensifies. The watershed event is the 1952 Republican convention, which permanently alters the balance of power among the rivals and sows the seeds of battles to come.

A clear understanding of the rivalry first requires a short discussion of the unique aspects of California politics in the 1940s and 1950s that made the success of the four men possible. That will be followed by a brief description of their early lives and careers prior to their victories in 1946.

## *The Rivals and Postwar California Politics*

Few years in American history were as hopeful as 1946. The surrender of Germany and Japan a few months earlier had brought to an end a long national crisis. The country had weathered not one but two existential threats. The Great Depression of the 1930s had severely shaken the capitalist economic system, and the world war of the early 1940s involved this country in a two-front struggle with the most militarized societies on earth. After much hardship, the economy recovered, and the war was won. Americans could breathe again.

The end of these trials marked the emergence of the United States as the world's leading power. Despite the economic strain and the loss of thousands of American lives, the country had been physically unharmed. The nation's factories, which had been turning out unprecedented numbers of tanks and airplanes, were now retooled to produce cars and refrigerators. As war-weary veterans returned from overseas, a grateful nation subsidized their education in the skills necessary to build a great consumer society. These men and women were the backbone of a boom without precedent in American history.

The rise of the California rivals paralleled the rise of their state in the national consciousness as a place of glamour, excitement and promise. With the challenges of the past fifteen years finally overcome, no state was better positioned for take-off. California had long been an agricultural powerhouse and home of the entertainment industry, but the exigencies of war had also made it a vital center of defense production. So many servicemen had passed through California on their way to the Pacific theater that the state no longer seemed as remote from the rest of the country as it had before the war. Americans in their increasingly mobile society were now lured west by the prospect of well-paying civilian jobs and lives of sunny contentment.

California had experienced growth spurts before, but following demobilization people came in unprecedented numbers. Between 1945 and 1947 more than one million Americans moved to the Golden State. By 1948 a million more had arrived. Two years later, the total number of Californians passed ten million — twice as many as in 1930. In the 1950s, the population increased again by almost 50 percent. The need for housing triggered a building boom. The state became a cauldron of economic dynamism.

Under these circumstances, it seemed natural to look to California for political leadership as well. The population growth triggered a leap in the state's share of seats in the House of Representatives and its number of electoral votes in presidential elections. The national media wrote endlessly about West Coast trend-setters and about the activities and aspirations of Sacramento's political establishment. A demonstrated ability to govern such a large and complex state, or to represent its many interests in the Senate, would henceforth be seen as a strong credential for the White House. Postwar California became a training ground for aspiring presidents.

## *The Progressive Legacy*

California's Republicans were especially well positioned to profit from the state's new political prominence. Though demographic change made them a minority party at some time during the Great Depression, they had still managed to dominate state politics long before Warren, Knowland, Knight and Nixon arrived on the scene.

The key figures in the Progressive movement of the early 20th century, in fact, were middle-class Republican businessmen, unhappy with the political dominance of the Southern Pacific Railroad. The Progressives elected the great reform governor Hiram Johnson (1911 to 1915), and he reshaped state government by making it more professional, nonpartisan and responsive to public opinion. But Republicans retained firm control of the reform process, and after Johnson moved on to the Senate, power in Sacramento returned to more traditional Republican governors.

Even as the country moved to the left in the 1930s, the first two California governors of the Depression years were members of the Grand Old Party. In 1938, at the height of the New Deal, the Democrats finally managed to elect a chief executive, but this brief Democratic interlude ended when Attorney General Earl Warren won the wartime election of 1942.

Republican electoral majorities were fueled by immigration from small Midwestern towns, particularly into southern California, and by the generally conservative farming community in the state's great central valley. The Los Angeles area was dominated by small businessmen and Protestants with an anti-labor bent, while San Francisco, with its long history as a cosmopolitan and pro-union city, was an island of liberalism. From an early date, these differences gave rise to sectionalism in state politics that often pitted the north against the south.

As a result of the state's rapid growth, much of it in the bigger cities, the proportion of Democrats rapidly increased until by the end of the war they held more than a 20 percentage point majority. By 1948, there were a million more Democrats than Republicans. In the 1950s, with the increasing size and power of labor unions, the Democratic advantage grew even larger.

And yet, somehow, Republicans continued to win the vast majority of state elections. They did so because party affiliation had little to do with the way most Californians voted. The flood of immigrants formed an unstable and rootless population — a society of strangers — who joined an individualistic community that placed a premium on personal freedom and enjoyment of the good life.

Under these conditions, people tended to forget their self-identifications as Republicans or Democrats. Former Democrats who moved into rural areas or anonymous housing developments were untouched by the ethnic, economic or academic affiliations that might have previously sustained their allegiance to their party. It was not until 1958, for example, that the growing strength of the state's labor unions translated into a sizeable Democratic vote. Each election brought many people to the polls who had never voted in their new home before and knew little about the candidates who were running.

It might seem that the absence of information about candidates and local issues would cause people to cling to past party ties, rather than abandon them. But a California institution called cross-filing made this difficult.

The cross-filing system was one of the most important political legacies of the Progressives. During the Johnson era, they passed legislation that allowed candidates for public office to cross-file, or run in the primary of the opposition party as well as their own. Even more important, it prohibited party affiliations on the ballots. The result was that voters often did not know which party the candidates represented.

The purpose of cross-filing was to break down the power of the political parties and promote the Progressive ideal of nonpartisanship. What it also did was increase the importance of name recognition. Extremely popular figures, like Earl Warren, often won both the Republican and Democratic primaries and thus were spared the necessity of running in the general election in November. Cross-filing made a shambles of party discipline.

## *Campaigning in California*

With name recognition outweighing party affiliation, candidates with money and media support had a huge advantage. Republicans most often had both. Then, as now, they drew upon the relatively wealthy business community for financial resources and regularly outspent Democrats during political campaigns.

Most important, Republicans controlled the major state newspapers, and those papers enthusiastically endorsed Republican candidates. In the 1940s and 1950s, newspapers were in their heyday, far more influential — and partisan — than they are today. The *Los Angeles Times*, run by Norman Chandler and his family, represented the farmers, ranchers, small businessmen and suburbanites who dominated southern California. In the more liberal San Francisco Bay area, right-of-center newspapers like the *San Francisco Chronicle* and the *Oakland Tribune* still held sway. The *Tribune*, in particular, was long a mouthpiece for the conservative views of its publisher, Joe Knowland.

In fact, most of the state's newspapers consistently backed Republicans for public office. A contemporary analysis found that 80 percent of California's one hundred twenty-five dailies endorsed Republicans 75 percent of the time or more.[1] When Earl Warren ran for a third term as governor in 1950, not a single daily paper in the state supported Jimmy Roosevelt, the Democratic candidate.

The most coveted endorsement was that of Chandler's *Times* and its political editor, Kyle Palmer. The *Times* was intensely partisan and by the 1950s was at the peak of its power. Palmer was often called the "Little Governor," or the political boss of California, and he did not hesitate to throw his weight around. A former *Times* reporter once saw Palmer berating someone in his office, as though he were scolding a child. Peeking through the door, he saw that it was Governor Goodwin Knight.[2]

Palmer passed judgment on the electability of political candidates, as well as their willingness to promote policies consistent with the *Times*' pro-business interests. "Anyone who wanted to run for office had to clear it with Kyle," recalled the paper's Washington bureau chief.[3] When in Los Angeles, even Democrats considered a visit with Palmer a wise investment of time. Seen emerging from the editor's office in the late 1950s, Governor Pat Brown quipped: "Just going by to kiss his ring."[4] The four rivals assiduously cultivated Palmer and were rewarded with invaluable publicity and support.

The *Times'* influence extended beyond endorsements and supportive propaganda. Palmer and his colleagues headed an informal network of conservative money men who helped finance the campaigns of candidates that Palmer favored. Thus, he had the power to bring failure or success to nearly any political venture. He was also privy to a wide range of information on the plans and strategies of prospective candidates, which brought politicians to his door in search of tips and gossip. As we will see, Nixon used Palmer as an intermediary with Earl Warren at a time when the junior congressman was hesitant to approach the governor directly.

Another California invention made possible by the weakness of parties—the political management firm—contributed to Republican dominance. Its job was to orchestrate mass media campaigns, including the use of billboards, newspaper and magazine advertising, direct mail, radio spots, and planted stories, on behalf of its clients. In attempting to engage undecided and often poorly informed voters, political management firms simplified the issues, appealed to the emotions, and engaged in what today would be called negative campaigning. Their techniques would not raise any eyebrows today, but at the time many Californians considered them cynical, unethical, and even a danger to democracy.

The leading firm of its type was Whitaker and Baxter, based in San Francisco and named for former newspaperman Clem Whitaker and his partner, Leone Baxter. Most of their clients were Republicans because they were both better funded than Democrats and more in need of the advantages a media services company could provide. After Whitaker and Baxter managed the successful campaign of incumbent Republican governor Frank Merriam against feared former socialist Upton Sinclair in 1934, they were in great demand. Earl Warren was the first of the rivals to recognize their value and hired them to manage his 1942 campaign for governor.

A final advantage for California Republicans over Democrats was superior organization. During the 1930s, they formed the California Republican Assembly, whose main function was to find and endorse candidates for state office. Once assured of the CRA's unofficial backing, such candidates were unlikely to be challenged successfully in the party primary and were free to focus their efforts on the general election. Nixon's run for Congress in 1946, though not promoted by the CRA, was similarly prearranged by a committee of Republican businessmen seeking a man of talent to oust the incumbent Democrat.

All of these factors—media favoritism, the cross-filing system, the influence of campaign management firms, ample financial support, and organizational skill—made possible the rise of the four Republican rivals. Despite being in a minority from the mid–1930s on, Republicans won 68 percent of all state elections between 1914 and 1956. In 1952, Republicans won all statewide offices but one, nineteen of thirty Congressional seats, fifty-four of eighty state Assembly seats, and twenty-nine of forty state Senate seats.[5]

But a real and growing danger lurked beneath these favorable statistics. In a world where media exposure and advertising rather than the individual efforts of party rank-and-file members won elections, Republicans were in constant danger of becoming politically unmoored. They needed media support and Democratic votes in order to get elected, so they had to keep their conservative media benefactors happy while appealing across party lines. This would not always be easy to do.

As long as they were successful, things went well, but a loss could cause the most talented California Republicans to "tumble instantly down trapdoors." As Garry Wills observed, there was "no latticework of party structure to catch men's fall or slow their climb."[6]

The careers of the four rivals were sustained not by the strength of the Republican Party in California but by personal momentum.[7] "What they've got isn't a party," a Democratic politician told journalist Teddy White. "It's a star system, it's a studio lot. They don't run candidates — they produce them, like movie heroes."[8] From 1946 to 1958, California's political heroes — Nixon, Knight, Knowland and Warren — coasted along on a cushion of money and praise. But if the Democrats ever got organized — and, especially, if they were able to abolish cross-filing — Republicans would be in serious trouble.

Before that time came, the California rivals would put on quite a show. Like California itself, the rivals were "restless, ambitious and in a tremendous rush."[9] And, as the politician quoted above added: "Sometimes you get swell fights on the studio lot."

## PART ONE: THE RIVALS IN 1946

# 1

# *Earl Warren: Going His Own Way*

Earl Warren had been governor of California for only a year in January 1944, but already the nation was taking notice. He had shown administrative skill and toughness in his current job and, earlier, as state attorney general, but he also had an appealing personality and a common touch. That January, *Time* magazine described him as a "perfect political candidate."[1]

Warren was certainly a good fit with the Golden State. His style was deeply rooted in California's Progressive tradition, in the state's peculiar demographics, and in his own almost obsessive independence. He was a big man, with a thick shock of blond hair and a gentle smile and manner. There was something reassuringly ordinary about him. He did not talk down to the voters and made no pretense of being an intellectual. He was a devoted Mason, and he had a large, handsome, active family, with whom all Californians could identify.

Though Warren ran for high office as a Republican and had been active in party affairs in the 1930s, in truth he transcended party — or was perhaps a party of one. Writer Roger Morris called him an "authentic genius of the new California method, a politician without visible politics, a candidate running above mere candidacy."[2] Warren never campaigned jointly with other Republican aspirants and hardly ever endorsed them. His avoidance of labels was due in part to his strong belief that neither Republicans nor Democrats had a monopoly on ideas for good government.

His policy preferences were derived from experience rather than ideology. When he came down with a serious case of the flu, he realized how a little bad luck could throw the average working man into poverty, and he made several attempts to get a government-sponsored health insurance plan through the legislature. Cries of "socialized medicine" and the vigorous opposition of the medical community killed these efforts, but they showed Warren to be years, even decades, ahead of his time. He also proposed to allow the federal government to sell power to publicly owned utility districts, a stance that alienated the private utility companies. And, in the midst of growing concern about Communist infiltration of government and academia, he refused to join calls for a loyalty oath for University of California faculty members.

Warren's often startlingly liberal policies complicated his relationship with conservative newspapers like the *Los Angeles Times*, whose endorsement was critical to his success. He managed to retain *Times* support of his campaigns for governor, but political editor Kyle Palmer and the Chandlers gradually lost their enthusiasm for him as more reliably Republican politicians, such as Richard Nixon, emerged in the late 1940s. The governor resisted (and resented) pressure from all quarters, including the *Times*.

Warren ignored conservative grumbling and dealt with the state's problems pragmatically. The main reality, as he saw it, was California's dramatic growth. So, reasonably enough, he defined his main tasks as planning for growth and dealing with its consequences, even if the best solutions required an expansion of state government. This approach captured the mood of the times. In the flush of optimism and dedication to renewal that followed V-J day, he was returned to office by a majority of both Republicans and Democrats in 1946.

## *From Bakersfield to Sacramento*

Earl Warren's upbringing was the most normal of the four rivals. The son of Norwegian and Swedish immigrants, he was raised in Bakersfield, then a dusty, rural town in California's great central valley. His childhood was conventionally middle class — he went on hunting and fishing trips, earned money with paper routes, and was active in high school sports. His grades were good enough to get him into the University of California at Berkeley, where he studied law.

Warren's work ethic and temperament were more important to his political success than his intellectual curiosity. He had been, by all accounts, an indifferent student who was teased for his ability to get by on as little work as possible. Great ideas were not debated in his childhood home.

The young Warren absorbed much of the outlook and style of his dour and uncommunicative father, who spent most of his working life repairing trains for the Southern Pacific railroad. The elder Warren was never fully able to throw off the effects of a difficult and deprived childhood and became increasingly withdrawn as an adult. But he was frugal and hard-working and selflessly financed his son's education. Like his father, Earl Warren would be described as a man who worked hard, went his own way, and had few intimate friends. As historian Kevin Starr summed it up, "a loner father brought up a loner son who made being a loner his foremost political principle."[3]

While in law school at Berkeley, Warren was attracted to the bracing climate and middle-class ambience of the east San Francisco Bay area and decided to pursue a law career there. Admitted to the California State Bar in 1914, he settled in Oakland, the largest city in Alameda County. His choice of where to live and work turned out to be a key factor in his later political success. The *Oakland Tribune*, one of the state's major newspapers, was owned by Joe Knowland, who in time would become Warren's most influential supporter.

After a few years in private practice and a brief Army enlistment, Warren began his long career in public life with his appointment as deputy city attorney of Oakland. In 1925, following a short apprenticeship, he was elected Alameda County district attorney. He held that job through three four-year terms while establishing a reputation as an unrelenting fighter of crime and corruption and turning his office into a model of independence and professionalism. By virtue of his obvious prosecutorial talent and the positive publicity his cases generated, he ran for California attorney general in 1938 and won.

Warren took an instant dislike to the new governor, Culbert Olson, a fiercely partisan Democrat. The feeling was mutual—Warren claimed that Olson spoke to him only once in the four years they served together. After attempting to persuade several others to run against Olson in 1942, Warren finally decided to do so himself.

That year, he became the first of the California rivals to use the services of Whitaker and Baxter, the campaign management specialists. But Warren's insistence on going it alone soon created friction. Whitaker and Baxter came under pressure from Republican lieutenant governor candidate Fred Houser to produce an endorsement from Warren. As related by Warren biographer Jim Newton, Clem Whitaker released a statement, which he may have regarded as harmless enough, suggesting that Warren and Houser were working together.

Warren flew into a rage. "I called Whitaker and told him to close the office and issue no more bulletins," Warren later wrote. "This was my last personal experience" with him.[4] Whitaker was the first of many people to be amazed at Warren's unwillingness to endorse fellow Republicans, and the bad feeling was mutual. Interviewed several years later, Whitaker's son said:

"My father felt very strongly that he didn't want to have anything to do with Earl Warren" after the 1942 campaign.[5]

Warren was also the first rival to employ a Beverly Hills lawyer and lobbyist named Murray Chotiner, one of the new breed of California political managers and an proponent of hard-ball campaign tactics. Three of the four rivals would at one time or another use the services of the shrewd but aggressive Chotiner. He would become closely linked to Richard Nixon in the years to follow.

Warren prided himself on his incorruptibility and believed that a public office was a public trust. Just because he had help from individuals or interest groups in winning elections did not mean that he owed them anything. Once, Lieutenant Governor Knight asked him how he could take money from organizations and then attack them. "They didn't contribute to me," Warren insisted. "They contributed to good government. And if they didn't know that good government meant no special treatment for anyone, they know it now."[6]

On the other hand, Chotiner believed in the political axiom that the winner deserved the spoils. After the 1942 election, in which Warren carried every county in California but one, Chotiner went to see the new governor about state jobs for many of his campaign workers and for help on a court case he was working on. Warren threw Chotiner out of his office. When his 1946 reelection campaign began, according to an intimate, Warren "made it very clear that ... Chotiner was to have nothing to do with it."[7]

## *A Team of One*

Warren's independence and self-righteousness, as reflected in his relations with Whitaker and Chotiner, were sometimes interpreted as arrogance, despite his earnest and appealing manner. Kevin Starr described him as a man with "an egotism so great as to be heroic, for all its unpretentiousness."[8]

Warren was hard to get close to. An associate declared that "there was always a glass wall between you and what went on inside him." Said another colleague: "Verbalizing his emotions was beyond him."[9] He preferred seeing people alone or in small groups and disliked giving speeches. He did enjoy the hearty male companionship of fraternal organizations, but more than anything else, he liked to be home with his family. "I don't know who his confidants were, if he had any," Pat Brown admitted. "He was not very close even with his personal friends."[10]

Many of Warren's contemporaries commented on his blandness and apparent lack of depth — a piece in *Time* called him a "bullheaded, plodding mediocrity"[11] — yet these failings did not reduce his potential appeal for national office. His speeches may have contained "heavy quilts of homilies"[12] and failed to inspire, but they conveyed credibility and conviction. "The effect that he gives is one of solidness and dependability rather than color and excitement," observed George Creel, a California official. "People like him."[13] The writer John Gunther observed that "he has the limitations of all Americans of his type. [He is] a man who has probably never bothered with an abstract thought twice in his life ... and a man who, passably and with luck, could make a tolerable President of the United States."[14]

Most politicians put their own interests first, but, even by that standard, Warren was regarded by many people who dealt with him as self-centered. A career setback or two might have corrected this tendency, but instead he had glided from success to success and was used to getting his way. He became sensitive to slight and criticism. He did not like to admit an error. When he made one, he became sullen and stubborn rather than contrite. His biggest mistake was probably the internment of California's Japanese population at the beginning of World War II, an act for which he never apologized.

As many former associates later testified, the governor had a temper and a long memory when it came to grudges. He could be "a very high-handed, hot-headed person," recalled an aide to Goodwin Knight.[15] "Warren was quite a hater, you know," confided veteran correspondent Earl Behrens. "When he had a falling-out with anybody, he didn't forget things."[16] Pat Brown, who considered himself a friend, agreed. "Warren was a man of great prejudice," he told an interviewer. "If you did anything wrong, he was an unforgiving man."[17] Gardiner Johnson, a lawyer and California Republican official, said he was on Warren's "enemy list" after opposing him on a single issue.[18]

Warren also could be difficult to work for. When his staff did not measure up, he exploded in a rage that spared no one's feelings. He was notoriously stingy with salary increases and compliments. "Flattery," said his press secretary, "was a habit to which Earl Warren was not addicted."[19] He gave little guidance to his assistants, telling them only to think things through and do what was right and fair. According to Merrell Small, one of his closest aides, the best way for an associate to find out what was on the governor's mind was to attend his press conferences.[20] Despite these failings as a boss, Warren's staff was uncommonly loyal and dedicated.

Warren had a cautious and deliberate decision-making style that his associates often viewed as procrastination. To him, it was not unnecessary delay but justifiable prudence. The governor "ponders issues and decisions a long time before he moves," Raymond Moley of *Newsweek* wrote in 1947.

"No one can hurry him. He explores all the evidence."[21] On several occasions, he waited until the last possible moment before deciding to run for a particular office. Warren once said: "I may sometimes walk slowly, but never backwards."[22]

Related to his refusal to be rushed was his almost obsessive secrecy. He once pointedly advised his attorney general, Pat Brown, to "play them very close to the vest. Don't let them see your cards.... Never lay your cards down and tell people what you're going to do."[23] It was a useful political strategy, but at its heart were the pessimistic assumptions that no one could be trusted and that the world was full of opponents who must be outmaneuvered.

A story about an encounter between Warren and outgoing governor Culbert Olson after the 1942 election provides an insight into Warren's personality. Upon stepping into an elevator, Warren ran into Olson, who said to him: "If you want to know what hell is like, just wait until you have been governor for four years." According to his memoirs, Warren responded sympathetically: "Governor, I hope it won't be that bad." But a Democratic official who was also in the elevator claimed that his actual response was far less gracious: "Hmmph—well, it depends on how you handle it." This official came away with the impression that Warren was a "stuffy guy."[24]

Despite this litany of negative observations, most people agreed that Warren was a fine governor. Among his most notable qualities were a strong moral streak, an infectious sense of mission, and a belief in the public interest. He had no patience for groups or individuals who promoted their own good above that of the people at large. If he drove his staff hard, it was because of his desire to make California a better place for its citizens.

Lieutenant Governor Goodwin Knight had many reasons for wanting his job, but a lack of respect for Warren was not one of them. "You had confidence in him from the beginning," Knight once said admiringly. "He knew what he was doing. We were aware that we were political amateurs and we knew that he was a real professional.... I disagreed with him over a number of things and over tactics quite frequently, but ... things look different when you have the responsibility."[25]

## *Warren's Republicanism*

Historians have long debated whether Warren was a Republican out of conviction or convenience. The issue is important to an understanding of his relationship with William Knowland and Richard Nixon, each of whom claimed to be a better Republican than he.

Warren began his career as a Republican Party stalwart. He would not have been mentored and advised by publisher Joe Knowland unless Knowland had perceived him as ideologically compatible. In 1934, he was elected chairman of the state party central committee, a job that placed him in charge of the nuts and bolts of party organization and campaign financing. In one of a series of notes to his friend Bill Knowland, also a party activist, he lamented the lack of interest in Republican legislative campaigns throughout the state.[26] His letters during this period also reflected a strong interest in Republican fortunes in national races. One of these, sent to New York governor Tom Dewey, affirmed that Republicans must oppose the New Deal "right down the line."[27]

Despite such evidence of his commitment to Republican values, he wrote years later that he became a Republican "simply because California was then an overwhelmingly Republican state,"[28] and doing so seemed the best guarantee of success in politics. If true, much of his early political activity was calculated and insincere. But it is more likely that, in looking back at his long career, he underestimated (or forgot) how much his views had evolved leftward through his years as a three-term governor and then as chief justice of the United States.

The *Los Angeles Times*, which in any event had little regard for Governor Olson, embraced his candidacy from the beginning. In fact, political editor Kyle Palmer helped to formulate Warren's nonpartisan strategy for the 1942 election, depicting him as a unifying figure who could bring the state together under the pressures of war. His landslide victory, said the *Times*, was "the best political news California has had in a generation."[29]

Later, to the chagrin of Palmer and publisher Chandler, what started as a strategy to win elections became a strategy for governing. Assuming responsibility for the entire state and its problems seemed to end Warren's career as a partisan Republican. His appointment of Democrats to state office and to his staff, his resistance to pressure from Republican Party officials in search of spoils, and his support of state entitlement programs made him a "maddening enigma" to California conservatives.

His growing neglect of his nominal role as head of the state Republican Party caused increasing disaffection. "A great many of your friends are sorry that you have been unable to attend our last two conventions," wrote the chairman of the state's Young Republicans in 1949.[30] Later that year, Warren called Republicans "the party of negation" because of their opposition to affirmative action programs proposed by Democrats.

By his third term in office, his move to the political center — and perhaps beyond — was evident. Republicans in the legislature complained that he seemed more interested in manipulating the state Republican Party than in strengthening it, and that they would be no worse off under a Democratic governor.³¹ Even before 1949, California conservatives were transferring their allegiance to Knowland, Knight or Nixon — men who spoke their language.

Many Democrats were convinced that the governor was craftily concealing his true mindset in order to win elections. Robert Kenny, who ran against Warren in 1946, admired Warren personally but dismissed him as a careerist who knew where the votes were. Liberal California historian Carey McWilliams called Warren "an expert politician, just this and nothing more."³² Democrats became so frustrated by his successful self-portrait as a centrist that they handed out cards saying "Earl Can't Fool Me."³³ "He *was* a right-wing Republican," one Democrat insisted unconvincingly. "He didn't *seem* like it, [but] he *was*."³⁴

The evidence for Warren's nonpartisanship is more convincing than any signs that he was a closet conservative. Merrell Small, one of his closest aides, described his personal evolution as a "flowering"— the result of facing up to the state's problems.³⁵ If he was masking his true sympathies, he managed to fool President Truman, who told Californians that "your governor pursues forward-looking, liberal policies.... The facts of the case are that he is a real Democrat and doesn't know it."³⁶

\* \* \*

The story of Warren's rise in politics would be incomplete without an account of his relationship with the Knowland family and Joe Knowland's son, Bill. It is fair to say that Warren could not have become governor without the Knowlands and that Bill Knowland could not have become a senator without Warren.

# 2

# *William Knowland: Smooth Ride to the Top*

Alone among the four rivals, Bill Knowland was born into a world of money and privilege. His family had long been a dominant economic and political force in the east San Francisco Bay city of Oakland. His father, Joe, was a political prodigy, elected to the California State Assembly at age twenty-five and to the U.S. Congress at thirty. He served six terms in the House of Representatives, but in 1914 he lost a bid for the Senate. The defeat soured him on politics, so he decided to buy a controlling interest in the *Oakland Tribune*, which he transformed into a mouthpiece for his conservative views. By the 1950s, the paper had become one of the three most influential dailies in California. Joe Knowland ran the *Tribune* for more than a half century.

Family members have testified that Bill Knowland, by far the youngest of three children, received preferential treatment from his parents. His mother died when he was a month old, but his stepmother and father lavished love and attention on him, at the expense of his seven-year-old brother Russ and twelve-year-old sister Eleanor. The elder Knowland took the child along on his political rounds, probably sensing a kindred spirit in Bill, who, even then, shared his father's conservatism and loyalty to the Republican Party. Russ was so resentful of his second-class status in the Knowland household that he became estranged from his younger brother.

The expectations for Bill of his high-achieving father must have been great, but, if anything, the youngest Knowland exceeded them. He showed a seriousness, purposefulness and discipline unusual for his age. He shunned sports and instead formed political clubs. He was campaigning — and giving speeches — for presidential candidate Warren Harding at the tender age of twelve.

Perhaps because of strong parental support and guidance, Bill Knowland did not seem to experience the doubt and uncertainty typical of most adolescents. While still in high school, he was a Republican precinct worker and the finance chairman of the local Coolidge-for-President committee. After graduation, he enrolled at the University of California at Berkeley, where he made his first foray into electoral politics, running unsuccessfully for class president.

It seemed inconceivable that Knowland could rise in Republican state politics faster than his father, but he did. As a college student, he participated as a foot soldier in Herbert Hoover's successful 1928 presidential campaign and accompanied his father to the Republican National Convention. He briefly worked at the *Tribune*, but, according to a family friend, "he was a young man with that look in his eyes. He liked politics and politics liked him."[1]

He decided to run for office himself in 1932 and won election to the California State Assembly by a comfortable margin — a genuine achievement in the year of Democrat Franklin Roosevelt's landslide victory over Hoover. At twenty-four the state's youngest assemblyman, he attacked his job with energy, introducing ninety-three bills. His performance attracted the attention of veteran Sacramento journalist Herbert Phillips, who called Knowland an "engaging, exceptionally able, straightforward and conservatively inclined young man" who was "forging smoothly toward the top."[2]

After only one Assembly term, he surprised his father by running for the state Senate. He won again, though his victory margin was paper thin. All the while, he took an active role in the internal workings of the state Republican Party. By the outbreak of World War II, barely thirty, he had become chairman of the party's national committee.

## *The Warren Connection*

From his Assembly days until 1953, Knowland's political career was inextricably linked to that of his patron and fellow Oaklander Earl Warren. The Knowland family had known the blond Swede from Bakersfield since his bid for district attorney of Alameda County in 1925, when he had made a cold call on the publisher to ask for his help. "Without any acquaintance with [Joe Knowland], I went to his office, told him the situation and asked if I could not get a fair break on the news from the courthouse," Warren recalled later. "Knowland said yes and I believe that was the beginning of his interest in me."[3] The elder Knowland was impressed with Warren's independence and integrity and watched approvingly as he improved the efficiency and professionalism of the local DA's office.

By that time, Warren had met Joe Knowland's politically-minded son, Bill. Though Warren was seventeen years his senior, Bill came across as wise beyond his years, and the two men quickly became good friends. When Knowland ran for the state Assembly in 1932, Warren publicly endorsed his candidacy, describing him as a "young man of energy and character [who] is possessed of the ideals that make an office holder a public servant in the true sense of the word."[4]

Warren exchanged a steady stream of letters and notes with the Knowlands during the late 1930s, revealing a close, almost familial relationship. "Enclosed herewith is my check for $5," Warren wrote to Joe Knowland in 1936, "to repay you for the sum you kindly loaned me the other day."[5] Bill Knowland, checking into the Biltmore Hotel in Los Angeles on one occasion, noted that Warren was there as well. "Have you a dinner engagement?" he scrawled on hotel stationery.[6]

They also shared a strong interest in Republican Party organizational matters. In 1936, Bill and Earl were among several young turks who founded the California Republican Assembly. Both men worked in the state Republican central committee, and Knowland was selected in 1938 to represent California on the Republican National Committee in Washington. Warren's interest in party affairs would wane as his perspective on state problems broadened, but the two men remained close. "I think Warren felt he could trust Bill," said a Warren confidant. "He admired Bill's ability and appreciated Bill's views."[7]

Warren's aggressive and successful prosecutions as California attorney general during the late 1930s, coupled with growing disappointment with the Olson administration in Sacramento, advanced him to the forefront of possible candidates for governor in 1942. A big push came from his friend Bill, who was then a state senator. "I talked with many people, north and south, and ... found a unanimity of opinion that you would be by far the strongest possible candidate," he wrote in late 1941.[8]

Characteristically, Warren did not allow himself to be rushed in making such an important decision, and Knowland fumed at the delay. "The time is rapidly approaching when the bridge will have to be crossed," he reminded Warren. A month later, he pointed out that "our friends are champing at the bit."[9] When finally convinced that he had a good chance to win, Warren entered the race.

Once Warren declared his intention to run, Joe Knowland became his point man, raising money around the state and traveling widely to promote his candidacy. Though labor unions tried to label him as a "conservative chip off old Joe Knowland's block," Warren skillfully crafted an independent

**Bill Knowland (left), a young political prodigy, enthusiastically supported his friend and patron Earl Warren's rise to national prominence. He led state Republican delegations in 1948 and 1952 pledged to Warren's nomination as president (California State Archives).**

image by running a nonpartisan campaign and refraining from endorsing Republican candidates in other races. The elder Knowland denied having a personal stake in Warren's election. "I lost several friends who asked me to intervene in some important matter with Warren, and wouldn't believe me when I told them I couldn't influence" him, he later said.[10]

The 1942 gubernatorial campaign provided a small but powerful example of the importance of Joe Knowland's support. With the shock of Pearl Harbor still fresh in the minds of all Californians, a former state attorney general, James Webb, gave a speech to a civic organization in which he advocated denying citizenship to all Japanese. Warren was in the audience.

Over at the *Tribune*, a report on the speech came in from the Associated Press. "I found that the AP had sent out a story mentioning Webb's talk," the elder Knowland later wrote to Warren, "but your name was not included. I took off the AP dateline and rearranged the story, putting you in with a few quotes which I remembered which I think were perfectly safe." The revised headline and article featured Warren's previously expressed views on Japan, though he had said nothing on this particular occasion. Buried toward the end of the piece was the subheading: "Webb also talks," with a brief summary of his remarks.[11]

Along with serving as Warren's chief propagandist, the elder Knowland was not above trying to intimidate his competitors. According to a story in a small California newspaper about a Warren opponent in the Republican primary, Knowland had gone to Los Angeles in an unsuccessful attempt to persuade the man to retire from the race.[12] Knowland also urged prominent California Democrats to come out for Warren and had some success in doing so. "Dad has talked to [George] Creel [a former New Deal administrator and unsuccessful candidate for governor in 1934] and Creel is going to make a public statement supporting you," wrote Bill Knowland to Warren as the election drew near. "This should help other Democrats follow the same pattern."[13]

Warren's November triumph prompted a congratulatory letter from Bill, who was by then in the Army. "I would have given all the tea in China to have been with you," he enthused. Knowland was convinced that his friend was destined for even bigger things. "The two Roosevelts in New York and [Woodrow] Wilson in New Jersey became national figures while occupying gubernatorial chairs," he reminded Warren. "Of course," he hastened to add, "you have been elected governor and your one and only aim is to do that job. Time and circumstances will take care of other things in the course of human events." He then advised Warren to cultivate Governor Tom Dewey of New York. "He likes you and is most friendly. He will not be a presidential candidate in 1944 but *will* carry lots of weight."[14]

Knowland was one of thousands of men whose careers were interrupted by military service after the Japanese attack on Pearl Harbor in December 1941. He pointedly avoided pulling strings and allowed himself to be drafted. On the day he was called up, he hurried over to Warren's house to give him the news.[15]

The Army private kept up a lively correspondence with the new governor during the war. Knowland's letters to Warren were consistent with his high seriousness; they focused not on mundane army life but on America's responsibilities in the world and the likely shape of the postwar order. Upon his promotion to captain in December 1943, he wrote from the School of Military Government, where he was studying, about the uncertainty of his next assignment. "Wherever I may be, it goes without saying that I will be pulling for you as you take each hurdle en route to the other big jobs you have ahead."[16]

As Warren became more consumed with the demands of being governor, he had difficulty holding up his end of their correspondence. Increasingly, Knowland's letters went unanswered, except by Warren's secretary. "I realize that what you would like to have is a letter from the governor rather than an acknowledgement from me," she wrote in April 1944, "but your letters are received and appreciated by him."[17]

Busy as he was, Warren soon showed that he had not forgotten his friend—far from it. In the summer of 1945, Senator Hiram Johnson, the legendary California Progressive, died in office, giving Warren an opportunity to appoint a successor to serve the final year of Johnson's term. Warren debated with himself for a week before awarding the post to 37-year-old Major William Knowland, who was then in Paris awaiting demobilization. Knowland rushed to Washington for the swearing-in, still wearing his Army uniform and combat boots.[18]

Most Warren scholars believe that this was the only time in his long career in government when he made an appointment purely as a political payoff. He owed the Knowland family a great deal, and the vacancy gave him an opportunity to even the score. If Warren felt any guilt about appointing the son of his primary benefactor to the Senate, it was lessened by his conviction that Bill would bring both ability and strength to the position. In making the announcement, he said he had known Knowland all his adult life and could vouch for his integrity, competence and fairness.

The importance of Knowland's appointment to the Senate cannot be overemphasized. Despite his early successes in state politics and national committee work, his resume was still very thin. Left on his own, it would have in all likelihood been many years—maybe a decade or more—before he could make a serious run for such a prestigious position.

## *A Flawed Politician*

In fact, high political office might have eluded him altogether. Knowland was the unlikeliest of politicians, despite his love of politics. He was seriously deficient in interpersonal skills, tended to be humorless, and often showed little interest in other people and their problems. He was shy and awkward in public. He "strains painfully in his attempts at casual conversation," observed *Time* magazine a few years later, "even with his family."[19] Journalist Mary Ellen Leary told an interviewer that Bill Knowland was "so gauche socially, so unable to relate to people, so uptight" that it was "heartbreaking" to watch.[20] He was a "very strange man," recalled a prominent California attorney. "He was not an appealing figure."[21]

With these deficiencies, Knowland did not bond easily with constituents, or with other legislators. He was not a warm person. A former Republican state treasurer noted that there was "no small talk, just yep, nope, yep, nope."[22] When he arrived in a room to make a speech, said a journalist, he had presence, and people would listen to what he had to say. But he was "awkward in the situation of just passing the time of day."[23]

Knowland also led a turbulent and troubled personal life, which may have adversely affected his performance as a senator and campaigner. He had married young, almost as though he wanted to get that decision behind him in order to concentrate on politics. At the age of eighteen, as he was about to enter the University of California, he eloped with Helen Herrick, a girl he had known since the sixth grade who was now a divorced schoolteacher. Both families were against the courtship, but his doting stepmother was especially upset. She had expected him to marry someone of his own exalted station—a governor's daughter, perhaps.

Unlike her husband, Helen was vivacious and imaginative, with a good sense of humor. It is easy to imagine Bill envying her ebullience and she his imperturbability. Helen admired and respected her husband's obvious abilities and believed he was destined for greatness. But she also had a volatile streak that would spell trouble for the couple later. Pat Brown recalled her presence at a debate with Bill Knowland during their contest for governor in 1958. "I thought she was going to have a fit or something she was so nervous when I was speaking. I thought she was going to throw something at me.... Everybody knew she was a very nervous woman."[24]

Anxiety and loneliness due to wartime separation is not easy on any marriage, and World War II certainly put a strain on the relationship between Bill and Helen. After Bill was drafted into the Army in 1941, tensions began to develop. Helen faced the challenges of raising their two children alone back in California and making financial decisions for the couple, while the watchful presence of Bill's stepmother made her life even more difficult. Letters between Bill and Helen contained declarations of loyalty but also references to the presence of other people in their lives.

In 1945, while Helen was doing volunteer work, she met Blair Moody, then a reporter for the *Detroit News*. Both were lonely and bored, and she was charmed by his wit. Soon they became involved. Bill was apparently none the wiser when he returned home later that year to take up his duties in the Senate. Helen, in fact, was said to be delighted with the news of his appointment and eager to begin a new life in Washington.

Despite his limitations, there was much to like and value about the young Knowland. He was a serious student of politics and knowledgeable about the issues—a man of substance. If he ignored people or was brusque with them, it was usually because his mind was occupied with current events and the finer points of policy. In the days before television, his lack of charisma and social discomfort were not fatal flaws.

Early on, he built a deserved reputation as a man of principle, though he was so sure of himself that he often came across as stubborn and uncompromising. Capturing well both the positive and negative aspects of his style, one journalist wrote that his "stiff, unyielding integrity" gave him an "odd, indefinable weightiness," even as it frustrated his associates.[25] "He is the rudest man I know," said one of his friends. "I often wonder why I like him so much."[26]

## *Winning on His Own*

Knowland's 1945 appointment gave him a valuable year of incumbency — then as now an overwhelming advantage — before he would have to win an election on his own. Charismatic or not, he would be very difficult to beat running in a state dominated by conservative newspapers, including his family's *Tribune*, while having access to ample financial resources and enjoying the blessing of the state's popular governor.

It was his additional good fortune that Will Rogers, Jr., son of the famous humorist, was his opponent in 1946. At a time when an aggressive Soviet Union was becoming a serious concern, Rogers, a liberal Democrat, was pilloried by *Fortnight* magazine as a "Communist, fellow traveler, and crackpot."[27] In reality, he had a distinguished record and was no radical. However, he seemed a half-hearted adversary who often did little campaigning before evening. "He wasn't, maybe, interested enough," said one of his staffers.[28]

As Earl Warren had four years earlier, Knowland hired Murray Chotiner to manage his campaign. The senator did not seem bothered by the fact that Chotiner had in the meantime become persona non grata at the executive mansion in Sacramento. Chotiner resisted the impulse to tinker with Knowland's public face. Many people in the campaign urged the candidate to loosen up. "Well, you know, you may be right," he conceded, "but that is the way I happen to be. If you start changing me, you are apt to get a worse product than when you started."[29] Chotiner agreed.

Rogers had little chance against the wiles of Chotiner and the clout of the *Los Angeles Times* and *Oakland Tribune*. Knowland had not wanted to do any negative campaigning, but without his knowledge, Chotiner launched attacks on Rogers until he was "made to appear a menace to the very foundations of the republic."[30] The *Times* was, of course, firmly behind the Republican and portrayed Rogers as the candidate of the far left. Cross-filing, Knowland ran in both the Democratic and Republican primaries. He won both handily and thus secured his Senate seat without having to compete in the fall general election.

\* \* \*

The 1946 Senate campaign put Knowland into the electoral arena for the first time with three other victorious Republicans. Warren, of course, was about to be reelected governor. Knowland ordinarily would have been unaware of and unconcerned with the political debut of Richard Nixon, who was trying to unseat six-term Representative Jerry Voorhis in the twelfth Congressional district east of Los Angeles. But Murray Chotiner served as campaign manager for both men that year. When Knowland won his two primaries in June, Chotiner was able to shift all his energy and cunning to the task of defeating Nixon's liberal opponent.

The winner of a fourth 1946 contest, for lieutenant governor of California, was a southern California judge and radio personality named Goodwin Knight. He would provide the rivalry with its best example of undiluted enthusiasm.

# 3

# *Goodwin Knight: Charisma to Spare*

A celebrated American journalist described Goodwin Knight as "one of the most instantaneously charming men in American public life."[1] That much was obvious to anyone who saw him sweep into a crowded room, tell a humorous story, or break into a spontaneous tap dance. If Knowland was successful in spite of his stiff personality, Knight captured votes with his gregariousness, bonhomie and "whirling, all-out showmanship."[2] *Time* magazine called him a representative of an "old breed: an adroit practitioner of the crushing handshake, the baby kiss, the bellowed platitude, the remembered name."[3] He was, in short, a natural politician.

Knight made a memorable appearance. He was built like a prizefighter — with a large chest, wide shoulders, and narrow waist — and had a rugged, expressive face. His brow was furrowed by deep wrinkles "etched by great roars of surprised laughter at his own jokes."[4] He was a backslapper who emphasized points by poking listeners in the collarbone — so vigorously, it was said, that people often came away black and blue. He carried on his conversations at a high decibel level, loaded with superlatives, exclamations, whistles of astonishment and cries of delight.[5] Listening to him one night as he unleashed his vast repertoire of stories, gags and dialects, comedian Bob Hope deadpanned: "This man's got to go."

Knight's wise-cracking ebullience and spontaneity gave the impression that he lacked gravitas. When Richard Nixon, the least spontaneous of politicians, called him "one of California's best known comics," the comment seemed dismissive rather than complimentary. "Just because I'm a good-natured guy, they say I'm a lightweight," but "I've always been a serious student of public affairs," Knight said in his own defense.[6]

And he had been. In hundreds of speeches to Republican groups over the years, he had displayed an understanding of American history and politics worthy of an academic. The journalist Theodore H. White was impressed with Knight's extensive library, which showed that he was a "scholar of American politics in the deepest sense." In fact, White viewed Knight's buffoonery as protection against a more dangerous charge in mid-twentieth century America than lack of seriousness — that of being an egghead. He was always more inclined to see the big picture than to get lost in details.

In front of a group, any group, Knight was in his element. Constant practice had made him "the most mellifluous and willing orator since [William Jennings] Bryan," one of his early heroes. In perhaps Knight's finest hour on stage, then Governor Knight was introducing President Eisenhower at the Hollywood Bowl in 1954. The time allotted for his introduction was three minutes, but just before he took the stage, he was told that the live television feed was not ready and that he would have to fill twenty-eight minutes instead of three. Without batting an eye, he advanced to the podium and ad-libbed one of his most entertaining speeches while Ike looked on in open-mouthed amazement from the wings. At the exact moment the television crew was ready, he brought out Eisenhower, who quipped to an aide: "This is like sending the bat boy in after Babe Ruth."[7]

Unlike Nixon, Warren and Knowland, Knight was an emotional man who displayed rather than hid his feelings. He got more excited and more angry than most people, and his intensity led to health problems that would ultimately cut short his career. He once told an aide to Warren that he became so agitated over the prospect of succeeding to the governor's office in 1948 that he suffered a perforated ulcer, requiring surgery that he almost did not survive.[8] Though he also had a larger capacity for enjoyment of life than his three rivals, he tended to be "oddly sensitive," a worrier, especially under pressure, and "a good hater."[9] He was the only one of the rivals who was, at one time or another, bitterly at odds with all of the other three.

Knight put a higher priority on his relationships with people than the other California rivals did. Aide Milton Polland observed that his positions on issues "would be swayed by a lot of friendships and heartstrings."[10] When he asked his daughter why she did not join a sorority at USC, she replied: "Unlike you, father, I feel no need for mass adulation."[11]

His unwillingness to make enemies raised questions about his toughness throughout his career. He seemed to take more pleasure simply in being a political leader than in achieving specific political goals. A veteran Sacramento journalist who covered Knight when he was governor attributed the lack of progress on the key issue of water distribution to his tendency to be nice to all sides and to seek a compromise that would not alienate some important constituency. Overcome by his own eloquence, one journalist observed that

Knight "stands too erect to portray obsequiousness," but lacks "enough steel in his backbone to keep him fully unbending."[12]

## *Early Promise*

As a young man, Knight showed an unusual breadth of interests and talent. He was easily the most well rounded and personally popular of his Republican competitors. He was also the only one of the four who was not a native Californian. He was born in Utah in 1896, but his father, an attorney, moved the family to Los Angeles in 1904. There, he made a comfortable living as a road builder and, later, as a mining speculator.

Goodwin — or Goodie, as he became known at an early age — uttered his first word before he was eight months old, according to an admiring profile, "and hasn't shut up since."[13] His family's affluence allowed him to spend most of his boyhood in middle-class ease. While he was still in elementary school, his father pulled together a series of tales the boy had written and had them published under the title *Good's Budget of Boys' Stories*. Knight bought a pony with the royalties.

Later Knight attended Manual Arts High School in Los Angeles, where he "rose like a bubble in a glass of beer."[14] Displaying the versatility and high energy that would later become his trademark, he was a cheerleader, composer of school songs, star debater, glee club member, actor, and student body president.

Like Knowland, he showed an early interest in politics, campaigning as a student for Progressive icon Hiram Johnson during the gubernatorial election of 1911. He once cut school and bribed a janitor to allow him into a political rally in Pasadena, where the former Democratic candidate for president, William Jennings Bryan, was on the program. Before he had cast his first vote, he had managed to hear in person not only Bryan and Johnson but also Theodore Roosevelt, Woodrow Wilson, and William Howard Taft. Mesmerized by the quality of the oratory he heard, he resolved to become a skilled public speaker.

After graduation, Knight did hard physical labor in the lead and zinc mines of southern Nevada — an experience to which he later attributed his broad shoulders and burly physique — and then worked for a time as a newspaper reporter, saving money for college. In 1915, he was accepted at Stanford. He left school during the last year of World War I to serve on a sub-chasing vessel. Afterward, he returned to Stanford and continued to attract attention — as a tap dancer, rugby player, prize winning orator, and ladies' man. "Everyone knew he was around," was one classmate's wry comment.[15]

Knight later won a graduate scholarship to Cornell, where he studied political science and law and campaigned again for Hiram Johnson, who was then running for president. When his scholarship funds dried up, he left Cornell, became a law clerk and passed the bar in 1921 without earning a law degree. He then set up a practice in southern California, forming a partnership with a former Stanford classmate. By the time the practice was dissolved in 1934, it was one of the largest in California.

In 1932, near the height of the Great Depression, Knight decided to invest $6000 in a gold mine in Kern County. The price of gold shot up after the Roosevelt administration took over, and the mines began to make large profits. Soon, Knight was able to sell his stake for over $400,000. This windfall, along with his successful law practice, gave him considerable flexibility in the years ahead and allowed him to pursue his real interest — politics. "With my luck," he once said, "who needs brains?"[16]

## *A Republican Jurist*

Knight continued his active support of Republican candidates throughout the 1920s and 1930s. His colorful personality and his conservative politics made him a popular guest speaker at Republican gatherings around Los Angeles. Classes in oratory had added another dimension to his natural gregariousness and charm. He had a deep, pleasant voice, an animated face, a light, humorous touch, and deft timing. Though many of his speeches were highly partisan attacks on Franklin Roosevelt and the New Deal, he also showed a command of history and a talent for political analysis. In time he was considered one of the state's outstanding orators.

In 1934, Knight's heightened visibility brought him to the attention of the California Republican Party, which asked him at the last minute to replace the scheduled keynote speaker at its convention. Party officials hoped that his close association with the Progressive wing of the party would give the Republicans a more moderate image in their battle against the ultra-liberal Democratic candidate for governor, Upton Sinclair.

Knight came close to backing out, believing that he did not have sufficient stature for the assignment, but he delivered the speech and went on to campaign extensively for Frank Merriam's reelection as governor against Sinclair. In appreciation, the victorious Merriam honored Knight's request for an appointment to the Los Angeles Superior Court. "I asked for the job," Knight freely admitted. "Any man who wants a political job gets it because he asks for it."[17]

After that, they called him the "mender of broken hearts."[18] Day after day, estranged Hollywood celebrities approached his bench at the Los Angeles Superior Court seeking divorces and a just distribution of assets. Though barely forty, Judge Knight handled the opposing parties with such a disarming blend of humor and empathy that they often reached a settlement in his chambers, or were persuaded to give their marriage another try. "Where did a judge so young in years and actual experience get his knowledge of the law, his wisdom, his patience and, most of all, his deep understanding of human nature?" asked a Los Angeles newspaper.[19]

Though he dealt with some of the most famous names in the movie industry, he cut them little slack. When actress Mary Astor wrangled endlessly with her former husband over child custody rights, Knight served notice that he would not brook further delays. The public was impressed by his sense of fairness, and he easily won reelection in 1936 and 1942. A local newspaper praised him as "one of the best known jurists in Los Angeles County with a large, enthusiastic following."[20]

As the 1930s drew to a close, however, Knight was becoming restless and dissatisfied. Being a Superior Court judge might have been an enviable position and a worthy career goal for most men, but Knight found it limiting and predictable. "I knew exactly how the cases I was trying were going to come out an hour before they began," he reflected later. "I used to sit on the bench and write letters, or anything, just to keep occupied."[21] The anonymity also bothered him; he hungered for a more visible role.

In 1941 he was invited to take part in a radio public affairs show called *Open Forum*. After sitting through one ponderous program, he told the producer the show was dull and needed a moderator to keep things moving. "How about you?" asked the producer. He jumped at the opportunity.

For the next four years he took charge, choosing the guests and issues himself, and injecting his wit and personality into the discussion. His work attracted the attention of a San Francisco station, and he was invited to put on a show there as well. From then on, he took the train to the Bay Area every Friday and staged the KQW Roundtable, returning to Los Angeles in time to run the *Forum* on Sunday.[22] He also became involved with a program that allowed him to make use of skills developed in the courtroom. As the flamboyant host of *Knight Court*, he refereed the personal disputes of his callers.

## *Entering Politics*

All of this media exposure increased his name recognition and, in a state that worshipped celebrity, positioned him well for a political career. In

1944, after receiving promises of support from several Republican leaders, he declared his candidacy for the party's U.S. Senate primary. Favorable press coverage ensued. He was praised as "the greatest since [1930s Governor] Sunny Jim Rolph at the highly political business of never forgetting a face." However, most state party bigwigs felt that Lieutenant Governor Fred Houser had a better chance to win in the general election, so Knight decided not to make the effort after all. When Houser lost to Democrat Sheridan Downey in November, Knight went back to the bench and Houser went back to being lieutenant governor.

But Houser was dissatisfied with his job, and by 1946 Governor Warren was dissatisfied with him, so Knight saw another opportunity to enter politics. According to a *Saturday Evening Post* profile, Knight and Houser commiserated about their mutual unhappiness, and Knight said he thought he might enjoy being lieutenant governor. No, said Houser, "you'd be buried and forgotten." Unpersuaded, Knight said, why don't I run for your job and you run for mine? This struck Houser as a good idea.[23]

By then Knight had caught the eye of Kyle Palmer. A Warren biographer later wrote that Knight was "a creation of the *Los Angeles Times*, plucked from the backwaters of the Los Angeles Superior Court by the paper's political editor,"[24] but in truth Palmer was only one of many influential Knight friends. Knight paid a visit to Whitaker and Baxter, the campaign management specialists, introduced himself, and said he wanted to run for lieutenant governor. They liked his candor, personality and showmanship and were willing to help. They built a close relationship with Knight that lasted for twelve years.

Knight took leave from the bench, and in a whirlwind campaign, he visited all but eight counties in the state. He won by 330,000 votes. According to *The Nation* magazine, his plurality was the largest of any candidate for state office up until that time.[25]

Later, he called his decision to run for lieutenant governor the smartest political move he ever made, because it put him in a position to reach his ultimate goal — that of becoming governor. He would spend the next seven years in single-minded pursuit of that job.

* * *

The success of Warren, Knight and Knowland in the elections of 1946 made them — along with Sheridan Downey, the state's other U.S. Senator — the most important public officials in California. That same year, in the Los Angeles area, the race for Congress in the 12th District marked the political debut of an obscure but ambitious young attorney whose success would soon enough upset the plans and dreams of all the others.

# 4

# *Richard Nixon: A New Kind of Politician*

All of his life, Richard Nixon evoked strong feelings in other people, both positive and negative. His obvious intelligence and analytical ability, combined with iron self-discipline and a facility for oral self-expression, inspired confidence in many Americans and got him elected to the House of Representatives, the U.S. Senate, and the presidency. The public valued his competence and seriousness of purpose and was inclined to overlook or downplay the significance of his brooding nature, social awkwardness and introverted personality.

Yet a great many — perhaps most — of the era's most important national leaders harbored an intense dislike of Nixon. Presidents Harry Truman and John Kennedy, two-time presidential candidate Adlai Stevenson, and Speaker of the House of Representatives Sam Rayburn each spoke of him in bitter personal terms. In their view, he was not merely a formidable political opponent but also an unscrupulous and manipulative one. President Dwight Eisenhower rewarded Nixon for eight years of loyalty and widely acknowledged competence by telling friends that he was too partisan and that he had not grown in his job.[1]

Even before the Watergate scandal destroyed his presidency, Nixon's up-and-down career, comebacks and reinventions, and polarizing personality had already been the subject of numerous articles and books. More than a decade after his death, historians and psychologists still mine the data on his hardscrabble beginnings and cheerless family life in an attempt to understand the personal journey of this politician who seemed singularly unsuited to politics.

## "A Plain, Exacting Life"

Of the four rivals, Nixon had by far the hardest childhood. His father, Frank, grew lemons in the southern California town of Yorba Linda until his orchard failed and then worked as a laborer for an oil company. He was often unsuccessful as a provider — all of the Nixons had to work hard and do without. Hannah, his mother, found employment in a packinghouse to help make ends meet. When Richard was nine, the family moved to rural Whittier, where his father ran a combination gas station and grocery store. Richard and his two brothers were expected to help out in the store and do chores after school. It was not poverty, but it was a "plain, exacting life."[2]

Nixon got used to lacking material possessions and never developed a taste for luxury. He had within him a Celtic strain of asceticism, according to author Garry Wills. "Neither Dick nor I care a bit for creature comforts," declared Pat Nixon years later. Nixon even elevated self-denial to a success strategy. "One has to be uncomfortable to do one's best thinking," he once observed.[3]

Nixon's father was a difficult person, hot tempered, combative and frustrated, a man who yelled at his children and had to be treated with kid gloves. Hannah was calmer, gentler, and more refined than her husband, and she tried to compensate for Frank's volatility. Some of her friends said that she had married beneath her. She was a serious and private person — an acquaintance called her an "iron fist in a velvet glove." It is not an exaggeration to say that Nixon was a child of emotional, if not financial, deprivation.[4]

In contrast to his more outgoing brothers, Richard was a quiet, serious, diligent student with a rich interior world. He soon began to distinguish himself academically and to show a competitive streak. His father's volubility actually aided the boy's development. Thriving on the clash of ideas, Frank instilled verbal aggressiveness in Richard, who became a skilled high school debater. He had an ability — considered disturbing by one of his teachers — to "kind of slide around an argument instead of meeting it head-on" and take any side of an issue with equal skill.[5]

Despite his shyness, Nixon entered fully into high school life. He acted in school plays, tried out gamely for the football team, and ran unsuccessfully for school president. He was more admired than liked. His academic record was excellent, but his economic circumstances ruled out applying to expensive Eastern universities. He settled for nearby Whittier College.

The family endured tragedy as well as hard times. In 1925, when Richard was twelve, his younger brother Arthur, to whom he was very attached, became ill and died. Both Richard and his mother grieved deeply. For weeks,

Nixon later wrote, "there was not a day that I did not think about him and cry."⁶ Only two years later, older brother Harold contracted tuberculosis. Though the family sacrificed much to care for him, he finally succumbed in 1933, while Richard was in college. "This death had a deep effect on him," Hannah later recalled. "He sank into a deep, impenetrable silence. From then on, it seemed Richard was trying to be three sons in one."⁷

Nixon channeled his grief and energy into college life. Already evident were two contrasting aspects of his personality. On the one hand, he was stiff, tense, aloof and serious, and he impressed many of his friends as lacking in self-confidence. But instead of avoiding social situations and sticking to his books, as brainy but introverted students tend to do, he plunged into school activities. Though he was not especially popular, he sought elective office and finally succeeded in becoming school president his senior year. He was a skilled actor in dramatic productions and a mainstay of the debate team. He showed great tenacity as a bench warmer and tackling dummy for the school's football team. Then, as later, he sought leadership roles that were less than natural for him but that undoubtedly provided important psychic rewards.

During his first year at Whittier College, Nixon helped to organize a student society, called the Orthogonians, as an alternative to the more patrician Franklins. The Orthogonians posed for their class picture in open-necked shirts, because they could not afford tuxedos like the Franklins. "They were the haves and we were the have-nots," he recalled.⁸

Years later, Nixon reflected with rare candor on the deep-seated resentment that drove him during those years and afterwards. "What starts the process, really, are laughs and slights and snubs when you are a kid.... But if you are reasonably intelligent and if your anger is deep enough and strong enough, you learn that you can change those attitudes by excellence, personal gut performance, while those who have everything are sitting on their fat butts."⁹ William S. White speculated that controlling his rage required an "immense and sustained effort."¹⁰

Nixon graduated from Whittier College in 1934, at the height of the Depression, and headed for law school at Duke University in North Carolina. He did well at Duke, according to a classmate, because of his "iron butt"—he studied harder than anyone and managed to qualify for a full scholarship his final two years. He graduated near the top of his class but was rejected by the East Coast law firms to which he applied. In disappointment, he returned to California in 1937 and joined a law practice in his home town.

Though he was soon productively employed in his chosen profession and made a full partner in his firm, it was something of a let-down for Nixon to be back in small-town southern California. While he was puzzling over his future, he considered running for the California Assembly and became involved in an abortive business venture.

The most significant development from this period was his long and patient courtship of Pat Ryan. He and Pat were married in 1940. Nixon was never a warm husband and in fact showed little regard for women in general, tending to view them as a "different species." Author Blema Steinberg speculated that he feared strong women and tried to keep them in their place.[11] If he had such feelings, they might have colored his aggressive campaign against Helen Gahagan Douglas for the U.S. Senate in 1950.

By the early 1940s, Nixon had decided he did not want a career as a lawyer in Whittier. In casting about for alternatives, he was offered a job with the newly formed Office of Price Administration in Washington, D.C. He worked at the OPA for several months, but by then the country was at war. In the middle of 1942, he decided to enlist in the Navy rather than wait to be drafted. He spent most of the war years in the Pacific theater, loading and unloading transport aircraft. While in service, he became known as an excellent poker player, with a cool, analytic approach to the game and a willingness to bluff.

## *A Driven Man*

From an early age to the end of his political career, the pattern of Nixon's life remained the same — "weakness and failure turned into strength by dint of sheer persistence and hard work."[12] He sought to take advantage of all available time. As a Washington politician, he never left the office for the airport until the last possible minute for fear of having to sit around a terminal. Once, when he missed a plane, he went back to the office for an hour rather than have nothing to do.[13] In 1950, a magazine article described Nixon as having "no social life at all, no hobbies, and no interests outside of his family and working, working, working."[14]

Along the way, as part of his personal strategy for success, Nixon, like Earl Warren, learned to keep his own counsel. Few of his associates claimed to know him well or understand him, either in college or later in life. "Dick Nixon would never show his emotions. He was always to himself," recalled San Francisco mayor George Christopher.[15] Another California Republican, future Defense Secretary Caspar Weinberger, testified: "Although I've been acquainted with him for years and years, I didn't have any feeling that I ever knew him well or knew anything about what might be called his inner thoughts, or what he really had in mind. He masked his thoughts.... He talked about issues and all, but he never talked about himself personally."[16]

According to a psychobiography, based on a detailed study of his childhood, Nixon had a narcissistic personality, which allowed him a limited repertoire of feelings toward others. According to this analytic framework, he was unable to feel remorse or empathy, which aided the development of an aggressive, sometimes ruthless campaign style. Repeated frustrations during his childhood bred great ambition, while the need to maintain his "grandiose self" required constant reassurance, approval and praise.[17] Another psychological study of Nixon concluded that his emotional deprivation as a child led to bitterness, self-pity, and suspiciousness in later life. He was said to be a sad, depressed individual who was dissatisfied with himself and thus was unable to form healthy relationships with others.[18]

Whether or not Nixon had a narcissistic personality, his driven nature combined with his emotional unavailability provoked suspicion and hostility in many people. Acquaintances from his early years forward detected what Bela Kornitzer, in an otherwise sympathetic biography of Nixon, called an "indefinable defect" in him. "I don't respond to him emotionally," admitted Justin Dart, a California fundraiser. "Don't get me wrong. I like Dick — he could be very friendly — but the sparks don't fly around him in terms of political magnetism." A Whittier businessman agreed: "I couldn't warm up to him. Maybe he is OK, but I don't trust him, and, mind you, I am a Republican from way back."[19]

Dorothy Chandler, the influential wife of *Los Angeles Times* publisher Norman Chandler, was among those who found something "tacky" about the young man from Whittier. In an anecdote related by David Halberstam, she recalled a Nixon victory celebration at which all the Nixons ordered milk, but Dick Nixon ran after her and asked for a straight bourbon. "I don't want my mother to see me drinking it," he admitted. She did not like the idea of a grown man hiding a drink from his mother.[20]

Nixon was aware that he seemed distant to many people and often made them uncomfortable. Like Knowland, he was especially bad at small talk. He was "always concerned with serious world issues that he would rather discuss, even at inappropriate times, than indulge in conversation about everyday trivialities."[21] He referred to himself, accurately enough, as "an introvert in an extrovert's profession."[22]

Yet a number of people found his shy, awkward and sincere manner appealing, especially when coupled to his formidable intelligence. The fact that he was not smooth and charismatic ironically gave him more credibility with many Californians than outgoing but less capable politicians. Unlike his California rivals, he rarely spoke ill of other Republicans, which made him appear selfless. Early on, he attracted to his side a corps of dedicated loyalists who appreciated these qualities, who saw him as presidential material from the beginning, and who worked long hours with uncommon zeal over many years to promote his political success.

## The Voorhis Campaign

The idea of running for Congress in 1946 might not have occurred to Nixon had it not been for a letter from an old family friend and Whittier businessman, Roy Day. He and other local entrepreneurs were looking for an attractive Republican candidate to back for Congress, and he remembered Nixon as "a very aggressive individual." Nixon had been discharged from the Navy and was in Washington at the time finishing up some business, and he was planning to return to his law practice in California. He jumped at the chance to meet with the group.

Though several others were interviewed, Nixon made the best impression. As he left the room, Day turned to a colleague and said: "You know, that is saleable merchandise."[23] Running for Congress was Nixon's first foray into the world of elective politics. As it turned out, it was also a launching pad to success beyond his wildest expectations.

Going up against a seasoned opponent like Jerry Voorhis seemed a daunting assignment for a young attorney with no political experience or name recognition. The Democrat was seeking his sixth term and had all the advantages of incumbency. He had been voted the best congressman west of the Mississippi by a group of Washington correspondents. He was generally regarded as one of the hardest working, best informed, and most conscientious members of the House of Representatives. When Kyle Palmer, the *Los Angeles Times'* political editor, first met Nixon in 1946, he had the impression that the young navy officer was "out on a sort of giant-killer operation," destined to end badly.[24]

But Nixon had several things going for him. The 12th District at the time was primarily rural, middle class and conservative. The district's business community had become frustrated with New Deal policies and with negative postwar economic and social trends — the shortages of goods, lack of housing for returning veterans, and the growing power of labor unions. The angry mood seemed likely to benefit a Republican candidate.

Kyle Palmer's initial doubts aside, Nixon made a good impression on the overwhelmingly conservative southern California press, which was eager for a fresh Republican face. Though inexperienced, Nixon was attractive, well spoken and enthusiastic, with a solid resume, a charming wife, and a new baby daughter. After publisher Norman Chandler and political editor Palmer had a chance to sit down with Nixon, Chandler said: "This young fellow makes sense. He looks like a comer. He has a lot of fight and fire. Let's support him."[25] Palmer agreed. From then on, he considered Nixon his protégé.

Most of the other newspapers in the district backed him as well. An analysis of press coverage during the campaign showed that 26 out of 30 newspapers in the 12th District supported Nixon, and three of the remaining four were neutral.[26] This was a huge advantage during a time when nearly everyone read a daily paper, and journalists functioned more as propagandists than reporters.

Moreover, Voorhis was in many ways a vulnerable incumbent. A former socialist and a supporter of Roosevelt, he was much more liberal than the district he represented. Though he had managed to get elected five times, his success over the years had been due as much to lackluster Republican challengers as to his own abilities. His reputation as a hard worker had a downside — he divided his attention among so many issues that he could point to few legislative accomplishments after all that time in office.

Voorhis' intensity and air of grim determination led some colleagues in the House to refer to him sarcastically as "Kid Atlas," because he seemed to carry the weight of the world on his shoulders. His speeches were "serious expositions on complex subjects," often lasting well over an hour and devoid of any humor or wit.[27] His ten years in Congress had given him seniority but not much clout, since he was not one to "drink with the boys" or obediently toe the party line.[28]

Head to head against Nixon, Voorhis had other disadvantages. He was "rumpled, tweedy, and pipe-smoking, more professor than politician."[29] In contrast to his eager young opponent, Voorhis was not personally combative, had little stomach for political infighting, and often seemed lethargic. He relied on logic and reason, rather than emotion or demagogy, to win votes.

Nixon decided to mount an aggressive campaign that portrayed Voorhis as too liberal for the 12th District and to lure him into a series of joint appearances where the voters could compare the two men. His campaign started with little money or manpower, but the Republican candidate was a harder worker than his opponent. Though inexperienced, he proved to be shrewd beyond his years. An aide, Harrison McCall, marveled at how well Nixon could handle himself after only ten months in politics.[30] As he would throughout his career, Nixon prepared meticulously. "I was convinced that I knew Voorhis' record as well as he did," Nixon wrote later. "As it turned out, I knew it even better."[31]

An aggressive candidate needed an aggressive manager. Nixon found one in Murray Chotiner. One of the earliest proponents of mass-advertising techniques and market research in election campaigns, Chotiner believed that the best defense was a constant, hard-hitting offense. His approach was well suited to California's amorphous and disorganized electorate, but it was viewed as cynical and manipulative by many veteran politicians. Despite later suspicions that Chotiner determined the overall tone of the campaign, Nixon made key decisions himself and wrote all his speeches.[32] Still, Chotiner's zeal often led to tactical excesses — not only in 1946 but in years to follow — for which Nixon would be blamed.

It was Voorhis' misfortune, as a former socialist, to be running for reelection during a time of increased suspicion of Soviet policies in Europe and when the director of the FBI was warning of communist infiltration of government and labor unions. All over the country, in fact, GOP candidates were using the specter of the Red Menace to put incumbent Democrats on the defensive. Frustration born of so many electoral losses had given rise to near desperation among Republicans and a sense that in their attempts to regain power, this was an issue they could successfully exploit.

Voorhis was certainly a liberal Democrat. Like other mainstream members of his party, he was a supporter of the New Deal and favored policies that strengthened labor unions. He often took principled stands that were unpopular in his district, such as against legislation granting states title to offshore oil deposits. But he was far from a radical. He joined Republicans in criticizing Soviet moves in Eastern Europe. He was also a staunch Catholic with a strong Christian morality, and the author of a book called *The Christian in Politics*.

Nixon used the issue of communist influence in a way that later became typical of his campaign style. He was careful never to charge directly that his opponent was subversive or dangerous. He used an arsenal of debater's tricks — including oblique suggestions, false premises, body language, and innuendo — to leave the impression that Voorhis was hiding his true colors. And he left it to the combative Chotiner and his zealous campaign workers to raise doubts in the minds of 12th District voters about their congressman's suitability for the job.

One of Nixon's main lines of attack was that Voorhis had the support of radical labor groups. During the 1930s, the Congress of Industrial Organizations (CIO) had grown rapidly in size and power as the automobile and steel industries had grown. The deterioration in relations with the Soviet Union after the war made communist infiltration of the unions a concern, not only to the public but to labor leaders themselves. The CIO's Political Action Committee, or PAC, was the political arm of the CIO and took sides in national elections.

Nixon found a perfect venue for airing his allegations — a series of debates between the two men. It was Voorhis who proposed debates — a major miscalculation on his part. Nixon was a skilled and experienced debater who plunged into verbal confrontations with enthusiasm. Debating him, Voorhis was continually frustrated by time limits for responses as he tried to explain his intricate views, while Nixon was always ready with a quick and pithy, if oversimplified, comment.

At a dramatic moment during the first debate, he walked across the stage and showed Voorhis a document which he said proved that the CIO PAC had endorsed him. Voorhis appeared confused and shaken. In point of fact, the CIO PAC was not endorsing Voorhis in 1946, though it had backed his 1944 reelection bid. The document Nixon showed his opponent was a minority recommendation of an endorsement that had not been accepted. The Nixon forces had an easy time confusing the audience on the issue, because the allegation, if not exactly true, seemed true enough. Voorhis gave a convoluted explanation that only made matters worse.

As the campaign progressed, Nixon pressed his advantage. In a questionable statistical analysis of his opponent's voting record in Congress, he alleged that Voorhis had voted the "Communist-dominated PAC line" forty-three out of forty-six times. Voorhis later lamented that it took him a month to figure out which votes Nixon was referring to. When he did, he discovered that most of them were uncontroversial and that many Republicans had voted the same way, but by then the damage had been done.

Another of the challenger's campaign slogans was: "A vote for Nixon is a vote against the PAC and its Communist principles." The sentence suggested — but stopped short of claiming — that his opponent was supported by the PAC, or that the PAC was a Communist organization. It was a slippery statement, whose intent was to elicit an emotional response from the voter rather than communicate useful information about the candidate and his positions.

The Nixon campaign also aired a political advertisement claiming that Voorhis had admitted CIO PAC backing, but an article it cited as proof appeared not to prove anything. Toward election day, another Nixon ad warned, "Remember: Voorhis is a former registered Socialist and his voting record in Congress is more Socialistic and Communistic than Democratic." Voorhis spent most of the campaign shocked, disbelieving and on the defensive in the face of such charges.

In the final days, anonymous callers may have telephoned many 12th District voters and asked: "Did you know that Jerry Voorhis is a Communist?" This early version of a dirty trick was widely reported and condemned, though the Nixon campaign vigorously denied making the calls. Murray Chotiner told a columnist years later that no political manager in his right mind would organize such an effort, in view of its blow-back potential. The calls, if they were made, were certainly scurrilous. This may have been one of several times throughout Nixon's career when his fiercest adherents tarnished his legitimate accomplishments by crossing an important line.

The campaign also provided an early example of Nixon's polarizing effect on the electorate. For every person who loathed his style and personality, another was caught up in the passion of his argument and the urgency of his message. As the issue of communist subversion gained traction in the years to follow, this passion and urgency would fall on increasingly receptive ears. At the same time, a legion of Nixon-haters would reject his aggressive partisanship and self-promotion.

Nixon's unrelenting attacks suggested that he and his people believed the contest was closer than it really was. In the absence of reliable polling techniques, it was difficult to judge. When election day came, however, he won handily, by a margin of 15,000 votes out of 115,000 cast. He undoubtedly would have won even if he had not engaged in the kind of campaigning that later damaged his reputation.

## *A Blessing Withheld*

Earl Warren, running that year for reelection as governor, did not pay much attention to the political debut of Richard Nixon. But what he learned about the Nixon-Voorhis race, along with his interaction with the candidate and his representatives, left a bad taste in his mouth. Later this experience became known as "the opening round in a historical antagonism" between the two men.[33]

Nixon and Warren were in most ways poles apart. As Kevin Starr has written, they "embodied to perfection a contrast of generations, regions, values and styles that juxtaposed one California against another."[34] The governor was sunny and approachable — "the model of a friendly leader floating above the tumult of politics."[35] By contrast, the "neurotic and insecure" Nixon "had a tendency to hunch, clasp his hands, and shift his eyes nervously above a feral smile."[36] From Warren's perspective, Nixon brought something new and unwelcome to California politics — "not the gray, morally upright posture of ... other older Republicans but the no-holds-barred approach of a young battler."[37]

There were other differences. Though both men had been raised in middle class circumstances, Warren had glided confidently through life. Success and approval came harder to Nixon and required more of a struggle. Warren was focused on state and local issues while Nixon developed an interest in foreign policy and national affairs. Many saw Nixon as a representative of the "overreaching, conniving southern Californian who reinvented himself continually," while Warren, transplanted from the rural Central Valley, had developed the more sophisticated sensibility of a northern Californian. "Nixon was the kind of guy that Warren would instinctively distrust," Pat Brown said years later.[38]

Little of what the governor read or heard about the Nixon-Voorhis race pleased him. According to Warren's long-time aide, Merrell Small, Nixon's tactics offended his sense of fairness. Small recalled years later how much the governor "disliked the type of campaign that unseated … Voorhis."[39] Warren was particularly troubled by suggestions that hard-working public servants like Voorhis were somehow unpatriotic. "Warren's opponents were not, willy-nilly, Communists because they were his opponents," wrote biographer Leo Katcher.[40]

Warren may also have worried that Nixon's strong partisanship, if adopted by other Republicans, could unravel the inter-party coalition he had so painstakingly put together. Fulton Lewis, a popular right-wing radio commentator, embodied his concern. Lewis was one of many conservatives who praised Nixon for "fight[ing] it out on the issues, instead of compromising with a lot of me-too talk."[41] Positive reactions to Nixon's strident Republicanism marked the beginning of a disillusionment with Warren and his perceived collusion with Democrats that eventually found expression in the speeches of all three of his rivals.

Warren's customary aloofness from the Republican Party and its candidates was the immediate cause of tension between him and Nixon in 1946. Their personal relationship began with Nixon needing a favor. The outcome of his contest with Voorhis looked too close to call, and Nixon reasoned that it might easily be decided by a timely endorsement from the nominal head of the Californian Republican Party. It became a goal of the campaign to secure a public statement from Warren backing his candidacy.

Nixon did not believe this was an unreasonable request to make of a Republican governor. But, as he and other candidates throughout the state were fast learning, Warren was not particularly interested in helping other Republicans get elected. Accordingly, he kept his distance from the Nixon-Voorhis race. "Nixon's people were on their knees to Earl Warren, asking: 'For God's sake, endorse this boy,' recalled one California politician. "But Warren wouldn't endorse his mother."[42]

In fact, Warren may have preferred Voorhis. The congressman had supported Warren's very un–Republican state disability insurance plan, and the governor had written him a letter of praise for his efforts. During the campaign Voorhis pointed with pride to this evidence of Warren's favor. Worried about its possible effect on the voters, Nixon's press secretary, William Arnold, wrote a letter of his own to the governor complaining that the ambiguity of his gesture to Voorhis was hurting the Republican effort across the board and requesting (Arnold's recollection is "demanding") a statement from him that the letter was not intended as an endorsement. Warren refused to offer any elaboration, other than to say that Voorhis deserved his gratitude.[43] If he did in fact perceive Arnold's request as a demand, he may have been offended by the Nixon campaign's temerity.

There was a second bone of contention. Nixon received a telegram from the former Republican governor of Minnesota, Harold Stassen, with whom he had served in the Pacific war, offering to come out to California and make speeches on his behalf. According to Arnold's account, Nixon consulted with Kyle Palmer of the *Times* about whether or not to accept Stassen's offer. Palmer advised him to seek Warren's consent first.

Arnold realized that involving Warren in the decision meant, in all likelihood, that Stassen would never come. "We knew our Earl Warren," he recalled.[44] The governor sent word back through Palmer that he did not think it would be proper for a politician from outside the state to campaign in California for a local candidate. With both Warren and Stassen considering presidential runs in 1948, perhaps Warren did not wish to allow Stassen the extra exposure, or he may have seen it as detracting from his own reelection campaign. Whatever the reason, Nixon would not forget.

Nixon defeated Voorhis without the governor's backing. Warren sent him a warm telegram after the election. "I congratulate you upon your splendid victory and look forward to working with you in the service of our state during the next four years," he wrote. "I hope to see you anytime you are in the neighborhood of Sacramento." Nixon and his loyalists were unimpressed by this courtesy.

The 1946 campaign, Arnold noted, kindled a "slow burn" in the new congressman that in time became a blaze.[45] Nixon would himself later become known for the prodigious amount of work he did on behalf of Republican candidates everywhere—the kind of work that Warren was unwilling to do. He concluded from this episode that Warren was concerned only about his own ambition and his expedient coalition with Democrats.

So "for now, the two men shadowed each other, Nixon heading off to Washington, miffed that the governor had not helped him, and Warren settling in for a second term as governor, astonished that Nixon's people would even have asked."[46] Warren did not realize it, but the time was fast approaching when the support of Richard Nixon would be an indispensable asset in reaching his own career goal.

PART TWO: THE RIVALS IN
WARREN'S SHADOW (1946–1952)

# 5

# *"Defending California from Goodie"*

Goodwin Knight's election as lieutenant governor in 1946 on a ticket headed by Earl Warren was certainly not, as *Fortnight* magazine called it, "the sudden metamorphosis of a staid LA jurist."[1] He had been fascinated with politics since boyhood, and no one who knew him would call him staid. His campaign for lieutenant governor had demonstrated the success of his effort to become known around the state, rather than just in southern California. He arrived in Sacramento at the end of the year brimming with enthusiasm and high spirits.

But the job he had been elected to do, as his predecessor had tried to tell him, did not seem likely to keep an active and ambitious man challenged. Knight inherited a small office, a small staff, and few duties, one of which was the largely ceremonial task of presiding over the California Senate. Settling in, he faced the grim prospect of going from a bored superior court judge to a bored lieutenant governor.

If he wished, of course, Warren could invest the position with significant responsibilities, but Knight had no reason to expect Warren to welcome him into his inner circle. They had not known each other well before 1946, had not run as a team during the election, and personally had little in common. When Knight, the former entrepreneur, tried to tell Warren, the career public servant, about some stocks he owned, the governor was said to have fallen asleep.[2]

But they had complimentary strengths and might have made good partners. Knight was more serious than he pretended to be, and he was more likeable and sensitive to human values than the governor. Warren was the more thoughtful man, a better planner, and more purposeful. Knight could have handled liaison with the legislature, which did not always see eye to eye with Warren.

In fact, Warren did make an attempt to include Goodie on his team. He claims to have had a discussion with Knight at the beginning of his term — one that would have lasting consequences for their relationship. "If you will let me know anything you would like to do," Warren offered, "I'll try to find a place for you so you can be useful." According to Warren, Knight demurred. He felt that a definite assignment would "put him on the spot," and said that he preferred to act as a kind of "free agent."

Knight's unenthusiastic response eliminated any sympathy Warren might have had for him. If the lieutenant governor did not want administrative responsibility, Warren reasoned, he must have envisioned the job solely as a political platform from which to campaign for the governor's chair. This attitude did not square with Warren's concept of public service or being a team player, and it effectively banished Knight from the seat of power. From that moment, Warren later said, "I never paid any attention to what he was doing at all."[3]

At first Knight took on his formal role as presiding officer of the Senate and actively participated in the sessions, but not having a relationship with the governor made him easy to ignore. His relaxed approach to procedural detail and his outsized personality were a poor fit with the staid legislative chamber. On occasion, he would make a ruling that was greeted by groans of protest. After conferring with someone, he would blithely announce with an unconcerned shrug: "Well, my parliamentarian says I was wrong, so I hereby overrule myself."[4] At other times, he would reframe resolutions in such a puzzling way that senators did not know whether to vote yes or no.

In fact, Knight seemed less interested in the Senate's business than in playing to the galleries. If enough visitors were present, he might grab the microphone and explain the proceedings to them, or make an impromptu speech, complete with his characteristic grand gestures and wisecracks. Or he would interrupt debate to poke fun at individual lawmakers. "Ladies and gentlemen," he declared on one occasion, "I want you to know that just because your able and distinguished senators down here are sitting with their feet on their desks, reading newspapers, it does not mean they do not know what is going on."[5] His flamboyant approach to the job added color to the legislative give-and-take, but his antics risked his credibility as a serious future gubernatorial candidate. Warren's friends and advisors, in particular, saw him as a buffoon and an "amiable, lightweight hack."[6]

Whether or not he ever came to regret his rejection of Warren's offer, Knight's disappointment with his new job's limitations soon became evident. Resignedly, he said: "I get up every morning, go out on the front porch, unfold the paper, look at the biggest headline, and fold it up again. The only news a lieutenant governor could possibly be interested in would be that headline."[7]

He soon decided that he would spend his time doing what he enjoyed most — public speaking. Unlike Warren, who regarded speaking as a chore, Knight was a thoughtful student of oratory as it had been practiced decades ago. "Public speaking meant something in those days," Knight recalled. "Those men had to speak without microphones to huge crowds. It was a system that eliminated phonies.... We don't know our candidates like we used to."[8] Having already elevated the public address to an art form before coming to Sacramento, he was intent on accepting as many invitations as possible. He soon became one of the California Republican Party's most prominent spokesmen.

Traveling and speaking was more than just a way to keep busy. It served his long-term interests much better than sitting behind an empty desk in Sacramento. Knight had never made a secret of his ultimate ambition. As the author of a magazine portrait put it, he had been "busting his buttons" to be governor of California since about the age of five.[9] On a tour of the state capital in 1945, he was surprised to find that several areas of the governor's mansion were off limits to visitors. Not even a public official yet, he winked at a journalist and said that when he took over he would be more welcoming and friendly.

In 1946, that day seemed far off. Knight's friends encouraged him to run instead for the U.S. Senate in 1950, but as yet he had no interest in going to Washington, D.C.[10] He would just have to wait Warren out.

## *Clashing with the Governor*

Knight was not the first lieutenant governor of California to aspire openly to the governorship, but he must have realized that doing so would complicate his relationship with Warren. In the beginning, the two men appeared to get along reasonably well on a personal level. Warren poked fun at Knight's loquaciousness, sometimes calling him his "walkie-talkie," while Knight referred to the governor as "pearly Early."[11] An enthusiastic press account in 1947 noted that the two had become friends, and had even "gone grunion hunting together, swim shorts and all."[12]

In reality, of course, there was little warmth or communication between them. According to former aides of both men, neither visited the office of the other while Knight was lieutenant governor. Knight was a fine man, Warren once conceded, but he was a "will-o'-the-wisp." Warren assigned him occasional projects but only to "keep him busy, make his life worthwhile," as an aide put it.[13]

Knight's frustration was compounded by his awareness that Earl Warren was one of the most popular leaders in the history of the state. The job of governor seemed to be Warren's for as long as he wanted it. As the state's former attorney general and successful crime fighter, he impressed Californians with his air of strength and competence. Voters found him likeable, open, and down to earth, and they loved his vivacious family.

Warren's unattractive side was largely hidden from public view. Most significant for Knight, the governor had never been good at sharing the limelight — "as a consequence, if he saw anyone coming up from the ranks and developing power, he would devise ways to cut the fellow down."[14] It was clear that he would never embrace a lieutenant governor who openly coveted his job.

## *The 1948 Campaign*

To Knight's immense delight, however, Warren decided to seek the Republican presidential nomination in 1948. In this effort, he enlisted the help of his friend Bill Knowland and asked him to chair the California delegation — a role he would reprise four years later. Warren arrived at the party convention as a long-shot, well behind Thomas Dewey of New York and Harold Stassen of Minnesota. He did not improve his chances when he refused to engage in political deal-making and insisted on being nominated "in an orderly way, through direct and forthright action," or not at all.[15]

Dewey prevailed, even though he had been defeated by Roosevelt four years earlier. Once again, Dewey invited Warren to join him on the ticket. Warren was plainly reluctant to do so. In his memoirs, he claimed to have had little interest in presiding over the U.S. Senate, not to mention leaving a job that provided so many psychic rewards. Knowland advised him to say no and hold out for the top spot on the ticket in 1952.

But Warren felt that after two refusals to serve, the party would never extend him a third chance. So Warren joined Dewey in what most party professionals assumed would be a cakewalk over the struggling Democrats and embattled President Truman. Republicans had several reasons for optimism. It was commonly assumed (and polls confirmed) that the country was sick of Truman and that Dewey would win easily. The 1946 election had shown a conservative trend — Republicans had attained a majority in both the House and Senate for the first time since 1930.

When Dewey selected Warren as his running mate, Knight could hardly

At the beginning of Warren's second term as governor, he pretended to get along with his new lieutenant governor, Goodwin Knight (right), and they even "went grunion hunting together, swim shorts and all." But Warren and his advisors came to view the loquacious Goodie as an "amiable, lightweight hack" (California State Archives).

contain his excitement.[16] "It's no secret," Knight candidly recalled, "that I began making plans to move into the executive mansion."[17] The 1948 presidential campaign gave Knight an opportunity to help himself and his party at the same time. He worked hard for the Republican standard-bearers, logging thousands of miles and making dozens of speeches. As the campaign neared its end, he prepared to sell his home in Los Angeles and put finishing touches on a tentative list of senior appointments.

From the beginning, however, Warren was unimpressed with Dewey's complacency and bland speeches. "Maybe they know what they're doing," he said of Dewey's operation, "but I can tell you I never won any of *my* campaigns this way."[18] Nothing could be done to overcome Dewey's weakness or Truman's spirited attacks on the "do-nothing" Republican Congress.

In a stunning upset, Truman handed the Republicans their fifth consecutive loss in a presidential election. On that Tuesday evening in November,

Knight was rehearsing his inaugural speech. As the results came in, "the gloom was so thick in the usually gay lieutenant governor's suite that it could be sliced like salami."[19] Knight minced no words: "Some say that I'm a bitter man and desperately disappointed that I did not become California's governor. Well, they're right."[20]

After the election of 1948, Warren went back to work as governor. He "didn't talk about it, but for a while he was brusque and short," recalled Knight sometime later.[21] Warren's pride may have suffered a blow, but he could fall back on his untarnished prestige in California. If he wanted an unprecedented third term as governor in 1950, it was probably his for the asking.

Knight resumed his few duties without enthusiasm, increasingly frustrated and unhappy. The electoral debacle only added to his impatience, which in turn fed Warren's distrust of his second in command. Knight did not relish the prospect of running for the same job in 1950 and serving another term in Warren's shadow.

## Knight and the Republican Right

Administration harmony also fell victim to a growing split within the state Republican Party. Stung by the defeat of the national ticket and galvanized by increasing concern about an aggressive Soviet Union, the threat of world communism, and internal subversion, California's long quiescent conservatives began to stir. The immediate target of their ire was Warren and his liberal policies. They shuddered when he called himself part of the "vital center" of the political spectrum and argued for a universal health insurance program that looked to them like socialized medicine.

During this period, the national Republican Party was dominated by East Coast moderates, who adhered to a bipartisan, internationalist approach to postwar foreign relations and a middle-of-the-road domestic policy. Warren's nonpartisanship exemplified that kind of Republicanism. But when the United States experienced a dramatic series of setbacks in the late 1940s—including the Soviet acquisition of the atomic bomb and the victory of the Red Chinese over the Nationalist forces of U.S. ally Chiang Kai-shek—conservatives agitated for a harder line, both at home and abroad.

This split was no danger to Warren's political success. He did not need conservative Republicans to win elections. With the Democrats now the majority party in the state, he reached to his left rather than his right for the necessary votes.

In frustration, the party's right wing turned to Knight as a potential leader of its cause. Unlike Warren, he espoused core Republican positions on the important issues of the day. He decried the "creeping socialism" he saw taking hold in Washington and opposed Truman's controversial firing of General Douglas MacArthur. In 1951, Knight criticized Secretary of State Dean Acheson in unusually harsh terms, even for a conservative Republican, and ridiculed the secretary's "faltering, weasel words and doubletalk." Such passionate rhetoric made Knight a natural rallying point for anti–Warren sentiment.

Knight crossed an important line when he began to disagree with Warren in public. In 1949 the University of California came under pressure to ensure the allegiance of its faculty by requiring loyalty oaths. Warren opposed this idea as feckless, saying a Communist "would take the oath and laugh," but Knight sided immediately with the movement's supporters. When Warren, on the defensive, tried to insist that Knight was "100% loyal" to his administration, Knight commented: "Of course, that isn't a fact. The governor must know that I have never favored his compulsory health-insurance plan, and there are other points of difference."[22]

In private, Knight's comments about Warren revealed a certain amount of pettiness. Veteran correspondent Earl Behrens recalled that Knight would "criticize [Warren] very severely, on personal things, one thing and another." According to Behrens, the lieutenant governor sometimes alleged that Warren was in some way using his office for his personal benefit. He "peddled stories" that when the governor was in southern California, he would send the Highway Patrol back to Sacramento with his laundry and have it done there.[23]

After the election disaster, Warren increasingly perceived Knight as untrustworthy. "He personally worked against my father while he was lieutenant governor, which created considerable stress," recalled Warren's son, Earl Jr. "These things went on and on, and he was courting the ultraconservative elements of the party all the time.... So there was no great camaraderie between the two men."[24] Knight's increasing outspokenness did not cause an open break with the governor, but it ended any chance for an amicable relationship.

Unable to control the activities and statements of his second in command, Warren became concerned with preventing any damage Knight might do while he was out of the state. He claimed to have learned this lesson when the lieutenant governor, during one of the governor's absences, signed a San Francisco Bay bridge-building bill strongly influenced by special interests. He did so "believing he had accomplished a great political feat at my expense," said Warren later. Upon his return, he called Knight on the carpet: "Goodie, you may think you have achieved a great victory for yourself, but if so it has been at the expense of the people around San Francisco Bay."[25]

On another occasion as acting governor, Knight paroled two prisoners on humanitarian grounds, though he knew that Warren did not like to overrule judgments painstakingly reached by the courts.[26]

After these embarrassments, Warren never left the state without assigning someone to keep an eye on Knight. Once, while the governor was traveling in the East, his chief aide was given the task of "defending California from Goodie." He was to extend Knight every courtesy, but also to monitor his activities and keep pending legislation under lock and key.[27]

Knight's increasingly strident dissent from administration policies gave conservatives hope that he would challenge Warren in the 1950 party primary. Some of them formed a Knight-for-Governor committee, with backing from the powerful press tycoon and long-time financier of Republican politicians William Randolph Hearst. The lieutenant governor received praise (but not an endorsement) from the *Los Angeles Times* and political columnist Kyle Palmer. "Knight is a far better campaigner than Warren," Palmer wrote. "The party has never had a more personally popular leader."[28] According to the Los Angeles *Herald-Express*, it was "the consensus that Knight has [the allegiance of] a clear majority of [state] Republican officials."[29]

## Up to the Brink

The adulation clouded Knight's judgment about Warren's vulnerability. He decided to enter the race "if there should be a true indication that honest support will be forthcoming."[30] By mid–1949, the lieutenant governor was making three political appearances a day and looking for campaign financing. He hoped to become so well funded that Warren would see the handwriting on the wall and withdraw.

At a press conference in September, Knight declared confidently that the movement to draft him had reached "gigantic proportions."[31] He barely listened when *Times* columnist Palmer warned him to stay out of any "dogfight" with Warren and predicted that the result of a Republican split would be the election of a Democratic governor.[32] At a news conference, Knight said: "I'm a relaxed guy." Then he added a cocky prophecy: "And being governor won't change me."[33]

In fact, Warren had considered stepping down as governor after two terms, but Knight's attitude and behavior made him dig in his heels. "He is not a man to be pushed," said a Warren confidant.[34] The governor was clearly disdainful of what he called Knight's "self-conceived, self-financed, self-motivated, simulated draft."[35] In his memoirs, Warren stated plainly: "I might not have run for a third term had it not been for the intransigence of the lieutenant governor."[36] He may also have worried that a conservative Knight administration might reverse many of his programs.

For these reasons, plus an awareness that remaining in office would keep him in the limelight as the 1952 presidential election approached, Warren finally decided to run again in 1950. When his campaign workers reported difficulties in raising cash because of inroads made by Knight, Warren replied: "Well, if we can't get any financial support, we'll just have to run it without money."[37] Though his mind was made up, he did not bother to tell his lieutenant governor.

Knight, meanwhile, was calculating his chances of winning if Warren ran. He certainly would rather have avoided a struggle with the governor in the party primary, but his confidence was so high that he thought he could prevail regardless. Most of his friends disagreed. Long-time political reporter Earl Behrens warned him he would lose, and then echoed Kyle Palmer's conviction that, even if he somehow won, a Republican primary fight would guarantee a Democratic victory. Knight bristled at the prediction and pointed out that nine county Republican central committees had already endorsed him. Several political correspondents considered Knight's optimism naive and believed he had been used by conservatives who were trying to get at Warren.

Feeling momentum behind him, Knight somehow became convinced that Warren would not run again and began a bizarre negotiation with the popular San Francisco mayor, George Christopher, who he wanted as his running mate. Christopher liked Knight and was flattered by his interest, but he did not want to have to guess at Warren's intentions. So Christopher picked up the phone, called the governor, and asked if he was running. Warren assured him that he was. The mayor reported this news back to Knight, who said: "Well, I'm going to run anyway." Christopher then said: "You may, but I won't."[38]

Warren's declaration, which he soon made public, burst Knight's bubble and effectively put an end to his candidacy. Senior party leaders worked to avert the electoral disaster they felt would follow a Knight challenge and finally were able to persuade him to put the interests of the party first. Again Knight briefly considered running for the vacant Senate seat, but his real interest was in state politics. He would seek reelection in 1950 as lieutenant governor and continue waiting for Warren to move on.

Now having no significant Republican opposition, Warren coasted through the primary. In November, he had little difficulty beating the Democratic candidate, James Roosevelt, son of the late president. Even in victory, Warren remained bitter. He blasted Knight in his memoirs for "running for governor throughout his entire term of office" and blamed him for the conservative rebellion that threatened to undo his administration. "My lieutenant governor," he said, "devoted his four years in office to creating a schism in the party."[39]

In truth, Knight had been guilty of little more than opportunism. Warren was correct about his aspirations, but Knight had not provoked the growing division between Republican moderates and conservatives — he had merely exploited it. He may have disagreed with Warren's more liberal policies, but he did not envision a Knight administration as a departure from its predecessor. "I didn't really have any quarrel with Warren," he admitted later. "I just wanted to be governor. I was tired of being lieutenant governor."[40]

In the end, the personality and style of each man led to mistakes. Warren tended to be controlling and suspicious. Had he made additional efforts to include Knight in the affairs of government, Knight might have remained loyal and brushed off suggestions that he mount a challenge in 1950. For his part, Knight was indiscreet and impatient. Had he shown greater tactical flexibility in pursuing his ambitions, he might not have aroused the anxieties of the proud and sensitive Warren. Their lack of mutual trust and their inability to communicate led to conflict, wasted effort, and inefficiency, for which both men, as well as the people of California, paid a price.

The split with Knight and the growing rebellion within the state Republican Party were sources of great concern for Warren as he considered his chances for president in 1952. He needed to be seen as a unifying rather than a divisive figure if he wanted to attract attention as a potential national candidate. Still angry over Knight's apostasy, he now had to worry about the loyalty of the California delegation to the party's convention in Chicago, even though it was pledged to support him. One of his least favorite politicians, Richard Nixon, would be a member of that delegation.

# 6

# *The Rivals and the Nixon-Douglas Race*

Richard Nixon served two terms in the House of Representatives. By any measure, he turned in a strong performance. His energy, shrewdness, persistence and discipline propelled him to national attention less than two years after taking office.

With his party in the majority upon his arrival in Washington in 1947, Nixon was given choice committee assignments — for education and labor. *Newsweek* called his first speech in Congress "intensely sincere" with "a quality of steel behind the voice," yet all delivered in "calm, measured tones."[1] He would continue to attract mostly positive media treatment throughout his two terms.

## *An Impressive Debut*

Nixon took a serious and thoughtful approach to legislative matters. A profile in *Fortnight* magazine called him a "scholarly — but unstuffy — man of assiduous work habits, with a reputation for thoroughness and integrity."[2] He struck up a friendship with John Kennedy, who contributed a modest amount to his reelection campaign. During his first term, he stayed in close touch with his constituents, wrote a weekly column, and worked without letup.

At considerable risk to his young political career, Nixon parted company with a large number of Republicans, especially conservative isolationists, by supporting the Truman administration's Marshall Plan for European recovery. A trip to Western Europe convinced him of the importance of American economic aid in reducing the attractiveness of Communism to countries rebuilding after the war. The people in his district were skeptical of such a large financial commitment, but he spent a month in California selling the plan and was so convincing that his popularity at home actually increased. Despite a lack of foreign policy experience, his stand showed that he was developing a well considered and independent view of America's security interests abroad.

Nixon also displayed skill as a legislator. He played a minor but not insignificant role in the writing and passage by the House of the Taft-Hartley bill, which modified the mostly pro-union National Labor Relations Act of the Roosevelt years. He summarized the issues so smoothly in an essay for his constituents and fellow congressmen that thousands of reprints were ordered. Nixon and John Kennedy staged a debate on the bill at a local political gathering. He also associated himself with an effort, led by Karl Mundt of South Dakota, to place limitations on Communist activities in the United States.

## The Hiss Case and the Elections of 1948

The coming of the 1948 presidential campaign reawakened his uneasy relationship with Earl Warren. Nixon was still an admirer of his friend Harold Stassen of Minnesota and considered him the most electable of the possible Republican nominees. But he was also impressed with Warren's efforts to become a viable candidate. He wrote to an associate that the governor was "playing his cards very cleverly in his bid for the nomination."[3]

The Warren forces tried to enlist Nixon as a delegate to the convention in Philadelphia, but Nixon refused, out of loyalty to Stassen. "My own opinion," he wrote to Roy Day, "is that Earl Warren would do well to have some understanding with Stassen because I think by convention time, Stassen will be the strongest single factor there."[4] In sum, Nixon was "something less than an ardent Warren supporter," as one of his friends put it.[5]

When Dewey finally prevailed, Warren accepted the number-two spot. Though he had backed the wrong horse, Nixon recovered quickly and joined Bill Knowland in posing with Warren as the convention came to a close. Nixon publicly expressed pleasure that Warren was on the ticket, calling him a "great asset as a vote getter in California and other states where the battle will be close."[6] Warren thanked him for his help.

Beginning that summer, Nixon found himself taking another big career gamble. He decided to pursue allegations that Alger Hiss, one of America's most impeccably credentialed public servants, had been a spy for the Soviet Union. His role in the effort was made possible by his unsought membership in the mostly moribund House Un-American Activities Committee, whose work until then had mostly been an embarrassment.

Nixon's leadership in the committee's dramatic confrontation with Hiss during the last half of 1948 has been exhaustively described elsewhere. It is enough to say that by dint of his usual dogged persistence and his skill as an interrogator, he trapped Hiss into making inconsistent statements, which ultimately revealed that he had been passing state secrets to the Russians in the 1930s. By mid–1950, when Hiss was convicted, the case had become a national sensation. It made Nixon one of the best known members of the House of Representatives and a hero to many on the Republican right.

The apparent guilt of a man who had accompanied President Roosevelt to Yalta in 1945 shocked the country's Democratic establishment, especially the Truman administration. Nixon may have done the country a favor by exposing Hiss, but his aggressive prosecutorial manner and disdain for Hiss' defenders infuriated leading liberals. Instead of recognizing the issue of Communist infiltration as a serious problem in need of a bipartisan solution, Truman and the Democrats reflexively labeled the Nixon investigation a red herring. Writer A.J. Liebling observed that "it is un–American not to convict anybody Congressman Nixon doesn't like."[7] The conduct and outcome of the Hiss case would color the views of many leading Democrats toward Nixon for years to come.

In October 1948, Nixon made a speaking tour in support of the Republican ticket. Privately, he worried that the party leadership was "rolling in complacency," though he wrote that "Warren is *very* well thought of every place I go ... probably more popular than Dewey."[8] At the same time, he criticized the level of effort Warren was making. He confided to an aide that he "might as well be sitting on his butt in Sacramento for all the help he has given us."[9] When the press wondered why he had little praise for the vice presidential candidate, he replied weakly that people "would have thought I was unduly biased if I had built up a fellow Californian too much."[10] On election day, he watched in dismay as Dewey went down to defeat and the Republicans once again became the minority party in the House of Representatives.

Nixon had little trouble with his own campaign that year. He ran for reelection against an under-funded, little-known opponent. He was well enough known by then to strike an above-party pose, while his operatives again aided his cross-filing effort by mailing out literature addressed to "Fellow Democrats." Financial aid from Stassen found its way to Nixon's campaign — a blatant violation of Warren's non-interference doctrine and a continuing irritant to the governor. Nixon spent most of the fall in Washington, focusing on his congressional duties. In general, he avoided the exaggerated statements that had marred the Voorhis campaign and, cross-filing, easily won both the Republican and Democratic primaries.

## 6 — The Rivals and the Nixon-Douglas Race

In the aftermath of an otherwise discouraging year for Republicans, Nixon basked in favorable publicity. *Newsweek* called him the "most outstanding member of the present Congress." Raymond Moley, an original member of Roosevelt's brain trust, described him as a rising star. Conservative commentator Fulton Lewis, Jr., told an audience that Nixon was "one of the truly great youths to cut a swath across Congress." The congressman was especially proud of a cable from FBI chief J. Edgar Hoover. "The conviction of Alger Hiss," Hoover wrote, "was due to your patience and persistence alone."[11]

In sum, as the elections of 1950 approached, Nixon had emerged as a figure of national importance.

### Considering the Senate

Despite his remarkable celebrity as a congressman, Nixon was becoming impatient with the slow pace of life in the House of Representatives and the frustrations of his junior status. "You come to Washington, you have great ideas, and there you are in the committees and on the floor of the House, and you have an inability to implement your ideas," he said later. He disparaged many of his colleagues as people who "know how to play the game" for their own benefit, or "Don Quixotes, who never accomplish anything."[12] He confided to a friend that he would "either become a Senator or return to Whittier and practice law."[13] His associate, Bill Arnold, believed that he had "a secret ambition" to seek the presidency someday.[14]

A big step in that direction would be a successful run for the U.S. Senate. Nixon began considering such a move after winning reelection in 1948, though he wanted his interest in the job kept secret. In a note to Roy Day in California, he wrote: "I see no reason ... why my name should not be discussed provided, of course, that there is no indication that I had been consulted."[15] Day replied that he was "throwing out feelers on the Senator deal and the reaction seems good."[16] Nixon's prominent role in the Hiss case gave him favorable name recognition throughout most of California, but he would still face long odds against incumbent Democratic senator Sheridan Downey. Nixon prided himself on being a risk-taker and was not worried by the likelihood of strong competition.

But he also knew that he was the junior man among California's most prominent Republican politicians and had to be careful not to be at cross purposes with any of them. So he cautiously explored the attitudes of Warren, Knowland and Knight toward his prospective candidacy. The interplay among the four men during 1949 provides a revealing insight into their relationship at this early stage of their rivalry.

The plans of both Warren and Knight were unclear in the first months of the year. Knight wanted to run for governor in 1950, but he did not know whether Warren intended to seek a third term. Knight also had the option of running for the Senate, in which case Nixon, if he ran too, would face an uphill primary battle against a popular, well known politician.

As he surveyed the political landscape in 1949, Nixon had to take into account the decisive influence of the media, particularly the *Los Angeles Times*, in determining Republican candidates for high office. Aide Frank Jorgensen, writing to his boss from California in March, predicted that "whoever the *Times* lays its hands on" would be supported by the state's three major papers. According to Jorgensen, the *Oakland Tribune*'s Joe Knowland had used up a favor four years earlier, when he appealed to the *Times* to endorse his son Bill for the Senate. The *Times* had gone along then — now it was in the driver's seat. Jorgensen urged Nixon to continue cultivating *Times* political editor Kyle Palmer, "who is favorable to you," in hopes of getting the paper's blessing.[17]

In June 1949, Nixon decided to have a talk with Bill Knowland about the Senate vacancy. In view of Warren's well known reluctance to endorse other Republicans, he suspected that a Knowland endorsement might be crucial. He paid a call on the senator and asked if he could count on his backing. The response he got was not reassuring. "[Knowland] left me with the impression that in the event I appeared to be the strongest candidate, he would be very glad to give me every support," he wrote to Jorgensen. In other words, Knowland was also waiting to see what Knight and Warren were planning to do.

In the conversation, Nixon let Knowland know that he did not wish to antagonize Warren or Knight. "I told him that I did not intend to get into a fight with the party leaders in California, and I would not run unless I felt that it was with their approval," he said to Jorgensen. "Incidentally," he continued, "I wish that Kyle [Palmer] could some way get that same information to Warren." He concluded on a determined note. "My own feeling," he wrote, "is that if they give me the green light, I should like to do it."[18]

His letters reveal that, despite his ambition, Nixon was irreproachably deferential to his California political elders. The fact that he would attempt to use the political editor of the *Los Angeles Times* as an intermediary between himself and the governor of the state on such matters illustrates Kyle Palmer's inordinate influence on the political process. With the largest and most influential newspaper in the state a key player in Republican Party circles, it is no wonder that Republicans dominated the state long after they were outnumbered by Democrats.

In fact, one of Jorgensen's letters to Nixon was a report on Palmer's views of the upcoming races. Palmer told Jorgensen that Knight would ultimately run for reelection as lieutenant governor and would thus not stand in the way of a Nixon Senate run. He also believed that Democrat James Roosevelt would go up against Warren for governor and Representative Helen Gahagan Douglas would contest the Democratic senatorial primary against the incumbent Sheridan Downey. All of these predictions came to pass. He also told Jorgensen what Nixon wanted to hear — that Warren had "definitely come around to the point of where he would support you."[19]

These messages show Nixon's understandable reluctance to communicate directly with either Warren or Knight about their plans — after all, he was only a junior congressman. But even Goodwin Knight felt uncomfortable asking Warren a direct question about his candidacy for governor in 1950 and allowed himself to be kept in the dark for weeks. Both facts say as much about Warren's aloof, imperious — and perhaps somewhat intimidating — political style as they do about either Nixon or Knight.

Nixon was even willing to give up a significant source of funds if he thought it would help earn Warren's blessing. A California oil executive had pledged a "substantial amount of money" and active involvement in a Nixon campaign for the Senate, but he did not get along with Warren. As a result, he was not offered any significant role on the Nixon team. "We must be most cautious of Warren's relationship," wrote Jorgensen.[20]

Another Nixon operative in California, Herman Perry, wrote a few days later with more intelligence from Palmer. "Kyle informed me privately Warren and Knowland had agreed to support you if and when you announced yourself as a candidate," Perry noted on June 17. "*I suppose, however,*" Perry continued, "*this will be a behind-the-walls endorsement* and not an open one."[21] In other words, their support sounded more like acquiescence than active backing. But it was close enough to the green light Nixon had been seeking.

Perry suggested that Nixon approach Knowland again to confirm what Palmer had told him. Nixon declined to do so, believing the ball to be in Knowland's court and being unwilling to embarrass him by pressing too hard. Despite Perry's assurances, Nixon "did not have the impression that the matter was settled."[22] Nixon's willingness to endure the uncertainty of Knowland's position for as long as necessary seemed to show that his relationship with the senior senator was still a formal and distant one.

The tentative news that Nixon did not have to worry about the opposition of Warren and Knowland shifted his concern to Goodwin Knight. "The rumors continue to reach me that Goodie Knight is giving very serious consideration toward running, [though he] also said that he didn't want to run against me," Nixon wrote to Perry. "My opinion is that if Knight decides to go it would be very difficult for me to run against him."[23]

For a while, a Knight attempt for the Senate seemed likely, although he clearly was more interested in Warren's job. Another of Nixon's California allies, Pat Hillings, wrote the congressman on July 20 that Knight had told him he was not going to run for lieutenant governor again, saying "you can draw your own conclusions from that as to what I'm going to do next year."[24] Hillings took that to mean a Senate run.

Nixon did not rule out a race against Knight in the Republican primary. His California staffers, in a series of letters that summer, assessed his chances against the lieutenant governor. One of them, Bernard Brennan, observed that Knight would have the edge in control of the state party machinery but that Nixon would be more electable if he could get past the primary. Jorgensen wrote that Knight "is the strongest man of those who have indicated interest today" but that "his strength results more from his personal popularity and loyalty to the party than it does to any confidence in his soundness on issues or his potential effectiveness in the Senate."[25] He told Nixon that he could cut into Knight's lead if he made an extensive tour of the state.

For the next several weeks Nixon continued to wait as matters sorted themselves out in California. Everything seemed to hinge on Warren's plans. Jorgensen and a friend of Hillings talked to Knight in mid-July and found him preoccupied with the governor. "He repeated the oft made remark that Warren confides in no one," Jorgensen relayed to Nixon. "It is obvious that Knight does not have completely high regard for Warren."[26] "He made some derogatory remarks" about the governor, one campaign worker told Hillings, "but is obviously afraid of him."[27]

The *Los Angeles Times* and political editor Palmer viewed a Nixon-Knight primary battle for a Senate seat as a potential disaster for the party and moved quickly to influence events. According to Roy Day, the *Times* was discouraging Knight all they could and "are for you definitely, but Bernie [Brennan] doubts if they would endorse anyone if you both ran."[28]

A *Times* writer then told Pat Hillings that the paper was considering an endorsement of Nixon once he decided to enter the race. "Apparently Kyle and Chandler like you a little more as of this date," Hillings wrote on July 21. Soon, Nixon learned from Jorgensen that Chandler had written a private letter promising the paper's support for a Nixon Senate candidacy. Nixon wrote back that he was glad to hear it. He tried his best not to alienate Knight as he groped toward a decision. Aware of this danger, Hillings strongly suggested that "you and Goodie should sit down and talk about this thing" in order to prevent any misunderstanding.[29]

At this point the lieutenant governor was well disposed toward the second-term congressman. Hillings, after meeting with Knight in California, wrote that he "seems to think a lot of Nixon." Jorgensen, too, came away from a conversation with Knight believing that "Goodie has a good opinion of our group."[30] Finally, Roy Day asked Knight point blank in early August if he would be willing to rule out a Senate run and back Nixon. "Well, Roy," Knight allegedly said, "can you get that guy [Warren] out of Sacramento and I'll take that and take my coat off and go to bat for Dick. I like him, he is a grand guy."[31]

Nixon spent the entire month of August on pins and needles, as Knight announced on the 4th that he could "be of no further service to the people in my present position."[32] Since few believed he would dare run against Warren for governor, Jorgensen again advised that "we should hold up until we know what Goodie will do."[33] Knight's indecision complicated Nixon's life right into the fall, as Knight announced for governor at the end of August and then backpedaled under pressure from party officials appalled at the prospect of a primary struggle with Warren. In the meantime, Nixon made a two-week swing through California to test the political waters.

After he returned to Washington, everything seemed to fall into place. Knight decided to run again for lieutenant governor, allowing Nixon to enter the Republican Senate primary without significant opposition. Chandler helped to persuade the editors of the largest northern California dailies, the *San Francisco Chronicle* and *Oakland Tribune*, to get behind Nixon's bid. With the *Tribune's* backing came word of Bill Knowland's now unqualified support — news that "cleared the atmosphere considerably."[34]

This episode clearly illustrates the interrelatedness of the rivals' career decisions. If Knight had opted for the Senate in 1950 and Nixon had opposed him in the Republican primary, Knight may well have won. He was a popular lieutenant governor with a strong following in the state party, though he would have had to overcome the opposition of the *Times*. Without his Senate seat, Nixon would not have been considered a candidate for vice president in 1952, and his career would have followed a different trajectory. He might never have been president. But things broke his way.

Even so, his decision to run for the Senate was taken with due regard for the equities of all his rivals and in full recognition of his status as the junior man in the relationship. He showed himself to be ambitious but also patient and prudent. Though he had the valuable endorsement of the *Times* in his back pocket, he decided not to flaunt it. Warren may well have been unenthusiastic about his candidacy, but the arguments of Palmer, the support of the *Times*, and Nixon's correct behavior had left him no good reason to oppose it.

Nixon seemed to be putting the interests of the Republican Party ahead of his own. He voiced a willingness to take a back seat to Knight in the Senate race, writing early in his decision making process that someone has to put on a "vigorous, fighting campaign" and Knight is "the only one who could fill this bill." Of course, his view of his own chances changed later, but neither Warren, Knight nor Knowland had any reason to be critical of his conduct.

## *The Nixon-Douglas Campaign*

In early June, as Nixon was weighing his options, he received a note from California congresswoman Helen Gahagan Douglas with a clipping attached. "Dear Richard," the note began, "Have you seen this? I thought it would amuse you." It was an article from a local newsletter, the *Alhambra Legionnaire*, urging the two of them to run for the Senate. "I'll pay two bucks anytime to hear these two representatives talk," the author concluded, "and so will you." In view of his agonizing that summer, Nixon may have been more startled than amused by the Douglas note.

In the end, the *Legionnaire* writer got his wish. Nixon and Douglas found themselves running for the Senate a year later in a campaign whose bitter legacy would follow Nixon the rest of his career. Much has been written about the Nixon-Douglas campaign by historians seeking the roots of Nixon's later conduct as president, but the campaign was equally important in shaping his relationship with the other California rivals, especially Warren.

Nixon was the beneficiary of good fortune from the very start of his Senate run. He expected his opponent to be incumbent Sheridan Downey, a well-regarded conservative Democrat seeking a third term. But Downey, facing a left-wing challenge from Representative Douglas, retired from the race, citing health reasons. Nixon breathed a sign of relief. "Her entry," he later wrote, "brightened my prospects considerably."[35]

Helen Douglas was not only a congresswoman but also a beautiful actress, the wife of actor Melvin Douglas, and a liberal Democrat. A Senate race in the nation's fastest growing and most glamorous state, involving Douglas and the man whose persistence brought down Alger Hiss, was bound to attract national attention — and it did. *Newsweek* wrote a feature article in August 1950 about the importance of the contest as a referendum on the performance of the Truman administration and an indication of how the country might trend in the presidential elections of 1952.

Early on, Nixon decided to focus his campaign on foreign affairs, in view of his acknowledged expertise on the threat of world communism and Douglas' perceived vulnerabilities in that area. This choice of a battleground was almost by itself an election-winning strategy. Every time Nixon sounded the alarm about Soviet or Chinese intentions, the theft of atomic secrets, or the possibility of security compromises at the top levels of government, dramatic world events seemed to validate his concerns. Immediately after the 1950 primaries, for example, North Korean troops poured across the demilitarized zone into South Korea, eliciting an energetic response from President Truman. The timing could not have been worse for Douglas.

And she could easily be portrayed as soft on the kinds of threats that were dominating headlines in 1950. She was widely known as a bleeding heart liberal, even among Democrats. She had voted against aid to the Greek government when it was in danger of collapsing under communist pressure and against the continued existence of the House Un-American Affairs Committee which, in truth, had seemed feckless before Nixon energized it. But such votes looked shortsighted in retrospect and caused many to doubt her toughness.

Douglas was further weakened by disarray in the state Democratic Party. She faced a primary challenge from Manchester Boddy, a local newspaper publisher, who questioned her anti-communist credentials even before Nixon did. His reference to her as the "pink lady" was later copied by the Nixon forces.[36]

Outgoing Democratic senator Sheridan Downey made matters worse by questioning her ability and qualifications and calling her an "articulate spokesman for the Soviet line."[37] He also declared that he would vote for Nixon in the general election if Douglas won the primary. Nixon's people watched with undisguised glee and amazement as Boddy and Downey provided arguments against Douglas that they could later recycle. Despite these blistering attacks from fellow Democrats, Douglas managed to beat Boddy in the primary.

The Douglas general election campaign against Nixon, once it got under way, was riddled with amateurism. "When compared with the surgeons of the Nixon camp," said Nixon biographer Earl Mazo, "Mrs. Douglas' operators performed like apprentice butchers."[38] Douglas had an ineffective statewide staff, no clearly defined strategy, and an inadequate fund-raising apparatus. The candidate, too, was a drag on the ticket, because she was unable to discipline her public performances. "She talked too long," recalled future Democratic governor Pat Brown. "She would talk very long."[39]

Defying logic, Douglas and her staff also decided to attempt to portray Nixon as more pro-communist than she was — she criticized him, for example, for opposing aid to Korea. To Nixon, who attained national fame by unmasking a Soviet spy, this attack from the right was a clear sign of ineptness and desperation. "The charge that I was a Communist sympathizer," he correctly pointed out, "had no public credibility whatever."[40]

Adding to his considerable and growing advantage, Nixon was assured of robust support from the *Times*. The newspaper gave him three times as much coverage as his Democratic opponent and never ran a picture of Douglas during the campaign. On the pages of the *Times,* Nixon was extolled as "young, forward looking, aggressive and able," while Douglas was dismissed as "the darling of the Hollywood parlor pinks and Reds."[41]

The rest of the press followed the *Times*' lead. According to one analysis, nine of eleven major papers in the state backed Nixon, and one of the remaining two was neutral. Put another way, a Stanford University study showed that Nixon was backed by newspapers having 1,323,000 readers while the readership of Douglas-supported papers amounted to 265,000.[42] Of the 235 statements about Douglas published by the Hearst-owned *Los Angeles Examiner,* another study noted, 67 percent were judged to be unfavorable and 2 percent favorable.

Nixon also had an unusually strong staff of operatives in California. Men such as Frank Jorgensen, Pat Hillings, and Roy Day were skilled organizers and political analysts, and they were dedicated to Nixon's success. As the candidate was making his decision to run, Jorgensen and others were setting up committees, getting promises of funds, and recruiting campaign workers. Nixon's Senate campaign, like all of his California campaigns, was far better planned and executed than that of his Democratic opponent.

Nixon took nothing for granted, however. He knew that Republicans in California were greatly outnumbered and that they had to sell their candidates aggressively. If he were to be elected, he would need the votes of a sizeable number of Democrats. As in previous elections, Murray Chotiner and his associates established "Democrats for Nixon" groups and issued leaflets titled "As One Democrat to Another." California Democrats condemned these tactics as "deceitful devices."

With Chotiner's help, Nixon mounted a campaign centered on fear of communism. The conviction of Hiss just prior to the June primary gave him an opportunity to lambaste the Truman administration for allegedly blocking the exposure of additional espionage activity. Suggestions that the administration, which had successfully ended the war and developed the Marshall Plan, was somehow soft on communism enraged the president. Without hesitation, he endorsed Douglas for the Senate, calling her opponent a "no-good sonofabitch who hopes to be president someday."[43]

The best known of Nixon's "deceitful devices" was the infamous pink sheet, in which he attempted to compare Douglas' voting record in Congress with that of one of the most outspokenly radical congressmen then serving — Vito Marcantonio of New York. It was a flyer, printed on suggestive pink paper, which pointed out that the "Douglas-Marcantonio axis" had voted the same way over 90 percent of the time.

As proof of ideological compatibility, the analysis was highly inaccurate, because the vast majority of votes were on uncontroversial bills (at least among congressmen who were left of center), concerning such subjects as school-lunch programs or labor relations. But, as Jerry Voorhis had found four years earlier, challenging the conclusions of such a claim bill by bill took time and effort.

Even Herb Klein, later an intimate of Nixon as president, considered the pink sheet a "smearing distortion.... I was glad I had no part in the idea."[44] Nixon aide William Arnold later claimed that when Nixon saw the pink sheet, he said it was going too far and ordered that the rest of the printing be done in blue.[45] In reality, the candidate had no such compunctions. In pointing out that the flyer was Boddy's idea, Nixon later wrote: "All we added was the mordant comment of the color of the paper."[46]

The Nixon tactic that most infuriated Democrats, as well as many Republicans, was his clever way of saying something without quite saying it. The technique required practice and planning — two of Nixon's strong suits — and great precision in language. Nixon was able to link his opponent with the darkest forces in American society in a very personal way without making a direct charge. He said of Helen Douglas that "if she had her way, the Communist conspiracy would never have been exposed and Alger Hiss would still be influencing the foreign policy of the United States." And he asked rhetorically: "Why has she followed the Communist line so many times?" Nixon knew that Douglas was not a Communist, and he did not say she was. But a listener might easily come away with that impression. Nixon nevertheless insisted years later that he had never questioned Douglas' patriotism.

In one of his numerous attacks on the Truman administration and its foreign policy during the campaign, Nixon denounced Secretary of State Dean Acheson's "spineless school of diplomacy, which cost the free world 600,000,000 former allies." He did not say Acheson was a coward or a communist, yet he clearly implied it. Also, he relied on the average voter's ignorance of the reasons for the fall of China to the communists in 1949, defining for rhetorical purposes every Chinese citizen as a U.S. ally and blaming the administration for an event that could not have been prevented by any diplomacy, spineless or otherwise.

It was not the content but the style of Nixon's campaign that distinguished it from other races around the country. Republicans everywhere were running on the same issues and accusing their opponents of being soft on communism. By 1950 the party was desperate to regain power and appeared to be willing to do or say almost anything to win elections. But most Republicans were able to criticize Democrats without evoking the same wrath that Nixon did. Journalist William Lee Miller compared the "stodgy, earth-bound" language of William Knowland, who was known for his civility, to the "higher flights" of Nixonian innuendo.[47]

Nixon's calculated approach to speechmaking and his rigorous use of language conveyed the impression that he was more interested in winning votes than in advancing a particular set of policies. It did not help his reputation for sincerity when he told journalists after the election that his apparent anger at Douglas and the Democrats was staged. "The only time to lose your temper," he told a political writer, "is when it's deliberate." It was during the Douglas campaign that Nixon's opponents began referring to him as "Tricky Dick."

In the years ahead, Nixon would — perhaps unwisely — reveal additional details of his technique. "An efficient off-the-cuff appearance, according to Mr. Nixon," one magazine reported, "entails many hours of preparatory work."[48] One analyst of Nixon's behavior noted the ultimate absurdity — that "he will even pretend to be angry when he honestly is."[49] Such revelations helped launch a critical reappraisal of his conduct in the Douglas race.

## *Seeking Warren's Endorsement (Again)*

Earl Warren's view of the Senate race that year was colored by Nixon's growing prominence as a rallying point for anti–Warren sentiment. By 1950, the grumbling of conservative Republicans against Warren's liberal administration had swelled into a full-fledged rebellion. They gathered around Goodwin Knight when the lieutenant governor thought of mounting a primary challenge, and his sudden withdrawal left them in a state of frustration. Now Nixon's Senate candidacy gave them another cause to support.

Though he had not been openly critical of the governor, Nixon found himself receiving encouragement from anti–Warren Republicans. In their eyes, he was now Warren's chief rival for control of the state GOP. Groups like the Partisan Republicans, made up of southern California conservatives, called Warren "wishy-washy and namby-pamby" and proclaimed Nixon as their new champion. The Hearst newspapers and the *Los Angeles Times* began to view Nixon as more authentically Republican than Warren and were excited by his energetic campaign style. It was easy for Warren to see Nixon's popularity as a negative judgment on his governorship.

Warren's stubborn independence had also alienated some of his longtime supporters. Bernard Brennan, who had backed the governor's 1948 vice presidential bid, jumped ship and accepted the chairmanship of Nixon's Senate campaign. In a way, Warren's success as a nonpartisan governor was helping Nixon succeed as a partisan Republican.

The mounting differences between them were both stylistic and substantive. Nixon's tendency toward excess in campaigning was unattractive because it seemed to show how important winning was to him. Warren, on the other hand, always said that if he could not win without making deals or compromising his principles, he would be content with just having made the effort. He had a preference for a "snug, uncomplicated kind of politics" in which civility prevailed and losing did not mean the end of the world. Nixon appeared to believe that was exactly what losing meant.[50]

The governor was also much more relaxed than Nixon about the Red Menace and was uncomfortable with Nixon's criticism of the Truman administration's national security policies. Warren sympathized with many leading Democrats who now found their patriotism in question. He had never used the Red Scare as a weapon in his campaigns, and he considered Nixon's apparent attacks on Douglas' patriotism "grotesquely unfair."[51] He recognized Murray Chotiner's hand behind many of the Nixon campaign's tactics. In a note to his assistant, Merrell Small, he wrote that Chotiner was "not content with defeating an opponent.... He wants to destroy."[52]

While Nixon was battling Douglas, Warren had his hands full with James Roosevelt in his bid to win a third term as governor. As usual, he was running on his own rather than in association with other Republican contenders. Nixon was willing to accept that reality in the beginning. A large percentage of his supporters had broken with the governor over his increasingly liberal policies, and Nixon calculated initially that too close an association with Warren might actually damage his chances. So he went to Sacramento to suggest to Warren personally that they run separate campaigns. The governor, cool and correct, agreed to do what he intended to do anyway. "Warren wasn't having anything to do with him, that's for sure," recalled party official Keith McCormac.[53]

Later, Nixon decided that he might need the extra votes a Warren endorsement would provide. So his representatives returned to Sacramento with the recommendation that the two men run on a "packaged Republican ticket." As Earl Warren, Jr. remembered, a testy exchange ensued. The Nixon people "demanded that they throw in together, and he said, 'I can't do it.' And they repeated the demand, 'You must do it!' and he said, 'I'm sorry, I won't.'"[54]

Many Republicans agreed with Nixon about the benefit of a coordinated approach to the 1950 elections and tried to get the governor to bend a little. One of them, Kyle Palmer, brought Warren and Nixon together at a dinner party at the Chandler's. According to one of those present, Nixon stood in front of a fireplace, told war stories, and tried to charm the governor into forming an alliance. After the party was over, an aide asked Warren if he had been persuaded. "Oh, let Nixon take care of himself," he said angrily.[55]

Nixon did not give up; instead, he pursued a different tack. His campaign workers anonymously attended several Warren rallies and asked him to clarify his position on the Senate race, hoping to embarrass him into saying something nice about Nixon, but he rebuffed their questions. "I don't make it a policy of endorsing candidates for other offices," he said. "I'm interested in only one campaign — my own."[56]

His personal feelings about Nixon aside, Warren had other reasons for maintaining his distance. According to Earl Jr., he believed that if he endorsed Nixon, other Republican candidates would wonder why he did not endorse them as well. He also felt that his support would not necessarily be helpful. He was cognizant of the uncertainties of trying for a third term as governor of a state that had rarely allowed an incumbent to serve more than one, and he claimed to fear dragging down other Republicans if he did not do well.[57]

But Nixon's backers found Warren's lack of support unfathomable. "There was always a feeling that the governor of the state should have endorsed the Republican nominee for the Senate," said Nixon ally Pat Hillings. "It was awkward, but, of course, that was Warren."[58] As Nixon biographer Ralph de Toledano pointed out: "From the start of the campaign, Governor Warren ... said openly that he would not raise a finger for Nixon — and he kept his word." Similarly, he neither privately nor publicly ever expressed approval of Nixon's part in unmasking Alger Hiss.

Finally, Douglas provided Nixon with a small opening — she formally endorsed Democrat James Roosevelt for governor. Warren's impulsive reaction showed that he was no ordinary Republican. He prided himself on his nonpartisan appeal to both parties, and her decision, predictable though it might have been, was a blow to his ego. Angrily, he exclaimed: "In view of [Mrs. Douglas' statement], I might ask her how she expects I will vote when I mark my ballot for US Senator."[59] The Nixon forces were exultant. They had what seemed to be a statement of support.

In fact, contrary to what Warren was trapped into saying in public, it is possible that he favored Douglas. In addition to his blunt denunciations of Nixon's campaign tactics, Warren did not object when several high-powered Democrats came to California to give Douglas a boost, even though he had been quick to express disapproval of Harold Stassen's offer to campaign for Nixon in 1946.

Warren's son claimed that his father was never pro–Douglas — he was simply appalled by the Nixon campaign. "The Nixon people were very arrogant.... They came and said, 'This is what we're going to do.'"[60] Earl Jr. dated the schism between the two men to the bad feeling generated by this episode.

Nixon's margin of victory in the 1950 election was the largest of any senator elected or reelected that year. Despite criticism of his campaign, many Americans considered Nixon a breath of fresh air — a bright young man in tune with the times. He received hearty congratulations from some prominent Americans. FBI chief J. Edgar Hoover wrote: "Your victory was the greatest good that can come to our country." Herbert Brownell, a future attorney general under Eisenhower and key political strategist for Tom Dewey in 1948, praised Nixon's "brilliant campaign."

## *Legacy of Distrust*

After the election, Nixon's supporters remained bitter about Warren's studied indifference to the Senate race, and they irritated the governor by continuing to ask the reason for it. Pressed for a response at a National Press Club luncheon in Washington, with Nixon also in attendance, he responded angrily: "I am sure Dick knows whose corner I was in." Glancing at the uncomfortable Nixon, he continued: "And I am sure that whoever asked that question is no friend of Dick's or mine."[61] This ambiguous answer did little to satisfy Nixon or his backers.

A few days later, Nixon allowed some of his resentment toward Warren to slip out. The third-term governor and new senator were making a joint appearance in connection with Nixon's official assumption of his new duties. In a pompous attempt at humor, Warren remarked that Nixon would probably call him every day for advice, at which point Nixon interjected: "Or vice versa." Onlookers said the governor turned pink.[62]

Nixon was once asked a direct question about his relationship with Warren, and he answered as diplomatically as possible. "We are not unfriendly," he replied. "We are two individuals going our own ways."[63]

Nixon defended his aggressive tactics as legitimate and even as in the public interest. It is fine to talk about the importance of being gentlemanly, he later wrote, but hitting hard on the issues gives the voters a clear choice while keeping the candidates on their toes. The important thing, he concluded, is not to allow political differences to become personal. Besides, Douglas gave as good as she got during the campaign, even resorting to name-calling and insults. Reading of her sarcastic references to him as a "peewee" and a "pipsqueak," Nixon would not have been overreacting if he considered them assaults on his manhood.

Among Democrats, however, the campaigns against Jerry Voorhis and Helen Gahagan Douglas nourished the perception that Nixon was a politician without principles and that the sole purpose of his campaigning was self-advancement. Reflecting years later on her defeat in 1950, Douglas concluded bitterly that "there's nothing in his record to indicate he has strong convictions about anything except success."[64]

Many influential public figures from both parties were disturbed by what they read or heard about the Douglas campaign, and Nixon paid a heavy price in their disapproval.

- Phillip Burton, later a congressman from California, said Nixon was the reason he went into politics. "I took a private oath after Helen was defeated by Nixon's despicable campaign that I was going to work to see the day that man would be retired from public life," he recalled years later.[65]
- One reason Lyndon Johnson accepted John Kennedy's offer of the vice presidential nomination in 1960 was to keep Nixon out of the White House: "I figured that because of the way he behaved toward Helen Douglas in 1950, he should not be president."[66]
- The Nixon campaign alienated many members of the Eastern establishment. Encountering the new senator at a Georgetown dinner party after the election, governor and diplomat Averill Harriman walked out in flamboyant disdain.[67]
- Legendary Speaker of the House Sam Rayburn believed that he saw an unctuousness and ambition in Nixon unusual even by the standards of Texas, his home state. During the Nixon-Douglas campaign, he told Helen Douglas that "his is the most devious face of all those who have served in Congress in all the years I have been here."[68]
- Following the election, Carey McWilliams, a liberal California historian, called Nixon a "third-rate Tom Dewey" and wrote of his "brazen demagoguery" and "astonishing capacity for petty malice."[69]
- Mary Ellen Leary of the *San Francisco News,* after covering the Douglas campaign, reported her "instinctive dislike and distrust" of Nixon. He struck her as a "manufactured person ... his personality implanted."[70]
- According to an aide, Manchester Boddy, Douglas' primary opponent, decided after one meeting with Nixon that he "despised the man's politics and personal ethics."[71]

A common reaction of many who lived through the race was that they never got over their hatred of Nixon. Several Eastern newspapers carried stories about his "shockingly abusive" campaign.[72] Together with the fallout from the Hiss case, the race against Helen Douglas marked the beginning of what became "enthusiastic loathing" of Nixon by liberals of all stripes.

Did Nixon deserve the hostility his Senate campaign evoked?

Douglas did not lose the election because of his rhetorical excesses or campaign tricks. She lost because Nixon was an attractive and articulate candidate, supported by a vast majority of the media, running during a period

## 6 — The Rivals and the Nixon-Douglas Race

of Republican resurgence, with a message that seemed validated by national and world events, against an under-funded, disorganized opponent who was considered too liberal even by members of her own party. He did not need to smear Douglas — he would have won regardless.

Nixon did not know how aggressive he had to be to win. Political polls usually showed him with a strong lead, but polls had been wrong in the recent past. One pollster said in October that the election was too close to call. If Nixon had realized he was a shoo-in, he might have eased up, but he did not feel he could take the chance. He thought he had to push the envelope, and in the process he resorted to exaggeration and hyperbole. "I was a very young man," he said later — the closest he ever came to admitting that the 1950 race had become an albatross around his neck.[73]

Nixon's flights of rhetoric underlined that the primary purpose of the words he used was not to educate or inform but to influence voting behavior. He had learned from his political and debating experience that the emotional power of words was more important than their literal meaning. He almost seemed surprised when someone misinterpreted his remarks. His tendency to distance himself from what he said led to charges that he was unprincipled — that he was as much an actor as a politician, or worse, a demagogue.

Of course, he was not the first or only politician to put getting elected ahead of strict adherence to the truth. But something about his operating style bothered people. He had a "perplexing and inscrutable personality" that threw many Americans off balance. Political observer Herbert Phillips called him a man of contrasts — inventive and farsighted, yet moody and high-strung; gracious and pleasant yet argumentative and aggressive; disarmingly modest yet a young man in a hurry.[74] Nobody could be sure who the real Nixon was, but everyone had an opinion.

Despite the campaign's legacy of distrust, Nixon's accomplishment was genuine. It gave Republicans hope that the national fortunes of their party were improving. Years later, he reflected on his decision to run for the Senate in 1950. He had surveyed his friends before throwing his hat in the ring, and all of them advised against it. But he had a gut feeling he could beat the odds. "I must admit that I was lucky," he wrote, "but it is only when you take big risks that you are around to cash in on the luck."[75]

PART THREE: THE RIVALS COLLIDE

# 7

# *The 1952 Republican Convention*

In July 1952, a frustrated Republican Party convened in Chicago to select a candidate for president in the fall election. After absorbing the blow of Truman's come-from-behind victory over Dewey in 1948, the GOP was desperate to put together a winning ticket. Republicans had not won a presidential election for 24 years. This year, the issues seemed to favor them, but that could have been said in 1948 as well.

Despite general optimism, many in the party despaired over the lack of a candidate with true star power. The front runner was Senator Robert Taft of Ohio, known in party circles as "Mr. Republican" for his pedigree (he was the son of a former president) and his long and honorable service. But his Midwestern brand of conservatism and isolationism and his lack of charisma worried the more moderate, East Coast–based party establishment, which feared another wrenching defeat. Many of these moderates considered General Dwight Eisenhower, the hero of D-Day, the best possible GOP nominee. But it had not even been certain until earlier in the year which political party he belonged to or how interested he was in the job.

By 1952, three of the California rivals, Warren, Knowland and Nixon, were among the Republican Party's most prominent figures and legitimate contenders for a place on the presidential ticket. All would have a central role to play in the drama about to unfold during the first several days of July in Chicago. None of them would forget the emotional week they spent together.

## Knowland Makes His Mark

After his election in 1946, Bill Knowland had quickly established himself as a serious and knowledgeable U.S. senator. "He sailed into Washington," wrote *Time* magazine, "with the enthusiasm of a man determined to stay."[1] At the beginning of his first full term, he was identified with the moderate wing of the Republican Party, much like Earl Warren, and even voted with California's senior senator, Democrat Sheridan Downey, on several of the most important issues before Congress. According to his biographer, some of the old-timers questioned his leadership skills and his maverick tendencies, but they also noted that he did not engage in headline-hunting opportunities, as many of his colleagues did.

The one constant in his life during his first term was his loyalty to Warren, the man who had made his Senate career possible. The two men continued to maintain a close relationship. "I've been in Bill's office, in the afternoons in Washington," recalled aide Mac Faries, "and *every* afternoon, there'd be a call come in from Earl Warren, talking about state matters." According to Faries, Warren borrowed silver from the Knowland family in Oakland when he wanted to put on a party in Sacramento.[2]

As we have seen, they also worked in tandem at the 1948 Republican convention. The governor headed a favorite son delegation from California, and Knowland served as the delegation's chairman and chief advocate for his friend's first presidential bid. The effort came up short and ended with Warren's release of his delegates to Dewey.

Back in the Senate, Knowland moved to the right, particularly in foreign policy. He became increasingly concerned — some would say obsessed — with developments in the Far East. Chiang Kai-shek's Nationalist Chinese government, a close ally of the United States in World War II, was fighting for its life against a stubborn and increasingly popular communist insurgency. Knowland's single-minded concern for the health of the Nationalist government prompted *The Nation* magazine to call him "the noisiest and often the silliest" member of the pro–China bloc.[3]

Knowland undertook a fact-finding trip to China and returned convinced that Chiang's survival was critical to U.S. security. When the Nationalist government collapsed and Chiang fled to the island of Formosa (now Taiwan), Knowland mounted such a bitter attack on the administration's Asia policymakers that critics began to call him the "Senator from Formosa." During 1950 alone, he made over a hundred speeches on Asian policy on the Senate floor.[4]

The North Korean invasion of South Korea that same year added fuel to his fire. After U.S. intervention in the conflict, Knowland became an advocate for the most vigorous possible response, even at the risk of provoking a military reaction from Communist China. When Truman fired General Douglas MacArthur for advocating an expansion of the war into China, Knowland came to the general's defense. In many speeches, he lambasted Truman and Secretary of State Dean Acheson's handling of the crisis in Korea as "catastrophic."

## *Liabilities as a Legislator*

His seriousness of purpose and strong work ethic aside, Knowland was burdened in his official duties by an unappealing personality and a cold, aloof style. His tendency to keep his own counsel made him seem out of place in a collaborative, convivial body like the United States Senate. The *Los Angeles Times*, which consistently backed him for public office, called him "one of the most self-contained, self-reliant and self-consulting figures in state and national politics — somewhat of a combination of political rhinoceros and sphinx."[5] An illustration in a *Collier's* magazine article on the California rivals during the 1950s depicted Knowland as a Roman senator, complete with toga and an imperious manner.

Because of his physical stature, Knowland could also seem intimidating. He was a big, well-built man, a wrestler in his student days, who "radiated physical power." He had a booming voice, and when he was upset, ropy veins pushed out of his head. He walked with a sense of mission. "You can almost hear the floor rumbling under his feet," noted one politician.[6] An associate who was also an admirer later called him the "Sherman tank of the Senate."[7] On one occasion, a writer watched as he plowed through a room full of staffers "like a battleship through a fleet of dinghies," speaking to no one.[8] His plodding gait made him the occasional object of ridicule by liberals. "He walks like he thinks," remarked Sen. Richard Russell.[9]

In the Senate, Knowland affected a grim, somber demeanor. "I wasn't sure that Bill liked the work at all," said Senator Clifford Case.[10] Knowland's seriousness apparently stood in marked contrast with his publisher father. "If Billy Knowland had had just a little bit of [Joe's] warmth, it would have been entirely different," observed fellow Californian Thomas Kuchel. In many ways, Bill was a contradiction: a man who had no fun in politics but lived and breathed it, who did everything a successful politician was not supposed to do, yet was successful.

Typical of the Army officer he had been, Knowland had a stiff, by-the-book approach to governing and to life. "Billy doesn't bend," said Tom Kuchel.[11] He once stopped a senator's wife from jaywalking and gave her a lecture in the process.[12] Like Richard Nixon, Knowland allowed himself few diversions from politics, though he was fond of movies and dancing.

He was only in his thirties and forties when serving in the Senate, but he seemed older than he was. His Army letters to his wife, Helen, had often consisted of lofty pronouncements on American national interests rather than the more typical comments on military life. Senate colleagues called him a "young fogey." He had "never been a young man," said Pat Brown. "He's always been an elderly man" and a "stuffed shirt."[13]

His rigidity and literal mindedness put him at a disadvantage in dealing with more nimble and flexible opponents. His biographers admitted that Democratic majority leader Lyndon Johnson "ran circles around" Knowland when the two men led their parties in the Senate.[14] Richard Nixon, with his more subtle intelligence and greater tactical flexibility, was much better equipped to deal with the high-stakes environment of presidential politics. "Knowland did not parry and feint as a Nixon ... might do," noted an article in a major news magazine. "He plowed into battle, preferring the ax to the rapier."[15]

As senators, however, Nixon and Knowland seemed to work easily together. Both men were especially interested in foreign policy, had similar views, and shared an impatience with small talk. Each supported the Marshall Plan and strongly criticized President Truman for firing MacArthur. Nixon publicly praised the "great service [Knowland] has rendered to his country in pointing up the dangers which the situation [in the Far East] presents to the very security of the nation."[16]

As he had with Warren, Nixon took pains to cede Knowland the deference he was due as the more senior politician. He also sought to minimize any perception that the two were somehow in competition with one another. He and Knowland both communicated to their constituents via weekly radio programs. Given an opportunity to publicize his own program, Nixon turned it down because Knowland did not advertise his — if Nixon did, "people will use that to drive a wedge between the two of us," he wrote to a colleague. When he was asked to speak at a California Republican convention in 1951, he declined, saying: "Bill is coming up for reelection next year, and I think it is best that he take the spotlight on such occasions."[17]

Nixon went out of his way to support Knowland's 1952 reelection campaign, which he considered one of the most important congressional races and a bellwether of party fortunes in the fall. He was "sure that [the Democrats] will leave no stone unturned in their efforts to defeat him."[18]

A source of concern to California Republicans was Knowland's obvious discomfort as a campaigner. Journalist Stuart Alsop described his smile as a "huge, unnerving grimace." He had the habit — unfortunate for a politician — of forgetting names. When he went into a crowd shaking hands, "everybody [was] embarrassed, including Bill," said a supporter. Watching his campaign style in frustration, an assistant summed up the problem by saying: "Bill, you don't kiss babies."[19] Added William S. White in the *Washington Star*, "Far from kissing the baby, he is more likely to stonily ignore it."[20]

The distraction of Knowland's marriage problems, along with his many deficiencies as a campaigner, might have been exploitable by a strong, experienced challenger. The fears of his supporters were heightened by his single-minded focus on Asian affairs in the campaign, rather than on matters affecting Californians more directly. "Maybe I am doing the wrong things," Knowland admitted, "but I believe I am concentrating on the overriding issue of our time." The government has no right to "ask Americans to fight," he declared, "and then deny them the right to win."

As in 1946, however, he was fortunate to have a little-known Democratic opponent. With Murray Chotiner in charge of his campaign and with the usual support of California's newspapers, he rolled to impressive victories in both the Republican and Democratic primaries. His total of over two million votes was the largest ever received by any candidate in a state primary. Asked to explain his decisive victory, a Republican official commented that Knowland was hardly an ideal candidate, but he was "a straight-thinking, forward-looking, hard-working, sincere kind of guy. What the hell more do you want in politics?"[21]

The easy win had an unfortunate side-effect, however. It gave Knowland a dangerous and unwarranted feeling of political invincibility.

## *Warren's Outside Chance*

Despite the impressive successes of Knowland and Nixon in Congress, Earl Warren still commanded the largest national following among the three California rivals in 1951. By then, he was the successful and highly respected three-term chief executive of the country's fastest growing state. His resume matched up well with that of any politician in the country. He now saw himself as a viable candidate for president. In November 1951, he tossed his hat in the ring for the following year.

Warren's ambition, as ever, was low key. He gave the impression that he would enjoy winning, but not if he had to compromise his fierce independence or make deals. Consistent with this view, he later claimed that he was not "hell-bent" on being the party nominee — that he entered the presidential race "without burning ambition or expectation of success."[22]

If true, he may have been caught up in the "next logical step" syndrome, in which an aging and oft-reelected politician tires of his current responsibilities and is neither ready to retire nor interested in a lower-wattage job in the private sector.[23] "Time to push on," wrote Kevin Starr, "lest one be forced to contemplate an unprecedented fourth term as governor, or go on the bench, or return to private life, in which Warren had little interest and next to no experience."[24]

In his memoirs, Warren justified his run for president by saying that if he had not entered the race, he would have become a "political nonentity," and that unless he actively sought the nomination, he would be accused of fronting for one of the two favorites. These reasons do not sound persuasive today. Warren was much more ambitious than he let on. Once he made the decision to run, his formidable pride and ego were fully invested in the outcome.

It was a decision he took against a backdrop of personal problems that must have weighed heavily. His vivacious daughter, Nina, better known around the state as Honey Bear, was slowly recovering from polio, the dreaded scourge of the age, and had only lately regained the ability to walk. Then he became ill himself. In the same month he announced for the presidency, he underwent surgery for colon cancer. While convalescing, he was obliged to stanch rumors that he was facing almost certain death. Herbert Hoover told Republican leaders at a dinner party that the surgery had failed to solve the problem.[25] Fortunately, both he and his daughter recovered. But mounting a campaign for national office at this stressful time suggests that he was strongly motivated to seek the presidency.

Warren was enough of a realist to understand that his liberal political leanings could be a problem in getting his party's nomination, but he did not try to minimize or obfuscate his differences with conservatives. In countering Goodwin Knight's charge that he was "nothing but a New Dealer,"[26] Warren defended the Roosevelt revolution. "We do not propose to deny the progress that has been made during the last decade," he declared. "Neither do we aim to repeal it."[27] He condemned "those who would freeze our nation in the status-quo, with whatever inequalities go with it, and ... have our country return to what they look back to nostalgically and affectionately as the good old days." In deflecting criticism from groups like the American Medical Association, he pointed out that "the American people are not socialists ... but they are definitely committed to social progress."[28]

As infuriating to conservatives as his nonpartisan policies was the identity of his friends and supporters. He associated happily with Democrats and even employed them in his administration. When President Truman visited California, Warren greeted him cordially and respectfully. He recalled later that "some of our Republican partisans thought this hospitable gesture could have been dispensed with." When Truman fired General MacArthur, Warren did not join the howls of protest from conservatives. He also raised hackles by forming close friendships with such Republican bete noires as California attorney general (and later governor) Pat Brown and presidential candidate Adlai Stevenson.

The upshot of Warren's policy apostasies and his lone wolf style of campaigning and governing was that many party officials — particularly the national Republican bosses — were never more than lukewarm about a Warren presidential candidacy.

Before the convention, Warren tested his national appeal by competing in two primary elections outside California — in Wisconsin and Oregon. Because he was unwilling to leave his state in the hands of Goodwin Knight for more than a few days at a time, he campaigned only intermittently in these states and with limited effect. He finished a strong second to Taft in Wisconsin, where Eisenhower was not a candidate, but lost badly to Ike in Oregon, where AMA spokesmen pounded him on the issue of socialized medicine. His foray outside California was, at best, a mixed success.

For the third consecutive time, however, Governor Warren planned to lead a favorite-son delegation to the convention — one that was pledged to support him for president, unless (or until) he released them to vote for someone else.[29] He commanded a huge number of delegates — 70. In past years, he had quickly yielded to other candidates, but this time, he would not give in so easily.

Even if he had done better in the Oregon and Wisconsin primaries, Warren would have started out far behind both Taft and Eisenhower. His slim chances depended on a stand-off between these two men. Should neither be able to prevail, Warren hoped that he would be everyone's second choice. He was depending on Knowland, again the leader of the California delegation, to keep the group voting as a bloc, at least through the first ballot. He knew he faced long odds. "My father realized he's riding a dark horse," recalled Earl Jr., "or at least a pretty gray one."[30]

Because neither Taft nor Eisenhower would be arriving in Chicago with a decisive advantage, the job of picking the nominee could easily come down to wheeling and dealing in proverbial smoke-filled rooms. In such an atmosphere, the rewards would not necessarily go to the most high minded or competent but to the man who could operate best in a fluid environment. Warren was prepared to put up a good fight for the nomination, but he prided himself on getting his way without compromising his principles. He refused to say who he might support if he lost.

## 7 — The 1952 Republican Convention

### Warren's Shadow Dissipates

Until his election as senator, Richard Nixon understood that he was as yet no match for Earl Warren politically. As a Nixon loyalist phrased it, the governor "called the tune and held the reins on the California Republican organization at all times."[31] Accordingly, Nixon had always taken pains to show Warren the respect and deference due a three-term Republican governor.

But his requests for assistance in 1946 and 1950 had been received with such coldness that Nixon could perhaps be forgiven for concluding that he had gotten little in return for his subservience. After defeating Douglas, he moved out of Warren's shadow for good. He was now playing on a national stage and emerging as a hot political property.

Even so, he continued publicly to acknowledge Warren's importance and his contributions to Republican success. "There are many of us in California," he said in several speeches in 1951, "who think that Governor Warren rendered a great service, not only to his state but also to the nation, when he defeated a man by the name of Roosevelt by over one million votes in a state which has a million more Democrats than Republicans."[32]

He also tended carefully his personal relationship with Warren. He wrote the governor in January 1952 to pass along the best wishes of a man he had met while traveling who had served with Warren's son in the Marines. In closing, Nixon wrote that he was "very glad to hear, in talking to Kyle Palmer on the phone yesterday, that you have completely recovered from your operation and are in fighting trim again."[33] The reference to Palmer may have also been a sly reminder that he was now the columnist's fair-haired boy.

As his horizons expanded, there was no question of his ambition — only of the direction it would take. At a critical time, he received encouragement from Murray Chotiner, who pointed out that being a junior senator "doesn't amount to anything," and, since Knowland was young and healthy, he would always remain one. "There comes a time," Chotiner said, "when you have to go up or out."[34]

Until 1952, Nixon's logical next move had seemed to be a bid for governor of California. His staffers took note of Warren's growing unpopularity and Nixon's high standing with the conservative movement in the state. "I honestly believe Dick ... [was] set on being elected governor in 1954," said one, "and then making his run for the national ticket about 1960."[35] Of course, pursuing the governorship would have brought him into a confrontation with the equally ambitious Goodwin Knight, who had been waiting impatiently for Warren to move on.

## *Nixon Makes His Choice*

Nixon had long been making sharply partisan attacks on Truman and his administration. As a senator, he took a passionate interest in the race for the Republican presidential nomination, taking shape throughout 1951. Battle lines were hardening between Robert Taft, who was still well ahead in polls of likely convention delegates the following summer, and a small group of men who were orchestrating the candidacy of a still uncommitted Dwight Eisenhower. Tom Dewey, the two-time candidate for president, was now a leading figure behind the Eisenhower movement.

Though Nixon had great respect for Taft, he was among those Republicans who viewed him as politically out of tune with the times — a man who, if nominated, would likely lead the party to a repeat of the Dewey disaster of 1948. He was repelled by Taft's cautious isolationism, and he later told an associate that he considered the Ohio senator's aloofness and abrasive personality a serious disadvantage in a presidential campaign.[36] Nixon exchanged letters with *Times* political editor Kyle Palmer about the prospect of a Taft candidacy. Taft "should not be our man," Palmer agreed.[37]

Nixon's negative view of Taft was no doubt influenced by his strong enthusiasm for Dwight Eisenhower. He had visited the general in Paris in May 1951, while on a swing through Europe. The hour-and-a-half meeting left him inspired. He felt he was "in the presence of a genuine statesman," he later wrote. "I came away convinced that he should be the next President. I also decided that if he ran for the nomination I would do everything I could to help him get it."[38]

Nixon often gave groups of friends his personal assessment of Taft and Eisenhower as Republican presidential nominees. He did so in the nuanced fashion that was becoming his hallmark:

> I have tremendous respect for Bob Taft. I like him personally and think he would make a fine president. I've seen Ike twice and I was impressed by him. But I think it narrows down to this: I don't say Taft can't win, but I do say that I'm not *sure* he can win. And I'm sure Ike *can* win. If I thought Ike was the wrong man for the job, none of this would make any difference. But I think he'll make a fine president — and I think the Republican Party has to win, if only to clean up the mess in Washington.[39]

The feeling between Nixon and the Eisenhower camp seemed to be mutual. High-level Ike backers believed that California votes were crucial to the Republican effort and argued for including either Nixon or Knowland on the ticket. Many of them gave Nixon the edge over the more senior Knowland because of his presumed ability to attract the youth vote, his experience in both the House and Senate, and his close identification with the likely most important issue in the campaign — the fight against international communism. The result was that influential Republicans began putting Nixon's name forward as a vice presidential possibility long before Eisenhower even entered the race.

But in mid–1951, Eisenhower's candidacy was far from a sure thing.

## Nixon's Balancing Act

With his commitment to Ike and growing involvement with the men around him, Nixon could not be expected to have much enthusiasm for Warren's presidential bid. Though he often spoke supportively of the governor in public, his view from the beginning was that he lacked the charisma, political outlook, and star power necessary to win this important election. He felt that Warren had an unrealistic view of his chances.

In fact, the favorite-son gambit looked more and more to Nixon and his allies like an ego trip. While Nixon was trying to keep relations with Warren on an even keel, he heard constant grumbling from his men in California about Warren's dictatorial attitude toward intra-party dissent. Unless the governor looked beyond his own long-shot candidacy, they feared that the state's Republican delegates would "wind up without much to show for their trip to Chicago."[40] Herman Perry fumed that he needed to show more flexibility. "For Warren not to do this," Perry concluded, "in my opinion brands him as one of the most selfish, unrealistic politicians of the day."[41] Apprised of the lack of Republican harmony, Kyle Palmer sighed: "You know Earl."[42]

Many Republican partisans, especially Warren's conservative opponents, were fed up with the favorite-son system, arguing that most favorite-son delegations played no role in choosing a president. According to Gardiner Johnson, a prominent lawyer who did not always see eye to eye with the governor, efforts had been made to bring "genuine candidates," like Taft, into the state to run against Warren. But there were objections — from the *Los Angeles Times*, in particular — that strong out-of-state opposition would produce disunity and disarray in the state Republican Party.

The rebellion against Warren on his home turf reached its climax when he was challenged in the California Republican primary by a rival presidential ticket, headed by a relative unknown, Thomas Werdel of Bakersfield. Werdel had little hope of winning, but conservatives hoped to embarrass the governor by mounting a state-wide campaign on Werdel's behalf, employing a half million dollars in contributions and radio and television speeches by such public figures as commentator Fulton Lewis, Jr., and actor Adolphe Menjou. "You have to admire them for their guts," Nixon observed.[43]

In his memoirs, Warren dismissed Werdel's candidacy as nothing more than a nuisance. The opposition consisted of "disappointed office-seekers, disgruntled legislators, and outsiders."[44] Not wanting to "dignify their effort too much," he mounted a "very modest counter-campaign, consisting of a few speeches, and spent very little money."[45]

In reality, the conservative rebellion angered and embarrassed him. He lashed out against what he called a "coalition of hate, backed by enormous sums of cash." He asked Bill Knowland, with his impeccable conservative credentials, to return to California to speak on his behalf. The senator complied, assuring campaign rallies that Warren "does not have an ounce of socialism in his makeup."[46] Warren won the primary by a two-to-one margin, but the Werdel challenge tarnished his image, made him look vulnerable, and weakened his chances for the presidential nomination.

Nixon had been tempted to side with the conservative California Republicans in their attempt to defeat Warren in the state party primary, and he was under considerable pressure from his southern California supporters to do so. Perry wrote to Nixon in May that "you will make a mistake if you make any special statement on behalf of ... the great white father."[47] Nixon worried aloud that Warren would "follow his usual tactics in California and try to go it on an every-man-for-himself program" as a presidential candidate. Instead, he said, the conservatives "want a candidate who will go all-out for the party, sink or swim."[48]

But even though Nixon may have had the political strength to risk a split with the governor, he hoped to avoid one. The reason had less to do with Nixon's presidential preference than with his own political calculations and those of Eisenhower's backers, who felt that Warren's control of the California delegation would at least deny its votes to Taft. Nixon reasoned that moderates and independents would form the bulk of Warren's delegation — the kind of people who would be inclined to throw their support to Ike rather than Taft if Warren's bid failed. So Nixon set out to maintain good relations with Warren while quietly promoting Eisenhower's interests. From the beginning, Nixon was playing a double game.

In private, he reassured Perry that he was "in substantial agreement with most of the sentiments" he had expressed regarding Warren's selfishness. A few days before the convention, he wrote to Perry again, speculating about who would place Warren's name in nomination there. He identified Knowland as the logical person to do so and confirmed that he had "neither the desire nor the intention of accepting such an assignment" should it be offered to him.

The effort to avoid an open break had even required that Nixon join Knowland and others in formally urging Warren to seek the Republican presidential nomination in late 1951. Warren announced his candidacy in November, but then Nixon quickly backed away from anything resembling an endorsement.

In a wide-ranging and typically calculated survey of the Republican field that same month, Nixon declared that many good men were available for the nomination, and "certainly Earl Warren is one of them." After Taft and Eisenhower, Warren would have to be the "strongest dark horse." The governor, he continued, is "electable by virtue of his warmth, his personality, and his family," and would "win handily" over any Democratic opponent. After this gentle beginning, Nixon turned to the negative side of the ledger:

> Actually, the country does not know too much of where he stands.... He lacks strength among the people who nominate outside of California. This may be partly because of his reputation for liberalism — which would certainly help him if he were nominated — and partly because the Republicans want a fighting drive. They want someone who will hit, and hit hard, on the major issues."[49]

The analysis behind these comments was fundamentally sound. Nixon had identified Warren's main assets and liabilities in a way that could not be construed as personal. (The only false note was the call for someone who would "hit hard" on the issues, which seemed more like sly self-promotion than a comparison with the campaign style of any other Republican candidate.) Still, Warren could not have been happy to read these comments. They should have put him on notice that Nixon was keeping his options open.

Nixon's public reservations about Warren's candidacy had the added benefit of keeping him in good stead with California's conservatives. The problem was that most of these anti–Warren Republicans were for Taft rather than Eisenhower. So he was trying to persuade the conservatives he was secretly for Taft while subtly undermining Warren's candidacy and hiding his real interest, which was in Eisenhower's success.

## Warren Appraises His Rival

As 1952 began, Eisenhower still had not declared himself a candidate for president. Concern grew among Nixon and Ike's other backers that the party would be left with the too controversial MacArthur, the too liberal Warren, and the too dull Taft as its best presidential prospects. Nixon toured California in February, alternately extending mild praise to Warren and exhorting Eisenhower to get into the race.

Few yet understood what Morris called the "intricate machinations" in which Nixon was engaged.[50] His public loyalty to Warren was increasingly hard to explain to the conservatives and even to his own activists in the state. "Hardly a day goes by but what I come across one of our enthusiastic supporters with whom I have to argue and reason relative to your present posture," wrote Herman Perry. "Everybody seems to think you have sold out your friends in California. I tell them no."[51]

Early in the year, Nixon calculated that Warren had strength enough to prevail in the primary against Werdel and the conservatives, and he considered declaring his intent to join Warren's delegation to the convention. The governor made clear he was welcome to do so, though he should have had no illusions about Nixon's dedication to his success. A Warren aide observed that Nixon was considered "no better than neutral."

Warren may not yet have recognized Nixon as a political challenger, but he probably viewed his growing popularity in California with concern, if not alarm. The governor could see that Nixon had become a rallying point for the state's disaffected Republicans. The international events of the past few years had made Nixon's warnings about Communist advances look prescient and Warren's rejection of the loyalty oath naïve. But if the governor sensed that the appeal of his message was dwindling and his advantage slipping, he did not let on.

He had decided, in fact, that he might be better off with Nixon in the California delegation rather than out. Attacks on him from the right were reaching a new level of intensity, and getting Nixon to join the favorite-son entourage might give the appearance of party unity. So he went "against some of the best political advice [he] could get, including [from] Knowland" and decided to try to control Nixon by recruiting him. The idea, Warren said later, "was to give Nixon a place ... and to have him satisfied with his place."[52] The belief that Nixon might really be neutral or be satisfied as a cog in the Warren machine showed either that Nixon had skillfully hidden his true agenda or that Warren had grievously misread it.

Nixon gave a clear sign that Warren could not count on his support by at first declining to join the delegation. The reasons for this are less clear. Was he trying to preserve his independence, so that he could work openly for the candidate of his choice? This course of action was the more honorable one, though Warren's feelings would have been bruised in the short term. Whatever his motivation, he was immediately set upon by Bill Knowland, at the Warren camp's behest, who told him it would be "unseemly" not to take part.[53]

After more conversations and "considerable arm twisting," Nixon agreed to join, but on the condition that he be allowed to select twenty-three of the seventy delegation members.[54] "It is essential," he wrote, "that we get the strongest possible group as members of the delegation so that it can do the right job at the proper time."⁵⁵ He also got Warren to agree to allow Murray Chotiner on the train to the convention as a manager of southern California's delegates.

From Warren's point of view, this arrangement probably looked harmless enough at the time, but it had far-reaching consequences. Nixon's men set to work adding loyalists and Eisenhower supporters to the delegation. Then, as some Warren delegates dropped out for mundane reasons, Bernie Brennan, a state Republican Party official and Nixon partisan, helped to identify "suitable" replacements. The Warren forces, distracted by weightier issues, were not paying attention. The result was that many of the delegates, though formally pledged to the governor, did not consider him the best candidate the party could put forward.

Mac Faries, a Warren aide, warned his boss about the slowly shifting composition of his delegation. "A lot of these people," he told the governor, "while they'll sign up to support you, are not definitely for *you*." Warren replied: "We can't help that. We want to get the best people, and if they sign up, I will trust them on their support." Faries concluded later, with some bitterness, that Warren was "a little bit ... naïve — he thought if a man gave his word in writing he would stand by it."⁵⁶

When the deadline for appointing delegates arrived, Warren read the final list of attendees, which contained several additional Nixon supporters, with mounting anger. "I felt very badly about it," Faries admitted, "because I hadn't put thumb screws on where I should."⁵⁷ Warren could have struck Chotiner from the list, but in a further attempt to be fair, he gave his approval. The episode was a wake-up call, if one was needed. "We knew from [that] ... time, we had to watch Nixon," said one of the governor's men.

Along with other delegation members, Nixon was obliged to sign a loyalty pledge, affirming that he personally preferred Warren and swearing to support his nomination "to the best of my judgment and ability." But he reminded his backers that many delegates were not Warren partisans. In other words, Nixon was going to support Warren while hoping to redirect his delegates to Eisenhower when the governor's candidacy inevitably collapsed. If successful, it would be an extraordinary balancing act.

## *The Courtship of Nixon*

Back on the East Coast, Nixon's star continued to rise. In a kind of audition before New York's moneyed Republicans, arranged by Tom Dewey in May, Nixon delivered a well prepared and particularly effective speech. In it, he argued that Republicans had to appeal to Democrats if they were to win the presidency and reaffirmed the importance of internationalism in furthering U.S. security interests.

Dewey went away impressed with this expression of Eisenhower-style moderate Republicanism and told a number of his political intimates what he had seen and heard. Then he began asking questions about the freshman senator. "Everyone whose opinion I respected said he was an absolute star, a man of enormous capacity [with a] fine understanding of the world situation," Dewey said.[58] He decided then and there to support Nixon for vice president.

Soon after, he arranged for other influential backers of Dwight Eisenhower, including Henry Cabot Lodge and John Foster Dulles, to size Nixon up. When asked later about these contacts, Nixon professed not to take them seriously. Perhaps on some level, he did not, even though he had been told for almost a year that his chances of getting on an Eisenhower ticket were good.

Eisenhower had spoken with Nixon on a couple of occasions, including the cordial meeting in Paris at which Nixon had first decided to support him. Nixon met the general's requirements for the position — he was young and dynamic, and his high standing among party regulars balanced Ike's centrist political views.

But Eisenhower left the scouting of vice presidential prospects to his advisors. According to one of his biographers, the possibility of a Nixon vice presidency was first broached by Lodge to Nixon in May, and Nixon responded with "natural warmth" to the idea. Others who discussed the subject with him came away with "the same impression of availability."[59] Lodge informed Ike about his tentative offer to Nixon, and the general was "entirely favorable." Milton Eisenhower later confirmed that the choice of Nixon was "pretty much guided by the advice of the people who had been in politics for a great many years."[60]

But the Eisenhower forces wanted something in return. Ike still lacked enough votes for the nomination — thus the need for Nixon to "hold the line for the general" in the California delegation, as Lodge explained. "It was Nixon's role to keep California from going to Taft."[61] The acceptance of this task did not change Nixon's plans but it did raise the stakes.

At this point, the Warren-Werdel primary contest had not taken place, so Nixon still had to hope that Warren's slate beat the insurgents. Eisenhower lagged Taft by over a hundred delegates in most counts, and a Werdel delegation from California, if seated, would be dominated by Taft. On the eve of the primary, Nixon prepared a press release that was both an endorsement of Warren and a reassurance of the conservatives. Though it pleased neither side, it would later be regarded as vintage Nixon — at once nuanced, clever, and maddeningly ambiguous.

First, he denied what seemed obvious — that Warren's slate was committed to Warren. "Anyone who knows me and my political career realized I would not have gone on the Warren delegation as a rubber stamp for the governor or any other man," he insisted. Then he complimented Tom Werdel and the challengers, underlining his respect for them and their views.

"But I honestly believe," he continued, "that the Warren delegation is better qualified to represent California." To make this conclusion palatable to the conservatives, he then looked beyond Warren's candidacy to how the California contingent might affect the outcome. "Once Governor Warren releases the delegation," he said carefully, "we shall be free to look over the field and select the man best qualified ... the very strongest possible nominee." As one reader of that sentence observed, "one would expect a loyal delegate to use the word 'if' [rather than 'once']."[62]

Though Warren won the primary handily, in many areas of the state he was considerably weaker than he had been just two years earlier. Nixon took some credit for the outcome, and he deserved it. As Morris observed, he had managed to endorse Warren's candidacy and to damage Taft's interests without openly alienating California's right wing. To ensure that the conservatives did not mistake his intent, after the primary Nixon said: "I don't believe that any of us should have any illusions on the possibilities of Warren being selected for the top spot."[63]

Now that a Warren slate was going to Chicago, Nixon had the place on the delegation that Warren intended him to have, but the governor would soon regret it. Nixon wrote to an aide that "it is much better to be on the inside of the delegation with some power to affect its action rather than on the outside looking in."[64] Soon there were reports that Pat Hillings, one of his more zealous supporters, was trying to get Warren delegates to switch their votes to Eisenhower on the first ballot, pointing out that the law provided no penalty for breaking their pledge.

Though Nixon must have known that his chances for the vice presidential nomination were good, he wrote years later that he "had not even bothered to pack a dark suit for the trip, since I did not expect ... to speak in the convention hall."[65] This was not the last time that he would dismiss speculation that turned out to be correct. Certainly his efforts to promote Eisenhower's candidacy would appear less self-interested if he could persuade others that he had no thought of being on the ticket.

## *Knowland's Loyalty*

While Warren wondered how much to trust Nixon, and Nixon calculated how best to advance his and Eisenhower's interests, Bill Knowland entered the picture.

As it became clear that he was going to cruise to an effortless and lopsided reelection victory in the June 1952 California primary, the national media launched a boomlet for the senator as the Republican running mate. "California's more promising figure now is Knowland," rhapsodized *Time* magazine. He "has the bark and grain of vice presidential timber."[66] A West Coast columnist thought him a "likely prospect for both Senator Taft and General Eisenhower."[67] His father, the publisher Joe Knowland, lost no opportunity to discourage his son from considering it. "I hope Bill don't accept that vice presidency," he was frequently heard saying.[68]

Knowland was the most severely conflicted of the three California rivals. He had long been committed to Earl Warren's presidential campaign and had helped to set up the delegate selection machinery. He had also agreed to head the delegation, a role requiring him to prevent defections to either of the front runners. He was doing this even though he and Warren disagreed on a growing number of policy issues.

But bonds of friendship and loyalty to the man who made him a senator remained his overriding consideration. He would back Warren not only out of gratitude but because he was accustomed to keeping his word. "Do you know Bill Knowland?" Kyle Palmer asked rhetorically. "If not, I can let you in on one important fact: he is an honorable man."[69]

At the same time, there was no question of Knowland's ambition. "That man wanted to be President of the United States," recalled his daughter Emelyn Jewett. "He never admitted it publicly, but that's what his whole career was shooting for. That's where he wanted to be. That's where he thoroughly expected to be at some point in his career."[70]

Given his long-term goal, his head must have been turned by thoughts of the vice presidency. Of the major Republican candidates, he was most in tune ideologically with Robert Taft. The Taft forces, in turn, made clear that the vice presidency could be his in exchange for help in delivering the California delegation. "Why, no, I won't do that," Knowland said. "As long as Earl Warren is in the picture, I will support Earl Warren."[71] Mac Faries got wind of the offer and reported it to Warren. "Well, of course," Warren said. "I knew that Bill would be that way."

Nixon well knew that his fellow California senator was a competitor for the vice presidential nod. Both out of respect for Knowland's seniority and as a smokescreen for his own ambitions, he took a deferential attitude whenever the issue came up in public. Before the convention, he said that "if it were a choice between him and Knowland, it should go to Knowland."[72] The statement, by itself, was disloyal to Warren. After all, asked a reporter, "who [ever] heard of two men from the same state on the same ticket?"[73]

Once he was on the delegation, Nixon was drawn into speculation about a Republican ticket not headed by Warren. "If it becomes clear that either Ike or Taft will win," he offered, "we will all press for Knowland as vice president." He continued to tout Knowland as a strong prospect for either place on the ticket in private communication with the delegates. "As a result of Knowland winning the [June] primary," Nixon wrote, "he has completely supplanted Warren as the vice presidential prospect, and several people have [even] been talking about Knowland as the best bet of a dark horse in the event of a deadlock."[74]

Knowland had actively supported Nixon in his campaigns for public office and as a Senate colleague. But on the whole, he had arrived at a nuanced view of the junior senator, one characterized more by caution than anything else. Like Warren, he saw something in Nixon that made him wary. Warren's deep hostility toward Nixon must have influenced Knowland's attitude, in view of their often daily communication over a number of years. "Let's be candid," his daughter Emelyn Jewett told an interviewer, "I think it's fair to say that ... Dad didn't trust Nixon even from the early years."

In general, Knowland seemed better able than Warren to moderate his distaste. As his daughter explained:

> He watched very carefully what Nixon was up to. I think they had a good working relationship.... You have to understand Dad and his sense of morality — that even if you don't trust or like someone, if they're getting a bad rap ... Dad doesn't feel they should be hung on that issue.... Dad was straightforward and honest and candid.... Nixon was a political expedient. I think my Dad saw through him and didn't admire him because of that, because Nixon would take sides on an issue based on what was going to help Nixon. [It] wasn't easily reconcilable.[75]

## *Nixon's Poll*

After the California primary, Nixon undertook another risky gambit. He sent a presidential preference poll to 23,000 people who had assisted his senatorial campaign of 1950. It began: "As you know, Governor Warren has announced that if it should appear that he cannot obtain the nomination, he will release the delegates to vote for whoever they individually feel is best qualified." Nixon went on to ask them to write in who they felt was the strongest candidate the party could nominate for president. He pledged to maintain absolute secrecy about their responses, which he described as for his information only. The poll showed Eisenhower with a lead over both Warren and Taft.[76]

When Kyle Palmer at the *Times* got wind of the poll, he thought Nixon had gone too far. He wrote a column that concluded with the pointed observation that "honorable men don't stab their friends — or enemies — in the back!"[77] According to Warren's memoirs, it was Palmer from whom he first heard of the poll. He was furious. "I told Palmer that was not consistent with the oath that all the delegates had taken to support my candidacy," he recalled, his written words showing less anger than he no doubt felt and expressed at the time. "The governor felt that this was undercutting him," Bill Knowland said simply.[78]

Warren delegates likewise considered the poll an act of betrayal. "If you're going strongly for the head of the delegation who is the candidate for the presidency," recalled Warren associate Thomas J. Mellon, "you don't ask each member ... who the second choice would be."[79]

Nixon knew that he had his hands on political dynamite, and he told his office staff to reveal nothing about the polling data. But the results began to leak almost immediately. Warren sent a strong message to Nixon through emissary Bernie Brennan, who was close to both men, demanding that the poll results not be published and that Nixon cease his efforts to undermine Warren's campaign. Trying to be impartial, Brennan warned Nixon that unless he honored both requests, he "would be finished as a man of honor."[80]

Nixon probably realized that he had overreached. He soon told a wire service that naming a second choice after Warren would be "improper" until Warren releases the delegation — hastening to add the words "if that time should come." Palmer wrote a conciliatory column, reaffirming Nixon's commitment to Warren and rationalizing the presidential poll as an attempt to "pierce the fog caused by conflicting claims of Taft and Eisenhower supporters."[81] Though a few newspapers reported the leaks from Nixon's office, outright publication of the poll and its results was prevented.

Warren inadvertently helped Nixon undermine him in another way. California had a seat on the convention's platform committee, and Warren decided to offer it to Nixon. He probably assumed he could do little damage in this role, but it gave Nixon an excuse to arrive in Chicago early and a vantage point from which to monitor the battle for delegates between Eisenhower and Taft. He lost no time in circulating among the arriving party officials and gathering political intelligence that he would later put to good use.

## 7 — The 1952 Republican Convention

### *The Train to the Convention*

Over the years, several witnesses have recounted the dramatic details of the train trip made by the California Republican delegation from Sacramento to Chicago in the days immediately preceding the convention. Some of these accounts are in disagreement. The following version is the most persuasive, best documented, and most consistent with events that took place both before and after the trip.

The Warren delegation set off from Sacramento on July 3 in high spirits. The governor had told the delegates that morning that he was "without any intention of making ... personal deals ... or ... to serve as a Presidential nominee-maker." He was "full of confidence," according to an aide, "not cocky ... but he gave you the feeling he was hopeful."[82]

He clearly believed that he was a better choice for president than Eisenhower. He had told an acquaintance a few weeks before that, as an experienced governor of a large state, he had more preparation for the White House than an untrained military leader.[8e] Asked about rumors of defections, he said solemnly that "it would be dishonorable for delegates pledged ... to leave him until he had released them."

On the second day out, the party-like atmosphere came to an abrupt halt when a report reached the train that Senator Nixon, who had been in Chicago for several days, would be boarding in Denver. A Warren associate, Butch Powers, saw the governor "visibly arch" when he learned of Nixon's imminent arrival. "It was very much a surprise," Powers recalled, "and I could see there was quite a bit of feeling between them."[84]

When he boarded, Nixon headed to the compartment of four of his closest allies. One of them, Frank Jorgensen, recalled him saying with some excitement that "Eisenhower was running very strong and that Taft had lost ground." Jorgensen added that "he even mentioned his own [vice presidential] candidacy."[85] Nixon spent considerable time with these men, and the Warren party was becoming irritated that he had not first gone to see the governor.

When he finally did, Warren managed to receive him cordially. He wrote later that Nixon "paid his respects to me and said that if any of his friends got out of line to let him know." A witness to the talks said that Nixon expressed "one hundred percent" support of Warren's presidential bid. The senator reported that it had come down to Eisenhower and Taft back in Chicago, but "he didn't get into saying that Warren couldn't win."[86]

What happened once he left Warren's compartment helped in time to cement his reputation for duplicity. Nixon wandered around the train, shaking hands and greeting people with such verve that, as one reporter said, "you'd have thought *he* was the candidate, not Warren."[87] Then he called impromptu meetings of groups of delegates, including some Warren supporters, to pass along gossip he had picked up while attending pre-convention preliminaries.

But the message he delivered to them was quite different than the one he had just given the governor. According to delegate John Dinkelspiel, Nixon told them that "Warren has very little if any chance of getting the nomination," and that Eisenhower's momentum appeared unstoppable. "The California delegation could effectively [e]nsure Eisenhower's victory," Nixon told them, "if they could be counted upon by the Eisenhower people." If California stays with Warren too long, it will be "left out in the cold."[88]

This statement electrified Nixon's allies, as well as many wavering Warren supporters, whose desire for victory in November was at least as strong as their loyalty to the governor. A young witness, Robert Finch, said that Nixon's report caused many delegates to ask themselves: "Had [Warren] done enough, was he an addition to the ticket in 1948? Was he really a salable candidate nationwide? That as opposed to Eisenhower's popularity was the thing that festered."[89]

When a delegate expressed concern about breaking his oath to Warren, Nixon assured him he could help Ike without violating his pledge. "It should be made publicly known," he proposed, "that the delegation would throw its strength to Eisenhower as soon as it could." Doing so, Nixon's men suggested, might carry a reward for California. As one writer summarized their argument, "If [the delegates] acted quickly and did not waste their votes, the delegation could suggest Nixon as vice president."

Nixon's assessment of the new political realities in Chicago threw the train into an uproar and the Warren people into a cold fury. Aides described the governor as angrier than they had ever seen him.[90] Even if Warren had not been the proud and sensitive man that he was, he would not have been able to view Nixon's behavior as anything less than a challenge to his authority. Some of the delegates believed they were witnessing a struggle between the two men for control of the California delegation.

Even worse from Warren's perspective, he was beginning to see that he was at a disadvantage in dealing with his young rival. Nixon was no longer a wet-behind-the-ears congressman from Whittier, but a well-plugged-in, highly regarded politician with powerful friends. If the delegates perceived Nixon as commanding more respect among high-level Republicans than Warren, they were bound to look to the senator rather than the governor for leadership. Some of them already did. Warren faced not only the end of his presidential bid but a considerable loss of face.

Later that evening, another dramatic scene took place, this one a heated discussion between Nixon and his supporters. The train's air conditioning had failed, and compartment doors had been opened to allow a breeze in. Even Warren delegates several cabins away were able to hear the raised voices. Nixon's men were demanding that he be much more aggressive in his challenge of Warren, even if it led to an open break. "They were working on Nixon ... to cut Warren up ... really putting the heat on him," Warren ally Thomas Mellon recalled. "They kept hammering on Nixon to be sure he didn't weaken his position in being for Eisenhower."[91]

Nixon argued for caution and for adjusting their tactics in response to developments at the convention. But his delegates, mostly southern Californians, did not care about subtleties — they wanted the governor out of the picture. Two of Nixon's closest associates, Frank Jorgensen and Pat Hillings, who had reminded Warren delegates that they would be breaking no law by violating their oath to the governor, were particularly "ruthless" in their arguments. According to Mellon, Nixon was thrown on the defensive. "Well, after all, I am a United States senator," he finally said. "We don't give a damn what you are," they apparently answered. "You wouldn't be anybody if it wasn't for us."[92]

If true, this anecdote suggests that Nixon was not so much a duplicitous schemer as a man caught between his convictions and his obligations. Mellon believed that Nixon tried at all times to steer a middle course between the venomous anti–Warren sentiment of his loyalists and the governor's refusal to give up his dream of being a compromise candidate. By this view, Nixon was more concerned about party unity and putting forward the best possible ticket than he was about his own prospects for high office.

Word of Nixon's debate with his allies filtered back to the governor. Years later, with restraint he undoubtedly did not feel at the time, he summarized the evening's events:

> During the night, the Nixon delegates — but not the senator as far as I know — held caucuses and urged other delegates to vote for General Eisenhower on the first ballot. Some of those who were importuned came to me and asked what the situation was. I told them what I had told the voters: that the delegation was not a front for anyone, and that no matter what happened it was obligated to vote for me on the first ballot at least.[93]

Warren seemed inclined to give Nixon the benefit of the doubt — judging that he was trying to honor the letter if not the spirit of his pledge. This would prove to be a distinction without a difference as the convention unfolded.

Warren had to endure still more aggravation before reaching Chicago. Nixon slipped off the train a few miles outside of the city — "furtively," as one observer described it. When the train pulled into the station, Bill Knowland had arranged a warm welcome, featuring a band and a large group of cheering supporters. As the Warren entourage made its way toward waiting buses, which had been bedecked that morning with "Warren for President" signs, an advance party discovered that the signs had all been replaced with Eisenhower banners. A panicked Warren assistant barely managed to pull them off before the rest of the group arrived. When the governor was told about the switch sometime later, "he was mad as hell," recalled a Warren supporter. "He thought that Nixon and Chotiner had pulled this fast one."[94]

Word of the turmoil in the California delegation had reached the Taft and Eisenhower campaigns. Even before the convention started, they were circling like hungry vultures, hoping to identify as many deserters of Warren's cause as possible. Nixon immediately began holding strategy meetings with his people and with Eisenhower's representatives — manning what biographer Roger Morris viewed as a "veritable command post of his vice presidential candidacy."[95]

Warren convened his delegation within minutes of arriving at the hotel. He made a brief statement to assure them that he was in the race to stay. "You trust me, and I'll trust you," he told them. But that first night, Warren went to bed deeply disturbed. Reflecting on what later was christened Nixon's "great train robbery," he asked an old friend almost plaintively: "How do you account for him doing a thing like this? I just can't understand anybody doing such a thing as that."[96]

## *Nixon and "Fair Play"*

One of the convention's first and most important orders of business was to decide which of several rival Southern delegations would be seated. The significance of the dispute lay in the fact that in each affected state, one slate of delegates was committed to Eisenhower and the other to Taft. A total of eighty-five seats were at stake.

Though many party officials tried to make the seating of one group over the other a moral issue, neither side was in reality more legitimate than the other — it was simply a struggle between two partisan groups claiming to represent the state's true Republicans. The credentials committee, which was controlled by Taft people, had decided to accept the credentials of the Taft groups, on the grounds that they were party members of longer standing.

With Taft still slightly ahead in the delegate count, the Eisenhower forces immediately saw that the seating of the Taft groups in the South could sink Ike's candidacy, and they challenged the Southern "steal." They prepared a motion for debate at the convention that, if passed, would seat the Eisenhower delegates instead. To increase its appeal, they christened it the "fair play" amendment and portrayed its opponents as intent upon the "rape of the Republican party." Then they applied all the pressure they could muster on the convention delegates to pass it.

Nixon quickly fell in line behind this effort. Even before the train trip to Chicago, he had reminded a group of reporters of the supposed moral consequences of the "fair play" issue and asserted that the Taft delegates had been improperly chosen. By accepting this choice as legitimate, he insisted, the convention would have no greater claim on the nation's trust than the Democrats they were trying to oust. "If the Republican party approves [this] grab," he concluded, "we will be announcing to the country that we believe ruthless machine politics is wrong only when Democrats use it."[97]

The California delegation held its first caucus on Sunday night. Bill Knowland opened with a joke that he hoped would defuse the tensions building in the group. There was no truth to the rumors, he said, that he and Warren were not speaking to Nixon. After the nervous laughter had died down, he said he was "not interested in being merely a bandwagon jumper."[98] He went on to argue that the delegation's best option was to split its votes on the "fair play" amendment, thereby preserving California's neutrality between Taft and Eisenhower and keeping Warren's chances alive. The Eisenhower forces knew that his desire for compromise would also keep Taft's chances alive, and likewise Knowland's chance to be Taft's vice president.

Nixon then took the microphone and reprised his earlier argument, urging the delegation to vote as a unit for "fair play." His appeal to principle seemed to persuade most of the delegates, but a word from Warren would have been enough to swing the group behind the Knowland formula. After all, he was still in charge. But Warren took the floor and seemed to agree with Nixon that the issue was a moral one. "You have to go back to the state of California and face the people of California," he said. "You vote your conscience."[99] After this short statement, the delegation voted sixty-two to eight to support "fair play." The unit rule gave all seventy votes to the amendment's supporters.

Why did Warren approve an action that, as it turned out, ultimately ended his candidacy? His supporters argued long afterward that he did so unselfishly, without regard for his presidential chances, because he truly saw it as a matter of conscience. As he said later, "I just couldn't go along with the way those Southern politicians manipulated the delegations."[100] Warren's detractors suggested that he was motivated by an offer of a Supreme Court appointment in an Eisenhower administration if he would ensure that California cast its votes for the seating of Ike's delegations.[101]

But the governor had what he felt were sound tactical reasons as well. He was already on record as supporting the seating of the Eisenhower delegates, in the mistaken belief that Taft had a sizeable lead. He may have believed that additional Eisenhower strength was needed to increase the odds of a stalemate. Because he and Eisenhower were more closely aligned ideologically than he and Taft, he had good cause to believe that if Eisenhower delegates could not nominate Ike, they would turn to him instead. Thus, he needed to ensure that Ike had more votes than Taft, but not enough to win.

The Eisenhower forces had better intelligence. Their counts told them that their Southern delegates, if seated, could bring Ike to the brink of the nomination. Nixon, on the inside, knew this too.

Knowland apparently saw the consequences of the "fair play" resolution more clearly than Warren did, because he tried to broker a compromise between the Taft and Eisenhower forces that would keep the issue from coming to an immediate floor vote. But the Ike backers smelled victory and pressed for a roll call Monday afternoon. The convention approved "fair play" by a 658–548 margin. As a consequence, Taft's lead over Eisenhower disappeared.

## *Traitor in the Delegation*

The next day, Warren paid a courtesy call on Eisenhower at his hotel suite. "Imagine my surprise," he wrote later, "when the doorkeeper who admitted me to the general's suite was Murray Chotiner, one of the managers on my train."[102] The reason for Chotiner's presence was not fully explained, but the bizarre scene certainly pointed to a strong link between Nixon and Eisenhower supporters. Warren, it seemed, could not take a step without being reminded of Nixon.

But the final straw was yet to come. That night, the controversial General Douglas MacArthur, who was still wildly popular among conservative Republicans, delivered the convention's keynote speech. Nixon acolyte Pat Hillings passed the word to the California delegation that headquarters did not want them to applaud his speech, because MacArthur might still be a compromise candidate. Several angry conservatives assumed the order came from Warren and clapped anyway. When they demanded an explanation for the order, Hillings admitted that Nixon had put him up to it.[103] The governor denounced Nixon's unauthorized action and then decided — far too late — to bar him and his aides from Warren's quarters.

# 7— The 1952 Republican Convention

Nixon (left) and Warren (right) confer with Republican presidential candidate Dwight Eisenhower at the 1952 Republican convention in Chicago. Nixon was pledged to support Warren for president but he worked behind the scenes for Ike's nomination and shocked his California rivals by emerging as the party's choice for vice president (California State Archives).

The next day, he summoned Paul Davis, a former Eisenhower associate, and asked him to convey a remarkable message "orally and confidentially" to the general:

> The problem is this. We have a traitor in our delegation. It's Nixon. He, like all the rest, took the oath that he would vote for me, until such time as the delegation was released, but he has not paid attention to his oath and immediately upon being elected [a delegate], started working for Eisenhower and has been doing so ever since. I have word that he is actively in touch with the Eisenhower people. I wish you would tell General Eisenhower that we resent his people infiltrating, through Nixon, into our delegation, and ask him to have it stopped.

"I tell you, but you needn't tell Eisenhower at this time," he said to Davis in conclusion, "that if he doesn't do that, we're going to take measures that will be harmful to his candidacy."[104]

"Well, I am not at all sure that his information is correct," Eisenhower responded somewhat evasively when confronted by Davis. "My understanding is that we are definitely letting the California delegation alone and not trying to interfere with it in any way whatsoever." In truth, all sides were maneuvering for position behind the scenes and offering deals for votes to anyone who would listen. When Taft heard how badly he had lost on "fair play" in the California delegation, his desperation became apparent. First, he went to Warren. "Taft begged me," Warren later told columnist Drew Pearson. "He said it was his last chance and I could have anything I wanted in his administration."[105]

Warren almost certainly considered working for Taft an unattractive prospect. In his memoirs, he criticized the Ohio senator's "sensitivity to human relations." And he was still nursing hurt feelings over Taft's failure to meet his train in Cincinnati when he was campaigning for the vice presidency in 1948 — an oversight that left him "really burned up."[106] So Taft's pleading left him unmoved. "No, Senator," he said firmly, "we will go ahead as planned."[107]

Then Taft went to Knowland. He believed that if he offered him the vice presidency, it could swing California's votes behind him. As usual, the senator was unwilling to negotiate. "I didn't feel that I could even discuss the subject without undermining the position of Governor Warren," he said later.[108] Knowland may have later regretted spurning Taft's overtures. Had he accepted either of them, and had Taft won the election, Taft's death in 1953 would have made him president.

Despite Eisenhower's assurances to Warren that he would not "interfere ... in any way whatsoever" in the California delegation, Ike's floor manager, Sherman Adams, also tried to feel Knowland out on the "situation." Adams later recalled that Knowland "hardly spoke to me. He only scowled, shook his head violently, and turned his back to me."[109] These rebuffs of both the Taft and Eisenhower forces left no doubt that Knowland was not for sale.

Having given both sides the cold shoulder, Knowland was said to be "peeved" over reports that his fellow senator from California might be Ike's vice presidential choice.[110] If this was the case, he realized, Nixon had been undermining Warren all along. "Nixon was conveying to Knowland that he was for Taft. And then he was conveying to the other people he was for Ike," remembered one party activist. "But he [Knowland] didn't grasp the situation as to what Nixon was going to do to him.... He believed that Nixon was an honorable man."[111] According to Knowland's biographers, his wife asked him: "Do you think Nixon double-crossed you?" "Yes, I think so," he replied.[112]

On Wednesday, stories began appearing in the press on the possibility of an Eisenhower-Nixon ticket. The *Chicago Daily News* went the furthest, flatly predicting and then endorsing such a ticket. Nixon ordered extra copies of the newspaper. "That will probably be the last time we'll see that headline, and I want to be able to show it to my grandchildren," he joked.[113]

On the eve of the presidential balloting, Warren felt his chances slipping away. "I couldn't help feeling sorry for him," wrote Drew Pearson in his memoirs. But Warren seemed resigned. "I haven't the money and I can't go out and make the deals necessary to raise the money to stage a real campaign," he lamented. "You have to hock your soul in order to do it."[114]

The three rivals played prominent roles at the final California caucus before the balloting. At this point, Warren and Knowland publicly showed their irritation with Nixon's divisive role. First, Knowland gave the group a pep talk, arguing that a Warren victory was not out of reach. In a veiled message to Nixon, who was sitting beside Warren on the platform, he warned against efforts to stampede the delegation and declared that it would not "engage in any kind of deal whatsoever." According to Knowland's biographers, he was "shaking with anger."[115]

As the Californians applauded, attention turned to Warren, who pointedly ignored Nixon and spoke of his "tremendous pride" in the loyalty of his delegation. Then he turned to thank Knowland, a man he would not trade "for any six chairmen of other delegations."[116] The obvious irritation of these two men was a price Nixon seemed willing to pay for his fast-approaching day in the sun.

As Eisenhower closed in on a first ballot nomination, he and his staff once again reviewed the vice presidential prospects. The talk was mostly of Nixon, but Knowland remained a possibility, despite his seemingly unshakable dedication to Warren. To be sure, he was a poorer ideological fit with Ike than he was with the more conservative Taft.

Looking for another way to view the choice between the two Californians, Ike adviser Herbert Brownell turned to none other than Murray Chotiner. The latter had, after all, managed the candidacies of both men for the Senate, so his opinion seemed worth seeking. "I gave him my candid opinion," Chotiner later said, "which was that Nixon had a shade as a campaigner and also appealed more to independents and young people ... just a shade in favor of Nixon." Brownell then asked him how Warren would likely react if Nixon were picked. His reply was a masterpiece of understatement: "I said I didn't know but that there had not been any warmth between the two."[117]

Then Brownell asked him what Knowland's reaction might be. In answering, Chotiner quoted Knowland's wife, Helen, who allegedly had said to him: "You tell Dick ... to go right ahead, and ... not to think for a moment how Bill would feel about it." Brownell apparently said: "Well, if Bill Knowland's wife feels that way about it, why that must be it."[118] Chotiner's comments succeeded in reassuring Brownell that, come what may, the Californians would be team players when it came time to campaign in the fall.

The next day, Knowland placed Warren's name officially before the convention. He proposed him "on behalf of the unanimous California delegation," in the conviction that "if nominated, he can be elected and if elected he would make a great President of the United States." Knowland was well aware that his words hid the true state of affairs within his contingent.

The balloting then began. Warren received only scattered votes from the other states. Eisenhower, as expected, closed in on a first-ballot victory. When he was only a few votes short of the nomination, the Minnesota delegation suggested to Knowland that the two groups switch to Ike to put him over the top — "as a means of healing party wounds," according to one listener. Knowland was brusque. "We don't want any credit or any responsibility for *that* nomination."[119] He also believed that Nixon would get the credit in Eisenhower's eyes if California's votes helped make the difference.

He later had second thoughts about joining Minnesota but could not find Warren in time to ask for permission. Not that Warren would have consented. "There were importunities made on me to turn our delegation over, which clearly would have done the job for [Eisenhower]," he recalled years later, "and I wasn't going to let it be said that I was a patsy for anybody else."[120]

## *Nixon Prevails*

In the chaos that followed Eisenhower's nomination, which left Taft supporters bitter and heartbroken, Henry Cabot Lodge found Nixon seated with the California delegation and asked him to be the vice presidential candidate. "Will you do it?" Lodge asked. Nixon said that he would.

Regardless of what Chotiner might have believed or Knowland's wife might have said, Knowland was unlikely to handle a Nixon nomination with equanimity. Warren aide Mac Faries was in the crowd with a friend waiting for Knowland after Nixon left the convention hall. "This is going to be awfully tough on Bill, let's get him out of here," one of them said. A strange scene then ensued. They grabbed Knowland, left the hall, and drove aimlessly around Chicago, talking of anything but the Nixon choice. Knowland did not speak of it either. Eventually, they had to stop at the hotel before returning to the hall, because Knowland's shirt was "as wet as a sheet."[121]

Back at the convention, the Eisenhower forces called a meeting of selected party leaders for the ostensible purpose of choosing a vice presidential candidate. Warren had long since seen the handwriting on the wall. "Believing that it was already a fait accompli, I declined [to attend]," he wrote years later.[122] The group went through the motions of considering several possible nominees, including Taft, but when Dewey spoke strongly in favor of Nixon, those assembled quickly agreed and adjourned.

Up until the last minute, Nixon worried that one of his California rivals would snatch the prize that now seemed within his grasp. "I knew that some of Eisenhower's more liberal advisors had preferred Earl Warren to me," he recalled, "and that some of his more conservative advisors had preferred Bill Knowland or even Bob Taft."[123] As the least experienced of the three contenders, and well aware of the fluid situation, he had every reason to be concerned. But it turned out that he was the only one of the three rivals actively interested in the vice presidency. And he had the good fortune to have chosen the winning side.

Eisenhower had still not talked to Nixon about being his running mate. That finally happened during the afternoon — a phone call from Brownell followed by a visit to the general, who received Nixon in what he considered a somewhat awkward and formal manner.

Knowland's enforced break from the convention probably helped him endure a final indignity. Dewey had planned to place Nixon's name formally before the convention, but at the last minute the assignment went to Knowland, as a gesture of unity toward the Taft people. Nixon later reported Knowland saying that he would be "proud and happy" to give the nominating speech.

His actual response was far less diplomatic. A Warren supporter heard Knowland ask: "I have to nominate that dirty son of a bitch?"[124] He managed to carry out the task, but his delivery was short on enthusiasm. Watching his speech on television back in California, Keith McCormac said: "Knowing Knowland like I did, you could tell that he would rather have been anywhere but there, nominating Nixon. I remember the look on his face."[125]

Not long afterward, Nixon, Eisenhower and their wives appeared in triumph on the podium. The cheers of the crowd climaxed a remarkable success story. Only four years before, Nixon was an obscure young congressman, but he now found himself running for the second highest office in the land. The headline in the *Los Angeles Times* that day added insult to the injury sustained by the man who had hoped to be a compromise candidate for president. It read: "Nixon Retrieves State Prestige Lost by Warren."

## Taking Stock

In piecing together an account of the dramatic events of 1952, one must make choices among many sources and versions. Depending on those choices, Nixon can appear as a selfless striver for Republican victory or a man who went back on his word in order to grasp the brass ring of the vice presidency. One can believe that there was a certain inevitability about his emergence as Ike's running mate, given the actions of Ike's backers and his growing reputation as a comer, or that his selection was due to his persistent effort to serve and impress the team around Ike.

In assessing Nixon's conduct before and during the convention and weighing the charge of duplicity, we must evaluate his claim that his loyalties were never a secret. At the time of his June delegate poll, Nixon characterized Warren's strongly negative reaction as "silly," because he had told the governor that he supported Eisenhower "from the beginning." In his memoirs, he described the moment when he told Taft that he was supporting Ike for the nomination. He also wrote without elaboration: "I had already informed Knowland and Warren of my decision."

Knowland called this claim "a definite misstatement of fact,"[126] and it probably was. But whether it was or not is immaterial. A careful reading of Nixon's public statements would have told Warren and Knowland all they needed to know. "You can't satisfy me that Warren wasn't perfectly aware of all of Nixon's ambitions, and Nixon's friends' ambitions," said Warren aide Mac Faries. "I think that the man [Warren] was so smart that he knew a lot of [the delegates] were not for him."[127]

But neither Warren nor Knowland grasped how fast their rival's influence in party circles had grown and how cleverly he could pursue his agenda. They certainly did not reckon on Nixon's talent for improvisation or, as Morris has written, his sheer political genius. If Warren believed that Nixon could be coopted and controlled, he seriously underestimated his independence and clout. If he did not know where Nixon's loyalties lay, he was not paying attention

From the perspective of Nixon and his allies, the goal was not so much to undermine Warren's presidential candidacy as it was to make him face reality — the "facts of life," as Pat Hillings put it. In a later interview, Hillings rejected any notion of sabotage. "I don't think that was ever the case at all. [Warren] never had a chance in the first place."[128]

Given Nixon's strong preference for Eisenhower, it can be argued that he could have pursued no other course. He balked at joining the Warren favorite-son delegation but was told his absence would be disloyal. He was therefore bound to his fellow California Republicans even though he believed that they were engaged in a losing cause. Under the circumstances, he probably saw no moral conflict in defining his role on the delegation as helping to maximize the state's influence on the nomination process and to win the election in November, rather than backing the favorite-son candidacy of a man who had never lifted a finger to help him.

At least one of Nixon's men insisted that the senator made an effort to honor his commitment to Warren. According to Frank Jorgensen, Nixon "tried to build something" during the first two days of the convention by talking to as many delegates as possible about the advantages of a Warren candidacy.[129]

But believing that he did so requires dismissing the many claims to the contrary, including one from an associate of Tom Dewey's that Nixon was a "fifth column" assigned by Henry Cabot Lodge to undermine Warren's control of the California delegation.[130] Nixon made a few lukewarm gestures of support for Warren — but only enough so that he could not be accused of overt disloyalty.

Jorgensen also denied that there was any deal to make Nixon the vice presidential candidate in exchange for his support of Eisenhower. It is true that Nixon could not be certain he would be chosen until the end of the convention. But if there was no deal, there was certainly an informal understanding. Dewey, Dulles and the rest of Ike's campaign managers could not guarantee Nixon anything, but he had reason to believe that his chances were excellent.

Some have concluded that there was a direct link between Nixon's personal ambition and his subversion of Warren's candidacy, but this does not seem to have been the case. Nixon decided to commit himself to Eisenhower long before any serious thought of the vice presidency entered his head. His protestations of being considered a candidate can be viewed as modest and prudent rather than evasive. His primary goal initially was an Eisenhower nomination. Anything else would be frosting on the cake.

Despite his youth and inexperience, Nixon had demonstrated political skills superior to those of Knowland and Warren. Knowland's stubbornness and lack of imagination proved a handicap in adapting to changing conditions. Warren, too, was bullheaded, and his egocentric aloofness distorted his view of political reality. As for Nixon, it is hard not to agree with Roger Morris that his 1952 balancing act was "one of the great, largely unseen prodigies of political positioning — a brilliant, audacious, sometimes reckless maneuver that would affect his life for better and for worse long into the future."[131]

## *Aftermath*

The Republican rank-and-file greeted Nixon's choice with enthusiasm. Even his fellow senator Democrat John F. Kennedy of Massachusetts wrote him a warm letter of congratulations. "I was tremendously pleased that the convention selected you for vice president," he enthused. "You were an ideal selection and will bring to the ticket a good deal of strength."[132]

Others reacted negatively to the new nominee. In the aftermath of the convention, Nixon attempted to gain the acceptance of Taft loyalists, including Taft himself. But bruised feelings would not be easily mended. The Ohio senator was conciliatory in public, but he soon described Nixon as a "little man in a big hurry," with a "mean, vindictive streak" and a personality that "radiates tension and conflict."[133] President Truman told the California press that the Republican Party should have nominated "your great liberal governor" but instead chose "another Californian who is not worthy to lace his shoes."[134]

The surprising outcome jolted both Warren and Knowland. They now had to reconcile themselves to Nixon's success. More than that, they had to recover sufficiently to campaign for the Eisenhower-Nixon ticket in California. If the election was to be won in the fall, the losers had to close ranks with the winners and present a common front to the public. It would not be easy.

Warren had the presence of mind to declare publicly that he was "happy to hear of the selection of Senator Nixon" and that his presence on the ticket was a "great honor to our state." Herbert Perry of Nixon's staff was impressed. Despite his misgivings about Warren in the past, he wrote, "I feel at the present time that he is honestly attempting to abide by the decision of the Chicago convention."[135]

In private, however, Warren's anger simmered. A while after his return to Sacramento, his secretary saw him staring out the window of his office and complaining of how Nixon had undermined his candidacy. "He was bitter, very bitter," she recalled.[136] Warren was prudent enough not to express his true feelings in writing. "The full measure of his unhappiness," observed biographer Jim Newton, "would only come to light in glancing admissions and occasionally unguarded remarks." Newton has noted that when aide Merrell Small read Warren's memoirs in draft, he wondered: "Have you not treated Richard Nixon with too kindly a touch? ... I have had the understanding that you believed [he] was ... prepared to cut your political throat."[137]

The shocking outcome of the 1952 convention moved Warren's attitude toward Nixon from annoyance to something approaching hatred. Governor

Pat Brown was one of several friends of Warren who later became privy to his thoughts about the events of that July. "He never forgave Richard Nixon," Brown told an interviewer in 1979. "You read the statements in the paper where he was said to have called him a crook and a thief. He told *me* that. He's told me that Tricky Dick — that's what he used to call him — he didn't like him at all."[138] In an interview three years later, Brown used stronger words. "When he hated people, he hated them, [and] the guy he hated more than anybody else was Nixon."[139]

Warren's supporters were equally angry. One writer reported that "many of them would forever consider Nixon's name roughly synonymous with treachery."[140] Ten years later, Warren's son, Earl Jr., let fly a tirade against Nixon that clearly referred to the events of 1952. Nixon, he said, had "wronged my father and the whole state" by "pulling the rug out from under us" and using "back-door tactics" undertaken for "political gain for himself."[141]

To his credit, Warren did not allow his personal pique to affect his public enthusiasm for the Eisenhower-Nixon ticket. Though he was not particularly active early in the fall — causing some Republicans to grumble that he was "sitting this one out" because of his dislike of Nixon[142] — he toured fifteen states in October and campaigned hard in California during the week before the election. Jerry Brown, the young son of California attorney general Pat Brown, was one of many Democrats who were amazed to see Warren stumping for Ike and Nixon. The Browns speculated that the governor was hoping to get a high-level appointment in return for his efforts.[143]

A call from Eisenhower shortly after the election would open a new chapter in Warren's life and remove him from politics for good. But he would spend the rest of his career rooting against Nixon from the sidelines.

Like Warren, Knowland put a brave face on the convention results, telling the press that Nixon was an "excellent choice" for the vice presidency. But when reminded years later that Nixon's "second choice" after Warren had been Eisenhower, Knowland bristled: "I was for Governor Warren, period. I didn't have a second or third choice."[144]

Still, Knowland did not seem to take the events of July 1952 nearly as hard as Warren did. Only a week after the convention adjourned, he penned a disarmingly friendly note to Nixon, along with a copy of the lead editorial from the *Oakland Tribune*, which included "a good picture of you, Pat and the youngsters." He suggested that Nixon get some rest. "Having made the trip around the country with Earl four years ago," he noted, "I have some appreciation of the problems and pressures you will be under, and even a fellow as young as you are will need to save your energy." He encouraged Nixon to contact him anytime for advice or assistance. "Helen joins me in sending our love to you and Pat," he concluded.[145]

The 1952 convention did not merely alienate Nixon from Warren. It also led to a distancing between Warren and his boyhood friend, Knowland. Warren himself observed after the events of that summer, they were never again as close. "Knowland was perfectly loyal to me," he recalled years later, "and held the delegation together as a solid unit throughout." He could have accepted Taft's offer of the vice presidency and become president soon after, Warren pointed out. "I mention this," he continued, "because thereafter my relations with Knowland, political and otherwise, cooled markedly — not to the breaking point, but noticeably."[146]

Knowland must have felt that his dedication to Warren's presidential campaigns in 1948 and 1952 had evened the score between them. Continued support of a man who was far more liberal than he would represent a sacrifice of his own career ambitions and send the wrong signals to the conservatives who formed his natural constituency. No longer having a sense of obligation meant that he could be his own person from then on. It also meant that the differences in their politics would no longer be hidden by personal loyalty.

\* \* \*

On the evening of July 28, Nixon was officially welcomed home to California. Republican national headquarters asked that the leading party office holders in the state be on hand to receive him. Of course, that meant Warren, Knowland and Lieutenant Governor Goodwin Knight. The three men waited next to the door of Nixon's plane as the vice presidential candidate disembarked. The cameras rolled as Warren said: "Welcome to California, Dick. All the people of California are rejoicing at your success."

The group then went by motorcade to the Whittier High School football field, where Nixon was reunited with family members and old friends. Mrs. Warren held one of the two Nixon girls on her lap during the festivities — a fact Warren cited later in denying any animosity between him and the vice presidential candidate.[147] As Nixon's wife, Pat, and mother, Hannah, looked on from the stands with "tears glistening in their eyes," Nixon told the crowd that it would have been "great" even if only Governor Warren or Senator Knowland had come. But all of them? "Well, for Pat and me this is the greatest moment in history."[148]

## *The Fund Crisis*

The task ahead seemed straightforward enough. With the tension and uncertainty of the convention behind them, the two Republican standard-bearers prepared for an intense two months of campaigning across the nation. Nixon had already begun to make the kind of slashing attacks on Democratic

## 7 — The 1952 Republican Convention

Nixon acknowledges the cheers of the crowd at his Whittier homecoming in July 1952. On stage, from left, Knight, Knowland and Warren lead the applause. A smiling Pat Nixon, at far left, holds flowers. Beneath the surface, Knowland and Warren were furious with Nixon because of his perceived betrayal of the governor at the Republican convention. Nixon's mother, Hannah, is just behind her son (Richard Nixon Presidential Library/National Archives and Records Administration).

nominee Adlai Stevenson that would evoke comparisons with the style and tone of his 1950 Senate race.

But in mid–September, disaster brought the campaign to a standstill. It began with rumors, which quickly gained traction in the media, that money from a private fund had been channeled to Senator Nixon to pay for some of his routine political expenses, such as postage, document printing, and extra clerical help. This expense allowance had been provided by several of Nixon's wealthy supporters, who understood that his meager income was insufficient to handle his nonofficial responsibilities.

Nixon freely admitted the existence of the fund. He insisted that it was not secret and violated no laws. Care had been taken to account for all disbursements, and favors had not been done in exchange for contributions.

At first, Nixon and his staff considered the story harmless, but after a front-page article in the *New York Post*, the allegation that Nixon had received improper financial support threw the campaign into turmoil. The dramatic episode, which Nixon later called "the most scarring personal crisis of my life," has been exhaustively described and analyzed — most notably by Nixon himself.

Less well known are the roles played by Earl Warren and, especially, William Knowland in the evolution of the scandal. To one or more of Warren's backers went the credit (or blame) for bringing the existence of the fund to light in the first place. The *New York Post* article that attracted so much attention had been written by an admirer and, later, a biographer of Warren's, Leo Katcher. Several days later, a *New York Times* reporter in California alleged that the scandal had begun with a leak from a "disgruntled Warren Republican," who had been "rankling over what happened in Chicago."[149] Warren himself, the *Times* said, was declining to pass judgment on the fund story "until all the evidence has been presented."

In time, reports reached Nixon that the State of California planned to review his income tax returns and those of his donors. The investigation would be headed by state Controller Thomas Kuchel, a Warren crony who was later appointed by the governor to fill Nixon's vacant Senate seat. Warren probably had nothing to do with any Nixon tax audit, but it is reasonable to assume that he was not sorry to see his nemesis thrown off stride by the developing furor.

Knowland was more than a spectator in the fund scandal — in fact, for a while he seemed likely to profit from Nixon's misfortune. As the crisis deepened, Ike staffers called him in Hawaii, where he was scheduled to deliver a speech, and asked him to fly back to the mainland immediately and join the Eisenhower campaign train. There he was to help advise Ike and his senior aides and serve as what Morris called a "Vice-Presidential replacement in the wings."[150] Though visibly excited upon his departure from Hawaii, he made light of the crisis and said he expected it to be overcome. As he flew off, he had to be struck by the irony of it all — he might wind up replacing the "son of a bitch" whose name he had reluctantly presented to the convention in Chicago only two months earlier.

When Nixon got word that Knowland had been summoned, he correctly assumed that Eisenhower's staff was debating his future. "Some of those who had supported other vice presidential candidates began to build up a dump-Nixon movement," he later wrote. Nixon saw his opponents divided into "those who thought I should be dropped immediately and those who wanted to wait and see how public reaction developed."[151]

Soon after, a telegram added to his anguish. It was from Harold Stassen, his former supporter, who now advised him to offer his resignation for the good of the campaign. If Eisenhower agreed he should withdraw, Stassen went on, "Earl Warren should be named to step in."[152] Nixon later called the cable a "severe blow,"[153] not least because of the gratuitous suggestion that Warren replace him.

His frustration mounted as days went by, media criticism grew, and calls multiplied for his withdrawal from the ticket. He was told that most of Eisenhower's senior staff wanted him to resign, and the general himself was certainly providing no help to his embattled running mate. Characteristically, Nixon perceived the attacks as politics, pure and simple. But Ike professed to see the fund as a moral issue and felt that any doubts about Nixon's probity had to be laid to rest. "Of what avail is it for us to carry on this crusade," he told reporters, "if we, ourselves, aren't as clean as a hound's tooth?" The remark dismayed Nixon and his staff. "It made me feel like the little boy caught with jam on his face," he later wrote.[154]

Nixon ultimately decided that the best chance to save his candidacy was by explaining himself to the American people on live television and hoping for a response positive enough to force Eisenhower to keep him. Exhausted, short tempered, and under almost unbelievable pressure, he prepared to deliver what came to be known as the Checkers speech.

Before going on the air, Nixon tried to get Ike to commit himself. "If I issue a statement backing you up," Eisenhower responded, "in effect people will accuse me of condoning wrongdoing." Would he decide after the speech?, Nixon asked. "I am hoping that no announcement would be necessary at all, but maybe after the program we could tell what ought to be done." Then Nixon issued his famous rejoinder: "General, a time comes in politics when you have to shit or get off the pot."[155] This was something Ike had undoubtedly never heard from his troops.

So effective was Nixon's televised portrayal of an honest, hard-working public servant struggling to make ends meet that it generated an outpouring of cards, telegrams and letters overwhelmingly favoring his retention. The *Los Angeles Times* showed its immense relief by giving the speech breathless coverage under headlines like "Dramatic Plea Stirs Nation" and "Documents Show Nixon Blameless."[156] Eisenhower's ambivalence was finally resolved by the calculation that the Republican ticket now seemed stronger with Nixon than without him.

In the end, Knowland's presence in the wings gave Nixon little to worry about. Few among Eisenhower's moderate team of advisers backed the conservative senator, and his selection in the event of a Nixon withdrawal was far from a sure thing. Just as important, his words and actions suggested that he was not interested in becoming a last-minute replacement for his fellow Californian, especially if the Republican ticket would not be stronger as a result. He later recalled that he stood up for Nixon shortly after joining Eisenhower's train. He told Earl Adams, a Nixon fund-raiser, that he said to Ike: "It's no go. You leave him alone and he stays on the ticket."[157] The popular success of the Checkers speech reinforced that conviction. After it was over, Knowland declared "full confidence" in his colleague.[158]

Once it was clear that the speech had been a hit, a day was spent in long-distance negotiations between a still anxious Nixon and Eisenhower over where and when the two men would get together to decide what to do. Nixon finally joined Ike in West Virginia. Greeting Nixon as he disembarked, the general said with a broad grin, "You're my boy."

The Republican contingent went on to a joint appearance in Wheeling that same day, and Knowland was among the many people who came on stage to shake Nixon's hand. He approached Nixon and said simply: "That was a great speech, Dick." As Nixon recalled later, "It was not so much what he said, or the sincerity with which he said it, but at that moment ... I had exhausted all of my emotional reserve. Tears rushed into my eyes. Knowland put his arm around me and I hid my face in his shoulder." That moment, he said, would forever "characterize the fund speech and my reaction to it."[159]

Tension is evident in the faces of the four rivals as they pose in the aftermath of the 1952 Republican convention. Warren (third from left) had the presence of mind to declare himself "happy to hear of the selection of Senator Nixon" as the party's vice presidential candidate, but his secretary recalled that he was very bitter (California State Archives).

Knowland remembered it as "quite a tense and emotional situation. I said: 'Everything is going to be all right, Dick' and he came over and said, 'Good old Bill.'"[160]

The fund crisis had ended well for Nixon, but it began his relationship with Eisenhower on a note of distrust that would be difficult to overcome in the years ahead. Nixon was angry at Ike's "needlessly belated benediction," and the men around Eisenhower reacted to the taint of the fund crisis with suspicion toward Nixon that continued when many of them joined the new administration.

The episode, especially Ike's withholding of support, scarred Nixon and his family deeply. "I had begun the campaign feeling vigorous and enthusiastic," he later wrote. "The fund crisis made me feel suddenly old and tired."[161] He noted that he seemed to age several years that week. His wife, Pat, was particularly upset.

The crisis appeared to serve Knowland's long-term interests. Eisenhower and his team needed the help of a cool head with good political judgment and a reputation for putting party above personal gain. Seeing those qualities in Knowland, they brought him into the campaign's inner circle, where he enjoyed frequent contact with the man who would soon become president. But Knowland would have considerable difficulty in the years ahead sustaining what began as a promising relationship with Ike.

It is not clear what Knowland thought of Nixon's emotional reaction to the crisis. Nixon had oscillated between anger and tears throughout the two weeks — understandable given the pressure he was under. But it was not the way the stolid Knowland would have handled it. In a photograph of Knowland and Nixon at Wheeling, Knowland seemed embarrassed as the vice presidential candidate collapsed in his arms. At that moment, he may have wondered about Nixon's steadiness as a national leader. He may also have begun to feel that Nixon was fragile and could be bested in future political combat.

# Part Four: The Rivals Under Eisenhower (1953–1958)

# 8

# *Knowland, Nixon and the President, 1953–1955*

### *Warren's Appointment to the Court*

In 1953, the chief justice of the United States, Carl Vinson, died, and President Eisenhower nominated Earl Warren to replace him. When word of Ike's decision came, it was hardly a bolt from the blue. Warren had long been interested in an appointment to the Supreme Court. The Truman administration had led him to believe that the job was within his reach — his name was floated as a possible replacement for Associate Justice Frank Murphy, who died in 1949. According to biographer Ed Cray, Warren was then telling friends that he was considering a court seat.[1]

In fact, before the 1952 Republican convention the charge surfaced that he was more interested in the Supreme Court than in being president. John Francis Neylan, an influential conservative journalist and attorney, speculated that the purpose of Warren's presidential candidacy was to allow him to "go horse-trading as a favorite son."[2] Warren felt it necessary to disavow publicly any intent to trade his delegates for a cabinet or Supreme Court post a week before boarding the train to Chicago.[3]

At the convention, there were more reports of deal-making. The Eisenhower forces needed Warren to stay in the presidential race so that Taft could not win a first-ballot victory. Lucius Clay, one of Ike's top lieutenants, recalled that he guaranteed Warren the federal office of his choice if he would not drop out. It was, Clay said, "the only commitment we ever made."[4] Warren did stay in, but not because of any agreement with Clay.

Speculation about a Warren appointment to the court began again as soon as Eisenhower became president. Ike had plenty of good reasons to pick him. The governor had a reputation for integrity, he was a moderate in the Eisenhower mold, he was one of the nation's most popular Republicans, he had helped swing the convention to Eisenhower by appearing to back the fair play amendment, he had campaigned hard for the Eisenhower-Nixon ticket, and, as a former California attorney general, he had the necessary legal qualifications.

But Warren's California rivals also had much to gain from his move to the bench. Most directly affected, of course, was Lieutenant Governor Goodwin Knight — a man who was tired of waiting in the wings. As *Frontier* magazine put it: "Rarely has one politician been so delighted at the advancement of another."[5]

Nixon was enthusiastic as well about the possibility of Warren leaving California. As chief justice, he would lose the power base that made possible his bids for national office in 1948 and 1952. With the governor politically sidelined, a major obstacle to Nixon's presidential ambitions would be removed. "You must get Warren out of California," Nixon allegedly said to Eisenhower. "He has control of the Republican party machinery and we can't do business with him."[6] To help Ike decide, Nixon also conjured up the threat of Warren running against the president in 1956 if he remained governor.[7]

But the man who had the greatest influence on Eisenhower's decision was William Knowland. According to political operative Mac Faries, the appointment "was just a friendship deal that Bill put through." Faries recalled that, even before the 1952 election, Knowland returned to California after a campaign trip with Ike and announced that he had "an understanding with Eisenhower that if a vacancy occurs on the Supreme Court, Warren will have it."[8] Several members of Knowland's family and staff also testified that he strongly recommended his former patron to the president. Knowland's daughter Estelle later wrote that her father's support of Warren for the court "had to be considered in some ways as an act of reciprocity."[9]

Though loyalty and gratitude were key motivators for Knowland, as they had been many times in the past, his recommendation was not entirely unselfish. Eliminating Warren from state and national politics improved his presidential prospects just as much as Nixon's.

So when Eisenhower, within a month of the election, offered Warren the court vacancy, all four of the California rivals were well pleased. The appointment ran into some opposition from conservatives in Congress, but both Knowland and Nixon issued statements supportive of Warren, and Senate confirmation promptly followed. At last, the long shadow of Earl Warren had been removed from California politics — at least, as long as he remained content with being on the Supreme Court.

With his departure for Washington, Warren would no longer be an active participant in the rivalry of the California Republicans. His place was taken by Goodwin Knight, whose assumption of the governorship made him preeminent in state politics. He would attempt to consolidate his control over the state Republican Party while Knowland and Nixon, as key members of the national political leadership, would turn their attention to compiling records strong enough to support eventual bids for president.

But Nixon and Knowland could not afford to let Goodie have free rein out west — their base of power was in California too. Though as a practical matter they were obliged to cede day-to-day primacy in California affairs to the new governor, their loyalists in the state worked to ensure that Knight would not interfere with their ambitions. Thus were the seeds of future conflict sown.

Eisenhower's election in 1952 introduced a new twist into the rivalry. Ike would get to know Nixon and Knowland very well over the next six years, and his opinion of their abilities would greatly affect their chances for political success during the 1950s. As leading competitors for national leadership after Ike, they found themselves drawn into a tense and complicated relationship with a president who never warmed to either of them.

## *Knowland and the White House*

Following Knowland's overwhelming victory in the senatorial election of 1952, his prestige grew with his appointment to the Senate Foreign Relations Committee. Then, in the summer of 1953, Robert Taft's sudden death catapulted him to the post of Senate majority leader. At the age of 45 he had become one of the most powerful politicians in the land. His presidential prospects seemed at least as good as Nixon's, and perhaps better.

Despite Knowland's increasingly conservative views, his ascendance was at first considered a setback for the party's right wing. Observers described the new majority leader as "middle of the road," "a little to the left of the Republican party," or a "liberal young Turk."[10] Many considered him "Ike's candidate," and the *New York Times* agreed that his success was a victory for the president, though the White House had taken a hands-off approach to the Senate vote.

The Republican majority leader needed to be a skilled handler of people. In that job, Knowland would be responsible not only for steering the party's legislative agenda through the Senate but also for liaison with the Eisenhower White House. The former task would test his ability to resolve differences, and the latter to carry out orders. Neither was his strong suit. He had always

## 8 — Knowland, Nixon and the President, 1953–1955

been "more inclined to tell people what they should do than to persuade them to follow a particular course."[11]

With his new prominence came media scrutiny, and the word written most often about Knowland was "stubborn." The *New York Times* gave his mulish quality a positive spin, calling him a "typical Senate man ... a man of strength and stubbornness ... a man who would not in any circumstances panic in the face of any internal Republican trouble."[12]

But Barry Goldwater, then a young senator, said in frustration: "I've never known anyone as headstrong — I don't like the words stubborn and obstinate, but they would apply."[13] Knowland was often depicted in political cartoons as a preening Roman senator, "wearing his classical toga of lofty defiance."[14] "He's never had to compromise," said his wife, Helen, "but he'll have to now, and that will be hard work. Billy will need a new technique."[15]

He never made a serious effort to find one. He continued to "plow his own furrow." His attitude seemed to be that if his views ran parallel to those of the administration, well and good, but if they did not, he would not worry about it.

His style and approach took a disastrous toll on his most important political relationship — that with Eisenhower. His weekly meetings with Ike to discuss pending legislation and foreign policy issues were a "torment from which Ike would emerge livid, exhausted and at times almost incoherent."[16] Knowland "tried to be president, in a way," recalled Senator Howard Baker. "He was always griping and scrapping with Ike.... He was never happy, never cooperative and never really sympathetic to the Eisenhower program."[17] Ike confided to his diary in 1954 that Knowland was the "biggest disappointment of my political life."[18]

His doubts about Knowland's temperament aside, Ike abhorred extreme partisanship of any kind. A man whose self-identification as a Republican was always tenuous, the president came to identify with the moderation and internationalism of the party's East Coast–led mainstream. Like Earl Warren, he did not automatically reject an idea just because it came from a Democrat. Once, when Knowland offered one of his typically narrow views of an issue, Ike blew up. "My God," he exclaimed, "you just can't sit back and assume the nation is safe from all harm because the Republicans won the last election."[19]

Knowland's opposite number in the Senate, the leader of the Democrats, was Lyndon Johnson. The aloof, unimaginative Knowland was mismatched against the smooth, wily extrovert from Texas. Before long, Eisenhower became so frustrated that he sometimes went around Knowland and worked through Johnson to get things done. In 1953 alone, the Democrats in Congress provided the winning margin for Eisenhower's programs over fifty times. Ike's reliance on Johnson only increased after 1954, when Democrats regained control of the Senate and LBJ replaced Knowland as majority leader.

Knowland's outspokenness on Asian policy added to Eisenhower's ire. Following the senator's threat to resign if Red China were admitted to the United Nations, the president fumed: "All he wants is attention, and he acts like a little boy at times."[20] When Knowland demanded military action to free eleven U.S. airmen held by the North Koreans, Ike's exasperation was apparent. "I can't understand that fellow Knowland.... As far as I'm concerned, this just confirms my impression that [he] is beyond the pale."[21] Some pundits used the word feud to describe their relationship. Adlai Stevenson joked that the two should sign a non-aggression pact.[22]

With the passage of time, Eisenhower became more dismissive and even sarcastic in his references to Knowland. He "means to be helpful and loyal, but he is cumbersome," Ike once said. "He does not have the sharp mind and the great experience that [Sen. Robert] Taft did." On another occasion, he cracked that Knowland's idea of foreign policy was to develop high blood pressure at the mention of China.[23] "I used to think Knowland was a good candidate for President," Eisenhower confessed, possibly referring to the earliest days of his administration, "but now I know he isn't."[24]

Knowland was generally aware of the president's attitude toward him, and his pride was said to be deeply wounded, but he was not one to "bleed in public." He tended to blame the people around Ike, who he believed had twisted his convictions to make him look like a warmonger.[25]

## *Estrangement and Betrayal*

Knowland's irascibility may have been aggravated by the continued turbulence in his personal life. Matters worsened when Blair Moody, his wife's lover, was appointed to the Senate in 1950, and soon the Moodys were drawn into the Knowlands' social orbit. Perhaps still unaware of the relationship between his wife and Moody, or perhaps in retaliation for it, Bill began an affair with Ruth, Blair's wife. That liaison was considered an open secret around Washington in the early 1950s, according to Knowland's biographers. They also gave credence to a bizarre allegation that Bill consented to a circumcision in order to please Ruth.

Helen Knowland wrote a novel around this time on the subjects of murder and marital infidelity, titled *Madame Baltimore*, in which her husband and Ruth were thinly disguised characters. Though he approved its publication, Bill Knowland looked with disfavor on any future literary activities she might be considering.[26]

Blair Moody died suddenly of a heart attack in July 1954. In her despair, Helen attempted suicide, after pouring out her feelings in a note to a friend. In a probable reference to the same event, a September newspaper article noted that she had been stricken with a mild cerebral spasm and rushed to the hospital. In the days that followed, Knowland received letters of concern from Earl Warren and Goodwin Knight, among others. Wrote Knight: "We badly need her vivacity and spunk."

This was by no means the only drama playing out in Knowland's life at the time. His biographers claim that, in addition to Ruth Moody, he had many lovers and "one-night stands" during the 1950s. He also had chronic money problems. Throughout his Senate career, his lifestyle was always "one rung higher than his income." In a letter to his father, he expressed the hope that dividends from the *Oakland Tribune* company might help him out of his financial bind.[27]

On another occasion, he complained that "running two households and doing what this job requires in a big state like California has required me to sell all my savings bonds and borrow on my life insurance."[28] Knowland's mounting personal problems formed a vicious circle, with financial and marital troubles leading him to seek solace in drinking and, especially later, in gambling.

As if this were not pressure enough, Knowland had a strained relationship with the rest of his family. He had never been close to his brother Russ, who resented his second-class treatment early in life. Beginning with his years in the California State Assembly, he had little time for parenting. While in the Army during the war, he was heard to complain that his kids were not writing to him. But their father was not a warm or inviting man. His son, Joe, once said: "The hardest thing I have to do is carry on a conversation with my father. Everything has to be just right or he won't talk."[29]

His close relationship with aide Paul Manolis compounded this estrangement. Manolis had been a college classmate and fraternity brother of his son, but through his close professional relationship with the elder Knowland, Manolis actually supplanted Joe in his father's eyes. Manolis later became the executor of Knowland's estate. Knowland once introduced Manolis at a cocktail party as "the son I always wished I'd had."[30]

Conflict in his personal life may have led to volatility and frustration on the job. Nixon described two examples in his memoirs. On one occasion, after an item unflattering to Knowland was leaked to the press from the White House, the enraged senator called the vice president, railed about "internal sabotage," and threatened to resign as minority leader. "I tried to calm him down," Nixon recalled. Later, agreeing with headline-seeking Sen. Joseph McCarthy about the apparently lax treatment of a left-wing

Army doctor, Knowland angrily ripped sheets of paper from his note pad while attacking Army conduct as inexcusable. "I don't know when I have seen him quite so stirred up on a matter as he was on this one," remembered Nixon.[31]

## Warren and Knowland: Growing Apart

Still another distancing added to Knowland's sense of isolation during the 1950s. Warren's appointment to the Supreme Court, which the senator had helped to engineer, seemed to mark the end of their active friendship. Knowland's daughter Emelyn noticed the change. Warren had been "as close to being a friend as Dad had," she pointed out, but her father found it difficult to understand or accept the socially liberal decisions of the Warren court. "They never had a falling out," Emelyn noted, "but they grew apart" in response to the apparent change in Warren's philosophy.[32]

Ideology aside, Emelyn believed that her father was simply unwilling to devote the necessary effort to nurturing his personal relationships, even those most important to him. "A friendship is a two-way street," she later observed. "You have to give as much as you get, and Dad only had time for his job, his country, his politics. He was not a good friend to people.... He did not open up and expose himself as you do to a friend."[33]

Warren agreed that he and Knowland no longer had much in common. According to a journalist who knew him well in Washington, the two men went from being close to very distant. Warren often said he did not understand what had happened to the man he had known so well since childhood. "I know deep down in his heart," the journalist guessed, "Earl Warren regrets that he ever named him to the US Senate."[34] Unlikely as this feeling might seem, Dr. Russell Lee, a Warren supporter in California, made an identical claim.[35]

Warren may also have been disappointed with his friend on a personal level. He was probably aware of the fragility of the Knowlands' marriage and the strains in his family life. Warren had a strongly moralistic streak and made judgments about people based on how they treated those closest to them. As governor, he once denied a recommendation from an aide that a prisoner be pardoned. "This is all eyewash," he said dismissively. "The man is not right with his family. Now, when a man is not right with his own family, he's not a good man. He's two-timing his wife, he's not treating his children properly.... Always look to how a man gets along with his family if you want to know what he's like."[36]

Whether or not this speculation is true, Knowland had to carry the burden of losing his best friend during a time when other pressures on him were mounting. Through it all, he managed to perform his duties as a prominent Republican senator and legislative liaison with the Eisenhower administration, speak out regularly on foreign policy, and attract notice as a possible presidential candidate. Such activity was a tribute to his ability to compartmentalize his life. But that life was full of unresolved problems and contradictions. If he had been more honest with himself, he might have realized that he was unlikely to reach his goal of becoming president.

## Nixon as Vice President

Vice presidents in American history had rarely made much of an impact before 1953, but Nixon was determined to be the exception. He quickly began to earn high marks for his energy and competence even as Knowland was wearing out his welcome at the White House. For a former congressman, Nixon had surprisingly good administrative skills, and these, combined with hard work and political savvy, made him in short order a valuable and respected member of the administration.

The range of his activities was so broad that the media began calling him the most relevant vice president ever. He presided occasionally over meetings of the cabinet and the National Security Council with what one observer called crisp efficiency. He helped conduct liaison with Congress, and began traveling overseas as an emissary. A trip to the Far East in 1953 earned praise, even from his critics.

Nixon's first year in office drew favorable reviews from the nation's major newsweeklies. In October 1953, *U.S. News and World Report* regarded Nixon's wide-ranging portfolio as evidence that Ike was grooming his vice president to replace him.[37] Days later, *Newsweek* noted that Nixon had smoothed over White House relations with obstreperous Republicans, such as Senator Joseph McCarthy, stepped into problem areas on his own initiative, and become Washington's most sought-after dinner speaker.[38] He was "proud of being the fastest dresser in the capital — eight minutes for formal clothes, two and a half for regular wear," wrote William Manchester.[39]

While he was gathering plaudits, Nixon was also dealing with the negative fallout from the campaigns of 1950 and 1952 and the accusations of wrong-doing that culminated in his Checkers speech. The fund scandal had convinced many in the media that Nixon's protestations of innocence "concealed a deviousness unmatched in previous politicians." Eric Sevareid, then a young journalist, wrote that the speech was the beginning of the "promptu impromptu, the calculated spontaneous, the general prepackaging school of modern statesmanship."[40]

Americans were beginning to divide into anti– and pro–Nixon camps, mostly along partisan lines. Democrats viewed Nixon as the Machiavellian figure of the era. His sincerity was constantly under attack. "He doesn't give a damn about the truth," said one representative Democratic critic.[41] Adlai Stevenson, the defeated Democratic candidate for president in 1952, showed an unusual depth of feeling about Nixon that no doubt derived from his losing campaign. He described a place called "Nixonland, a land of slander and scare, of sly innuendo, of a poison pen, the anonymous phone call, and hustling, pushing, shoving — the land of smash and grab and anything to win."[42]

Whether or not one accepted these harsh views of Nixon, they were a personal burden for him and his family. When he gave the commencement speech at Whittier College in 1953, half of the students refused to shake his hand. Officials at Duke University, where he attended law school, proposed to award him an honorary degree, but the faculty voted it down. He told a journalist that he stopped taking the *Washington Post* so that his daughters would not see the vicious lampoons by Herblock, the *Post*'s political cartoonist, who delighted in portraying the unshaven vice president slithering out of a gutter. The pervasive negativity bothered Pat even more than him. She extracted from her husband a short-lived promise to retire from politics in 1956.

Nixon's best chance of making people forget about the fund scandal and his campaign style was to focus on his responsibilities as vice president and to avoid attacking Democrats. Unfortunately, his main value to Eisenhower was as a partisan politician. Because Ike's views and policies tended toward the center, he needed Nixon's strong Republican credentials and fiery rhetoric to rally the party's base and to energize campaigns for Republican congressional candidates. By using Nixon as the hatchet man, Eisenhower could take the high road and build his image as a president who puts the interests of the country first. Thus, Nixon was sent across the country prior to the 1954 elections to lambaste Democrats and the "discredited Trumanism" they espoused.

While Republican audiences cheered Nixon's hard-hitting style, the 1954 campaign reignited concerns about his often harsh and inflammatory rhetoric. Brushing off Democratic attacks as "just politics," he launched his sharpest barbs at Adlai Stevenson, whom he labeled a "cheap opportunist" and a man with serious character flaws. He proclaimed that "thirty-four million Democrats, Republicans and independents were right when they found him unfit to be president in 1952." A careful listener might object to the assumption that losing the election meant that Stevenson was unfit for the office.

Nixon also made fun of the Illinois governor's reputation as an intellectual. Stevenson has a degree, all right, Nixon said — a "Ph.D. from the Acheson College of Cowardly Communist Containment." The sentence contained nothing of substance — it was ridicule, rather than a serious charge — but a reader could be forgiven for believing that Nixon was calling Stevenson (and, by extension, Dean Acheson) both a coward and a Communist without exactly saying it. Furious Democrats called Nixon "the leading practitioner of a cruel and malignant political weapon — the not-quite-libelous smear."[43]

As usual, Nixon's words were carefully chosen — the "polished weapons of the skilled debater who knows exactly what he is doing."[44] One of his applause lines noted that the Eisenhower administration had "kicked out the Communists and fellow travelers and security risks not by the hundreds but by the thousands." Later, when reporters had time to analyze the sentence and ask for clarification, Nixon aides were forced to admit that the thousands referred not to Communists or fellow travelers but only to the ill-defined category of security risks.[45]

Nixon often seemed unhappy that he had been cast in the role of the heavy. In his view, Republicans in 1954 were overly complacent about their prospects and were leaving the tough campaigning to him. Because he was carrying the fight, Nixon became the main target of Democratic attacks. In his memoirs, he claimed to resent being portrayed as a liar and demagogue.

Yet his work ethic and competitiveness would not allow him to coast. During the final week of the campaign, he was "so tired that I could hardly remember what it felt like to be rested." Impressed by his energy and stamina, *Newsweek* called Nixon the "sparkplug of the entire Republican campaign."[46] Though the Republicans lost ground that year — notably in the Senate where they once again became the minority party — many observers believed that Nixon single-handedly averted an electoral catastrophe.

Nixon's success did not cheer him, because it guaranteed that he would play the same role in 1956. "The prospect of having to go through it all again in another two years was depressing," he later wrote.[47]

## Nixon's "Problem"

During the 1950s, journalists of all stripes became fascinated by the sharp reaction of so many Americans to Nixon's public persona, and they wrote hundreds of column inches trying to explain it. What was it about Nixon that made Democrats "unite and fight and work and give and organize and vote with a passionate response"?

In person, Nixon did not seem ruthless or combative. Following an interview with the vice president, Stewart Alsop called him judicious, interesting and likeable, though shy, lacking in warmth, poor at small talk, and "oddly academic" in conversation.[48] He displayed an inquiring and retentive mind and discussed politics, his true love, with great facility. Journalist William Miller wrote similarly that he came across as a "nice guy" and that his mildly conservative voting record showed he was no extremist. He did his homework and was intelligent and persevering. What these men saw of Nixon did not seem to warrant the hostility directed toward him.

But they and others seemed to be reaching a consensus about what Nixon's problem was. In listening to him, one could never be sure where conviction ended and sheer artistry began. His arguments did not always seem linked to his known political principles. Behind the carefully prepared phrases, it was hard to tell where Nixon stood on the issues. He seemed slippery. As he showed in his fund speech of 1952, he thought it was better to speak effectively about an irrelevant matter than to meet criticism head on.

With the Eisenhower administration nearing the end of its third year in office, journalist Richard Rovere wrote an extended article for *Harper's* magazine assessing Nixon's status and prospects. He offered a cogent description of the 42-year-old vice president as "robust, intelligent, conscientious, ruthless, affable, articulate, competitive, telegenic, and breathtakingly adaptable." Rovere saw his youth and talent as a guarantee that he would "somehow or other be part of our lives—an influence, a force to be reckoned with in the affairs of the country for some time to come."

Rovere echoed the view of others that Nixon seemed more concerned about strategy than policy. No point of view could be identified as Nixonism, he maintained. The vice president could not be classified as either a right-wing or left-wing Republican. His views were "indeterminate and perhaps nonexistent." His overriding objective seemed to be the success of the Republican Party rather than any particular substantive goal. "More than anyone else," Rovere observed, "he has set the political style of the administration, with its heavy borrowings from the techniques of modern advertising and public relations ... with its mobilization of energies against the opposition rather than toward its own objectives."[49]

Administration insiders also noticed Nixon's focus on process rather than substance. Speechwriter Emmet John Hughes observed that he "never propos[ed] major objectives, but [was] quick and shrewd at suggesting or refining methods—rather like an effective trial lawyer, I kept thinking, with an oddly slack interest in the law."

Nixon was so much the dispassionate tactician that Hughes believed he could have served the Democratic Party just as well. "The philosophy of any policy interested him ... far less than its efficacy," Hughes noted. He judged any declaration or speech not by its content but by its impact." As Hughes put it, he was "the host obsessed with the setting of his table — but with no taste for food."⁵⁰ His obsession with tactics reinforced the view of many people that his Republicanism was little more than a vehicle for his own ambitions.

Stuart Alsop also saw "something mechanical, something faintly inhuman" about Nixon. "There is something of the too perfect quality of the very handsome girl, whose hair is always in place, whose slip never shows — and who is never led to the altar," he noted. Alsop thought that a hobby might help change his image — it would give him an excuse to appear more relaxed and down-to-earth in casual clothes. But Nixon waved away such suggestions. "You've got to be what you are, you can't pretend to be something different," he said.⁵¹

Rovere pointed out that some leading Republican officials — Earl Warren and Bill Knowland were surely among them — shared Democratic discomfort with Nixon's style and brand of politics. Looking ahead to 1956, he predicted "heavy opposition" to Nixon's renomination as vice president. If Eisenhower ran again, it seemed likely that Nixon would remain on the ticket. But Ike's advanced age and frequent frustration with his duties contributed to speculation that he would quit after one term.

A few observers saw positive change in the vice president between the elections of 1954 and the end of 1955. Alsop believed he was better at receiving criticism, more restrained rhetorically, and less aggressive than in the past. It was unclear to Alsop whether his behavior represented personal growth or was merely the result of a calculation that the American people would never elect a strongly partisan figure to the White House. The fact that this question even had to be asked was evidence of Nixon's continuing image problem.

## *Eisenhower and Nixon*

Rovere was only one of several political observers to assume with little evidence that Ike was grooming Nixon to be president, or even that Ike wished to retain him as vice president in 1956. Yet one of the most fascinating subplots of Eisenhower's presidency was Nixon's continuing inability to meet Ike's high standards. As we have seen, he was prepared to jettison Nixon when the fund crisis broke in 1952 and slow to welcome him back into the fold even after the success of the Checkers speech. Nixon would view Eisenhower throughout his vice presidency as an austere and remote father figure, whose approval he continually sought but never quite earned.⁵²

Sharp personal and political differences between the two men contributed to Eisenhower's inability to embrace his vice president. Nixon's extreme shyness and brooding nature probably doomed any real rapport with the more open and extroverted general. It did not help that several of Eisenhower's key advisers did not care for him. Sherman Adams, Ike's chief of staff, was a particularly strong critic. Emmet Hughes noted the staff's concern about "Dick running loose through the country" with no one to censor his impetuousness.[53]

The most predictable — and most ironic — source of Ike's dissatisfaction was Nixon's strongly partisan public persona. On the one hand, Eisenhower needed Nixon's red-meat rhetoric to secure the votes of conservatives, but, on the other, he was uncomfortable with the vice president's polarizing campaign style. He cringed when Nixon gushed in a television interview: "Incidentally, in mentioning Secretary Dulles, isn't it wonderful, finally, to have a Secretary of State who isn't taken in by the Communists, who stands up to them?" On another occasion, Nixon referred to Earl Warren as a "great Republican Chief Justice," a comment that no doubt irritated Warren as much as it did Eisenhower.[54]

Ike considered Nixon's focus on tactics to be a weakness just as serious as his overly partisan style. He told Hughes that Nixon was a "young man who managed at the same time to be 'too political' without holding a genuine point of view."[55] By doing Ike's "dirty work" during campaigns, Nixon only managed to confirm the president's feeling that that "he was not made for higher things."[56]

## *Nixon and Knowland: Cautious Rivals*

Given the identical career ambitions and high visibility of Nixon and Knowland, journalists and political pundits frequently speculated about the likelihood of conflict between them. In the middle of Eisenhower's first term, Knowland trailed the vice president in Republican presidential preference polls by some twenty points. Rovere's *Harper's* article on Nixon identified Knowland as his "dedicated, resourceful rival" and "bitter antagonist." If Eisenhower should decide to remove himself from contention in 1956, Rovere believed that Knowland would mount a strong challenge to any bid by Nixon to take his place.

By mid–1954, with Knowland and Nixon bound together in service of the Eisenhower administration, *U.S. News and World Report* saw evidence of competition between them. "In Washington and California, many are watching this little-publicized contest between the vice president and the majority leader," said the magazine. "California, a big state, may prove too small to accommodate the futures of two such men." It declared their rivalry a long-standing fact. "Two relatively young and highly placed Californians," it said, "are engaged in a simmering contest for political power and ... an eventual chance at the Presidency." In Washington, they seemed to be cooperating, but under the surface were "small indications of a widening breach."[57]

This alleged breach was the result of maneuvering for influence by proxy forces of both men back in their home state. Those forces were said to be rushing to fill the political void left a year before by the departure of Governor Warren for the Supreme Court. The prize was control of the Republican delegation to the 1956 convention. Media accounts said Knowland was trying to pull together former allies of Warren, while Nixon was banking on the support of his more conservative southern California loyalists. The result had been dissension and "much pulling and hauling" among state Republican officials.

Did the facts of their relationship support the contention that Knowland was Nixon's "bitter antagonist"?

Prior to 1952, the two men had been cooperative and friendly. Knowland made joint appearances with Nixon in both the Voorhis and Douglas campaigns and vigorously supported his young Republican colleague. In the Douglas race, he continually praised Nixon's role in the Hiss case — in stark contrast to Earl Warren.[58] Two weeks after Nixon was elected to the Senate, in what was admittedly a routine gesture of courtesy, Knowland proposed that they get together over lunch or dinner to discuss matters of common interest.

Little reason for antipathy existed at this stage — in fact, they had both an ideological and personal affinity. Knowland may have been as bothered as Warren by Nixon's tendency to go for the jugular, but he shared Nixon's concern about the spread of communism around the world and welcomed him as a rising star in the Republican firmament. "He makes a fine impression wherever he goes," his father Joe wrote to FBI chief J. Edgar Hoover. "His record on the Communist issue is so strong no one can doubt it."[59] By 1950 Bill Knowland probably agreed with Nixon on a wider range of issues than with Warren, who was by then trying to enable a variety of liberal social programs. Knowland and Nixon also had compatible personalities — both had few interests outside of work and preferred not to waste time with small talk.

Their direct competition began in earnest during the 1952 Republican convention. The events in Chicago resulting in Nixon's nomination for vice president angered Knowland, but he resolved not to let his personal feelings interfere with the imperative of Republican success in the election. His defense of Nixon during the fund crisis may have helped Ike decide to keep the ticket intact. But, as his daughter Emelyn said, he remained leery of Nixon even while offering his public support.

While the media portrayed a conflict that was growing in intensity, the principals steadfastly denied it. Nixon professed not to view the 1952 convention as anything more than an awkward moment between them. "Knowland was not only a personal friend but also the man Bob Taft probably would have chosen as his running mate," Nixon wrote in his memoirs. "[Yet he] said he would be proud and happy to nominate me."[60] Nixon almost certainly misread his colleague's feelings at that moment, but he did not doubt Knowland's basic good will. Knowland, too, claimed that the two men had always enjoyed warm relations. "The vice president and I are very good friends," he told the press later in Ike's term.[61]

Nonsense, said a *Look* magazine profile of Knowland in April 1955. "Nixon and Knowland can deny a split until hell freezes over, but it will still be there. Anything else wouldn't be natural. They're both from the same state. They both want to move into the White House. They both can't get there."[62] "Few men," columnist Drew Pearson added, "have more natural antipathy than they."[63]

Antipathy or no, they extended mutual courtesies and carried on a lively social interaction that cast doubt on any overt mutual hostility. Immediately after Nixon's triumph at the 1952 convention, Knowland wrote a note to Hannah Nixon that spoke volumes about his graciousness and ability to lay aside personal feelings in order to enhance a mother's justifiable pride. Mrs. Nixon had sent her congratulations to Knowland for his largely improvised speech at the convention nominating her son for vice president. "It was a masterpiece," she wrote. "You spoke so sincerely and convincingly I couldn't keep the tears back." Knowland replied:

> I have always had the highest confidence in [your son's] personal integrity and had no doubt in my mind that when he made his forthright statement [the Checkers speech] the public would respond. You can be proud of your son and the way he handled himself both on the television and at the meeting in Wheeling. I fully agree with Pat that he is a "wonderful guy."[64]

A few weeks later, Knowland extended an invitation to the new vice president and his wife. "Needless to say, I know [you are] going to have a heavy schedule of dining out, but perhaps somewhere sandwiched in between your formal commitments you and Pat will have time to come over to our apartment and relax for a quiet family dinner while we talk about children, grandchildren and other matters of major interest."[65] Among other examples,

## 8 — Knowland, Nixon and the President, 1953–1955

Many journalists considered Nixon and Knowland bitter antagonists in the 1950s, but they worked together in relative harmony under President Eisenhower. In truth, they were more concerned about their relationship with Ike than with each other (Richard Nixon Presidential Library/National Archives and Records Administration).

Nixon wrote to Knowland in response to his wife's illness in 1954: "You may be sure that I am looking forward to seeing you, if your schedule permits. Pat and I are so glad to hear of Helen's satisfactory recovery."[66]

During 1956, as the media continued to hype the Nixon-Knowland rivalry, the two men continued to speak and act like friends. Their correspondence also shows that they endeavored to keep each other informed of their activities. In January, Knowland took note of Nixon's birthday on the Senate floor, an act that elicited a thank-you from the vice president.

When the Nixons returned from a trip abroad in July, Knowland was at the airport to meet them. "This is just a note to tell you how much Pat and I appreciated your taking the time and trouble to welcome us home yesterday," Nixon wrote. "Since we were away such a short time, we were really overwhelmed to see so many of our friends when we stepped out of the plane. In fact, we both felt that our reception was the highlight of the entire trip." Knowland replied: "Needless to say, I was pleased to be with the Welcoming Committee ... and to see that you and Pat had survived the hard trip in such a splendid manner."[67]

Nixon and Knowland even mocked breathless newspaper accounts of their "natural antipathy" and jockeying for position. Drew Pearson alleged in August 1956 that Nixon had secured much needed political support from Knowland by agreeing to appoint him secretary of state when Nixon became president. Nixon sent a copy of the article to Knowland's office accompanied by a hand-written note: "I thought you might like to read this for laughs the next time you get a spare minute. I am glad that someone was present to record all the details of our deal!" Knowland replied: "I hope Drew Pearson was more accurate on some of his other stories than he was on this one."[68]

Despite their sometimes differing views of domestic and foreign policy issues, Nixon and Knowland worked together in relative harmony on the Eisenhower administration's legislative agenda. A *Newsweek* article in 1953 on Nixon's performance as vice president noted that "he has even managed to get on with Senator William Knowland, who has become majority leader, even though they belong to rival factions in home-state politics."[69]

As vice president, Nixon must have had many opportunities to undermine Knowland with Eisenhower. Ike was predisposed to view the senator as an irritant, and Nixon could have subtly reinforced those feelings. But in at least one case, Nixon was at pains to explain Knowland's actions to the president rather than condemn them. He observed that Knowland was "excited" about an issue of concern to the administration. "Yes, he's very emotional," agreed Ike. "This is only March — we have to live with him until [Senate adjournment in] July." Instead of echoing Ike's frustration, Nixon defended his fellow Californian, saying: "We must recognize the difficult position of the party leadership" on the matter.[70]

Knowland's strong views on Asian policy guaranteed a certain amount of tension between him and the more moderate vice president. Richard Rovere noted in 1955 that Eisenhower's annoyance at Knowland's "mutinous tendencies" had driven him to look to Nixon on occasion as the administration's principal point man in the Senate. For example, the vice president helped Ike win political support in Congress for the Korean War truce negotiations, which Knowland had dismissed as a "peace without honor."[71] Drew Pearson also took note of this tension but reported in 1956 that the two men had "made up."[72]

On balance, as the Eisenhower administration neared the end of its first term, Nixon and Knowland were enjoying a collaborative and civil relationship. In truth, they were far more concerned about their relations with the president than with each other.

At the same time, they became increasingly focused on developments back in their home state that would affect their standing at the party convention to be held the following year. *U.S. News and World Report* had been correct to observe in mid–1954 that California representatives of Nixon and Knowland were working to guarantee the two leaders maximum impact on the state's delegation to the 1956 convention. To complicate matters further, the new governor, Goodwin Knight, was attempting to round up enough delegates to mount a favorite-son bid.

In September 1955, however, an unpredictable and dramatic event threw the Republican Party and the country into turmoil and forced all four of the California rivals to reassess their plans for 1956.

# 9

## *The Rivals and the 1956 Convention*

The departure of Earl Warren in mid–1953 left a political vacuum in California. Though Goodwin Knight had achieved his long-deferred dream of occupying the governor's mansion in Sacramento, filling Warren's big shoes would not be easy. Also, Richard Nixon and William Knowland were keeping a sharp eye on the state and would surely contest any move by Knight to take over leadership of the California Republican Party. A leading Democrat likened the post–Warren transition to the breakup of Charlemagne's empire.[1]

### *Knight's Deferred Dream*

Knight's accession to the governorship coincided with the beginning of a happier period in his personal life. In October 1952, he had been devastated by the death of his wife, Arvilla, of a coronary thrombosis. While waiting for Warren to move on, he descended into loneliness and depression. Often unable to work, he processed his grief by talking to anyone who would listen about Arvilla and their two daughters.

He was restored to his more typical sunny, optimistic self by Virginia Carlson, an attractive widow he met while appearing on an interview program. After a period of courtship, the couple was married in August 1954. The relationship transformed Knight. Soon he professed to be the happiest man in the state. Virginia was a bright, charming and accomplished hostess for her governor husband, and a political confidant as well.

The advent of the new administration was marked by continued bad feelings between Knight and Warren. "When we moved in," Knight recalled, "the only piece of paper in the place was the calendar on the wall. Governor Warren had all his papers sealed and we had to start from scratch." Why did he do it? "I don't know; it's just one of the idiosyncrasies of the man."² For his part, Warren complained that his wife was not given enough time to move the family's possessions out of the governor's mansion. "Governor Knight was not too understanding about her task," he later wrote.³

Knight had the good sense not to allow his personal feelings to interfere with his political judgment. For years, he had billed himself as a conservative alternative to Warren and the creeping socialism his policies were said to represent. On nearly every important state issue, he had positioned himself well to the right of the governor. As soon as he moved into the executive mansion, however, he shifted to the center and began calling himself an Eisenhower Republican.

During his first year in office, he emphasized continuity with the Warren years by retaining nearly all of the former governor's appointees. Like Warren, he took a non-ideological approach to the state's growth-related problems, such as air pollution control and water resources development. He announced that his new motto was: "Moderation is best. Avoid all extremes."⁴

Knight even decided to risk a rupture with his Republican base by courting the state's increasingly powerful labor unions. He promised to veto any measure opposed by the unions, and he sponsored increases in unemployment insurance, workman's compensation, and disability insurance, earning him praise from the American Federation of Labor.

Knowing Knight as a staunch conservative, Democrats were surprised by the lack of a radical break with the Warren years. While lieutenant governor, he had "found it advantageous, I guess, to play up his more conservative side," observed Democratic Senate candidate Richard Richards, but "given full reign of his true beliefs, he, like Warren, showed himself to be more liberal in his basic approach to issues ... than we had heretofore thought."⁵

Knight's apparent transformation was less remarkable than it seemed. Though he had often attacked Warren's liberal views, he was, at heart, a pragmatic politician with a well-honed sense of where the votes were. He calculated that remaining on the right would not be a winning strategy in a state trending more Democratic with each passing year. He had to stand for reelection in 1954, one short year after taking office. He had only a few months to convince the California electorate that he was not all that different from his popular predecessor.

Over time, Knight's pro-union policies would jeopardize his political career, but in the 1954 campaign for governor, his moderation played well with the electorate. In a tricky balancing act, he "appealed vigorously for

Democratic votes but wanted it understood that he was campaigning strictly as a Republican."[6] The *Los Angeles Times* grumbled but endorsed him. He relied on his strong suits—boundless enthusiasm and personal dynamism, which contrasted favorably with his predecessor's Scandinavian restraint. He conducted a joke-telling, hand-shaking, whirlwind campaign, distributing pens, sewing kits and toy balloons. He had the good fortune to be running against a lackluster and little known Democrat who was required by illness to campaign for a while from a hospital bed. Knight won by half a million votes.

By virtue of his reelection, Knight found himself the subject of speculation about his ultimate political goals. Veteran Sacramento journalist Herbert Phillips wrote that the "governor of the nation's second largest and fastest growing state ... [is] almost automatically entitled to consideration for national office."[7] Would a man who only recently attained his lifelong ambition be looking ahead to higher responsibilities? On this issue he seemed unequivocal. "I would certainly like to be President," he said to an interviewer. "I am not going to lie to the people, and I'm not going to be coy."[8]

Despite this statement, Knight gave off conflicting signals to his associates on his national ambitions. Aide Douglas Barrett and Assembly Speaker Luther Lincoln were among his many colleagues who believed he had no interest in going to Washington. "I think he enjoyed the notoriety of it and basked in it a little bit," observed Lincoln, but "I don't think he ever expected it to happen. I don't recall us being asked to do any work in that direction."[9]

But several others disagreed. "Goodie lives in the future," observed a friend. "He is a first-rate example of the Don Juan complex in men: the pursuit is everything."[10] Paul Mason, another of Knight's staffers, thought that he already had the presidency in his sights before he became governor. Some saw him aiming only at the number-two position. Caspar Weinberger, then an up-and-coming California Republican, called Knight "very ambitious politically"—a man who "wanted to be vice president."[11] San Francisco mayor George Christopher once said—perhaps not intending to sound dismissive—that Knight was interested in the vice presidency because it contained duties, like hand-shaking, that he was good at.[12] Given Knight's mercurial nature, his goals probably changed with the political circumstances of the moment.

The 1956 Republican convention would provide him with an opportunity to stick his toe in the water. If he made a concerted effort, he seemed to have an outside chance for the vice presidential nomination. Richard Nixon was as controversial as ever, and it was not clear that his presence on the 1956 Republican ticket would help Eisenhower get reelected. Knight's labor adviser encouraged him to get involved, predicting that the unions would oppose Eisenhower if Nixon ran again. There was also talk that Ike might retire. In either case the vice presidency would be up for grabs.

## The Knight-Nixon Feud

While he was lieutenant governor, Knight had not shared Earl Warren's disdain for Richard Nixon. In 1949, he had called Nixon a "grand guy." Early in 1952, he and his first wife, Arvilla, returned from a visit to Washington, where the Nixons had been gracious hosts. "Goodwin so enjoyed being with you on our trip east," Arvilla wrote to Pat Nixon. "It is grand to know such fine Americans as you both are," Knight wrote to Nixon in similarly glowing terms.[13] When Arvilla died later that year, both Nixon and Murray Chotiner cabled the lieutenant governor with their sympathies.

While Warren was stewing about Nixon's perfidy at the 1952 convention, Knight was volunteering his support for the fall campaign. "I am writing this note just to let you know that I am interested not only in the party's success but in your own personal welfare," Knight wrote to the Republican vice presidential nominee in mid–July. "I will be glad to do anything in my power to be helpful."[14] After the victory, Nixon penned a note of thanks to Knight for his support. "Everything I did in the campaign was a pleasure," Knight replied. "I cannot emphasize too strongly how pleased we all are with your dignified conduct."[15]

Within a year or two, Knight would speak of Nixon in unprintable language and become determined to do anything in his power to stop him. How did Nixon manage to alienate him?

Knight's feelings had their origin in a series of perceived personal slights. The first took place after the 1952 convention, when Knight happily attended a homecoming airport ceremony for Nixon in Los Angeles. He claimed that, while on the tarmac, some of Nixon's southern California staffers brusquely shoved him out of a newspaper photo of the candidate being greeted by the welcoming party. He found himself standing on the sidelines "like a yokel" while the cameras snapped.[16] It was not until later in the day, when Nixon wanted a picture of the two men smiling, that Knight was finally able to meet with him.

Nixon campaign worker Frank Jorgensen remembered the incident differently. In Jorgensen's view, Knight was a prima donna who had an uncanny ability to get himself "smack-dab" in the middle of any photo that was being taken: "I've watched him work, and it was amazing.... He was an artist at it, he really was." As photographers took pictures of the group greeting Nixon, the VIPs jockeyed for position and Nixon, not Knight, was elbowed

The sensitive Knight (right) was excluded from several photographs of the other rivals during Nixon's July 1952 homecoming in Los Angeles after he was nominated for vice president. The perceived snub marked the beginning of his feud with Nixon (California State Archives).

out of one of the shots. He was "madder than hell," according to Jorgensen. He cut the photo session short, got into his car, and left.[17]

So, who was elbowed out of the picture? If it was Nixon, he would have had a right to be upset, since the purpose of the event was to honor his success and welcome him home. But Knight was only the lieutenant governor of California. Being excluded from a photo with the party's vice presidential candidate or being unable to meet with him did not seem to be a matter of great moment. Yet this trivial event remained emblazoned in his memory for years to come.

In another incident, which took place after the 1952 election at a governor's conference in New York, Knight believed that Nixon snubbed him in a way that was obvious enough to be reported in the press. Nixon had arranged private sessions with several governors but not with him — he "went out of his way to offend Knight, didn't want to do anything to build [up] Knight," according to an aide.[18] Former governor Tom Dewey later felt obliged to call him and apologize. "I told him that he didn't need to apologize for the vice president," Knight said. "Nixon is over twenty-one and can speak for himself."[19]

Knight felt Nixon's disrespect in other ways. Once, at a private gathering, Nixon described Knight as "one of California's best known comics." Another man might have taken it in stride, or even as a compliment, but the sensitive governor heard himself being called a clown. On another occasion, while visiting Washington, Knight claimed that he approached Nixon in the Senate dining room to say hello. Nixon apparently looked up, said hello, and then immediately resumed his conversation at the table.

Perceived slights aside, Knight also complained that he had received no expressions of gratitude for campaigning for Nixon in 1952, no condolences upon the death of his wife, and no congratulations on his remarriage. "I don't understand the man," Knight concluded.[20] On this score, his memory was clearly faulty. The first two of these charges, at least, were unfounded.[21]

Did Nixon intend these acts as signs of disrespect? Not according to a staff memorandum prepared in Nixon's office in response to the publication of Knight's grievances in a national magazine. The memo noted that Knight's account of the governor's conference ignored the fact that Nixon was a last-minute substitute for Eisenhower and had no flexibility to rearrange his schedule. "The governor has heard all of this many times," the staff memorandum pointed out. "No man who is obviously so small and who has such a thin skin should even try to get into national politics." In response to Knight's description of the alleged airport jostling, the memo commented tersely: "This man is supposed to be an adult."[22] Nixon did not choose to dignify the charges by responding publicly.

"Politicians are like children sometimes, or old ladies," Frank Jorgensen concluded. Nixon and Knight, he said, were jealous of each other, as politicians often are. They got incensed for no good reason, and a feud began.[23] Whichever perspective one takes on the airport event or the others, it is hard not to conclude that Knight overreacted and was overly concerned about his prerogatives.

## *Pre-Convention Struggle*

This bad feeling was the prelude to a contest for control of the state's Republican delegation to the 1956 convention — which Knight dramatically called a "fight to the finish."[24] Nixon, Knowland and Knight all had a legitimate interest in the composition of the group that would attend and vote at the party's quadrennial gathering, and they did not wish either of their rivals to have a dominant role. To achieve maximum influence on the outcome, Knight felt he had to lead a California delegation committed to him as a favorite son, as Warren did four years before. However, Knight gave

In another 1952 Nixon homecoming photograph, Warren and Nixon are flanked by several local officials, while Knight (second from left, behind man with bow tie) finds himself blocked out of the shot. He fumed later that he "felt like a yokel" (Richard Nixon Presidential Library/National Archives and Records Administration).

assurances that any delegation he headed would be committed to Eisenhower's reelection.

The stakes were raised when doubts continued to spread about Eisenhower's willingness to run for reelection. Ike had frequently told associates of his wish to be a one-term president. A headless Republican ticket in 1956 would catapult the California rivals into contention for one of the available spots. Knight declared that, in the event Ike retired, he would still lead a favorite son delegation to the convention, even if it meant confronting Nixon directly.

The focus of pre-convention squabbling in 1954 was the seemingly unimportant choice of a deputy chairman of the state Republican Party. Under the rules, however, the deputy chairman would automatically be elevated to chairman in 1956 and thus would be a key member of the delegation to the national party convention. Having the party chairman in his camp would be a valuable asset for any of the three rivals.

## 9 — The Rivals and the 1956 Convention

Proxy forces of Nixon favored Ray Arbuthnot, a Nixon supporter, for the deputy job, while the Knight people backed the governor's former campaign manager, Howard Ahmanson. Knight felt that Ahmanson was the better choice, having been "recommended by every responsible Republican leader whom we contacted," but he was also one of Knight's primary fund raisers. Ahmanson's opponents, he charged, were "a small and hard-core group who are determined to put over their own slate."[25]

After contentious negotiations between the two sides in August, Knight thought he had an agreement with Nixon agent Murray Chotiner that Ahmanson would get the job. In exchange for the Nixon concession, the governor's people agreed that Arbuthnot would move into the vice chairman position at a time when it might be more advantageous for Nixon to have him there.

With that issue seemingly settled, Knight and his new bride, Virginia, left on a honeymoon cruise to Catalina island, off the coast of southern California. While he was vacationing, the Nixon forces, headed by Chotiner, launched a telephone campaign against Ahmanson, alleging unspecified acts of corruption, and tried to persuade the committee membership to vote instead for Arbuthnot. Shocked that Chotiner would go back on his agreement, Knight cut short his honeymoon, sailed back to the mainland, and over four consecutive days made some 600 phone calls of his own. To each member, according to the *Saturday Evening Post*, he said: "This is Goodie. I have been double-crossed. I need your proxy."[26]

As the combative tone of Knight's remarks suggested, he was prepared to use hardball tactics in order to prevail. He told Republican legislators that anybody who voted against his candidate could forget about patronage or his signature on their pet bills. It seemed to Republican assemblyman Tom Caldecott that Knight was inordinately worried about the matter. "He was very afraid of the Nixon group," Caldecott recalled.[27]

Knowland appeared to share Knight's objections to the Nixon camp's attempt to steal the election of a vice chairman. He immediately flew to Sacramento to join the proxy fight. The pressure generated by these two heavyweights working in tandem quickly brought a majority of delegates back into line in support of Ahmanson.

The ugly split between the two factions could not be covered up. An angry Nixon ally, Pat Hillings, alleged that the Knight people had won by "brute force." And Knight's emotionalism about the whole affair led him to do some ill-considered crowing: "I had to demonstrate to them [the Nixon forces] that I keep my agreements, and that I am the governor."[28]

Correspondence between Nixon and his representative Frank Jorgensen in California left no doubt of the goal of Nixon's proxies or their resentment of Knight. "The big guns were definitely leveled on the southern California group, who are trying to the best of their ability to elect Ray Arbuthnot," Jorgensen wrote in an August summing up of the episode. Knight, he said, had misrepresented Chotiner's "agreement" with him: "Frankly, Murray took quite a beating and unjustly so. I have every reason to believe that ... the gentleman in Sacramento [Knight] deliberately lied to the newspapers in reporting the conversations he had with Murray."

Nixon-backers in California were becoming increasingly convinced of Knight's outsized ego as well as his mendacity. "I am sure that you recognize in dealing with our friend in Sacramento, we are dealing with a man who is so certain that he is top dog and that he is going to rule politics in the state of California without advice or interference," Jorgensen wrote to Nixon. He also admitted that Knowland's intervention on Knight's side had been decisive. "It was quite obvious that our senior friend from Washington [Knowland], when he came in on the floor and actively entered the proceedings, that we were licked in our move as far as Ray was concerned."[29]

Nixon recognized that the effort to overturn the agreement with Knight had caused much resentment, and he tried to distance himself from the whole affair. He conceded that his people had become a bit overeager but denied any advance knowledge of their activities. According to a magazine account, the Nixon team then asked Knight to join them in making a face-saving statement that Nixon knew nothing of the factional fight and, implausibly, that Chotiner had no authority to commit the vice president to an agreement. Knight was incredulous. "That's absurd," he exclaimed. "Why would I deal with Chotiner as an individual?"[30]

If the reasons for Knight's distrust of Nixon seemed inconsequential before, the Ahmanson affair added fuel to the fire. Part of Knight's pique was indeed directed toward Chotiner the man rather than the representative of the vice president. Caldecott recalled that "he was very outspoken in his opinion of Chotiner. He felt that he had been slighted on several occasions intentionally by Murray. I don't know if he had.... But he felt that Chotiner was very antagonistic to him."[31]

Nixon's men in the state may have been, as the vice president claimed, acting on their own. Caldecott, though he was a friend of Knight's, did not believe Nixon was behind Chotiner's shenanigans. "You never saw Nixon coming in and actually openly fighting.... He didn't want to. He had nothing to gain by it." He would send in his lieutenants, Caldecott said, and they would often get out of line. "I think they got a little overzealous and wanted to show their loyalty to Nixon by taking on some of the other California politicians. It actually caused trouble for Nixon and didn't help him one bit."[32]

Jorgensen claimed that the dust-up had taught them a tactical lesson only — that Chotiner was causing too many public relations problems and should no longer serve as Nixon's spokesman in California. It was time to "let some other people do the front work." He concluded that Nixon needed a "very few tight-lipped men, who will carry out the program of you and Murray."[33]

Though the vice president had a reputation as a micromanager, he was a very busy man in Washington, and he probably allowed Chotiner to decide day by day how to accomplish Nixon's goals out west. Nixon, of course, was ultimately responsible for actions taken on his behalf. And Knight, despite his distaste for Chotiner, did not distinguish between the words and deeds of Nixon's aides and those of Nixon himself. To him, Nixon was the evil genius pulling the strings. Whether Chotiner had acted on his own or not, Republicans in the state learned from this incident that any agreement with Nixon's representatives would have to be carefully policed.

## Resuming the Feud

Following his victory in the 1954 gubernatorial election, Knight began to express strong doubts about Richard Nixon's fitness for national leadership. In a conversation with Pat Brown, who was then the state's Democratic attorney general, he called Nixon "one of the most dangerous men in the world." Knight reminded Brown that Nixon had double-crossed him the year before and had done the same thing to Earl Warren in 1952. He would be the "worst man imaginable for the presidency of the United States."[34] Knight also told *Time* magazine that he regarded Nixon as a "political upstart."[35]

In his criticism of the vice president, Knight never argued that a particular Nixon policy preference was unwise or that he would pursue a different course of action. His opposition seemed strictly personal. During an interview with the governor, journalist Stewart Alsop reported that "Knight's stand was not based on logic. It was based on sheer bile. Nothing whatever that Knight said to me about Nixon in a long interview was repeatable on paper."[36] Knight associate Doug Barrett believed he "had a fixation that Nixon was a bad man and that [his] mission was to oppose him wherever he could and stop him wherever he could."[37]

In March 1955, Nixon arrived in Los Angeles to speak at a luncheon of the World Affairs Council. Knight reacted "with the warmth of an Arctic midnight." The governor was expected to preside over the sold-out event, but, as *Time* magazine put it, his reaction was more or less, "That's nice, but I'll have to look at my calendar." At the last minute, he told the organizers that he had a prior commitment. He neither showed up nor sent the lieutenant governor in his place, as protocol would dictate. His note of apology was so cool, according to *Time*, that the luncheon chairman would not read it to the press. In his speech, Nixon named and praised other state Republican luminaries such as Knowland and Senator Thomas Kuchel, but made only passing reference to "our present governor."[38]

Together at an event during 1955, Nixon and Knight professed publicly but ambiguously their mutual goodwill. Asked to comment on the apparent hostility between them, Nixon told the governor: "I want you to know that I have no such feelings toward you." Knight replied: "I see no reason for any such relationship." Knight agreed to accept Nixon's claim that his supporters, particularly Murray Chotiner, had become "overenthusiastic" in the past and engaged in activities of which he was unaware.[39] The exchange settled nothing.

All the while, Nixon was receiving regular reports from his allies in California on what they considered Knight's exasperating conduct. "In the opinion of so many responsible people of this state," one of them wrote in early 1955, "this particular party [Knight] not only is unpredictable, but at times positively unstable." Chotiner read this comment and told Nixon he was not surprised by it. Further, he told his boss that Knight was spreading the rumor that Nixon was anti–Semitic. "Perhaps, for the good of all," Chotiner concluded, "he ought to be made ambassador to some far-off country."[40]

Kyle Palmer at the *Los Angeles Times* also wrote to the vice president with increasing concern in 1955 about Knight's national ambitions. He ridiculed the governor as "His Excellency" and "the Great White Father in Sacramento." In another letter he observed that "friends do not know whether to call him Goddie, Gabby or Giddy." Well into 1956, he continued to express worry about Knight's "presumed plans and hopes."[41]

In June, Knight made headlines by refusing to endorse Nixon for vice president in 1956. After all, he noted, Ike had not made a public statement in support of Nixon as his running mate. "If President Eisenhower says he wants Mr. Nixon," Knight declared, "I'll support Mr. Nixon."[42] Until then, Knight would consider the job unfilled.

A month before, Nixon had held a party in Knight's honor in Washington, attended by several administration luminaries, including Eisenhower's chief of staff Sherman Adams, and California senators Knowland and Kuchel. When Nixon read in June of Knight's refusal to support him, he decided that the best strategy was to turn the other cheek. In a conciliatory letter, he pointed out to Knight how glad many of the guests at the party were for the chance to get to know him. Both he and Virginia had made a fine impression, he continued, and "Washington's California colony is literally bursting its buttons with pride."

Then he turned to the heart of the matter — Knight's comments to the media:

> The political dope stories have been coming out by the reams since you were here! As you can imagine, I was questioned quite vigorously on the stories which appeared in the *San Francisco* and *Los Angeles Examiners* yesterday. I didn't feel that it would be proper to disclose any communications that we might have had and, consequently, I simply said that our relations have been extremely cordial and I was confident we would have a united delegation in 1956.... You can be sure that I shall do everything I possibly can to knock down any stories or rumors to the effect that there is a Knight-Nixon feud.[43]

## *The Heart Attack and After*

Well into 1955, Eisenhower continued to leave open the possibility that he would not run for reelection in 1956. His ambiguous statements caused anxiety among leading Republican officials. If Ike left them in the lurch, only a limited amount of time would remain in which to close ranks behind a successor.

If Ike decided not to seek a second term, according to a Gallup Poll taken that April, Earl Warren was the first choice to replace him among Republicans and independents, leading Nixon by a three-to-one margin. A Warren candidacy, according to the *New York Times*, "terrifies" the Democrats. Senator John Sparkman agreed, saying: "I think Chief Justice Warren would offer the stiffest competition."[44]

For a while, it seemed that the Nixon-Warren rivalry was about to resume in full force. An intimate of Warren's believed that the former governor's negative feelings about Nixon were so intense that "Earl will run for president rather than see Nixon in the White House."[45] But Warren was not prepared to do so. To avoid raising any false hopes, he issued a statement ruling himself out of contention.

On September 23, the political landscape was changed dramatically by an event that jolted the Republican Party and the nation. Eisenhower was stricken with a heart attack while on vacation in the Rockies and was taken to a hospital in Denver. After a few days, as the country held its breath, Ike's condition stabilized and the immediate crisis passed. Still, the political establishment waited on pins and needles as the president remained at rest and in treatment over the next several weeks. Most people assumed that he would be unable to run again.

Eisenhower's illness began a period in which contention among the three remaining California Republican rivals reached its maximum intensity.

Prognosticators from across the political spectrum were sure that all of them would be in the running for a spot on the Republican ticket in 1956, and that one would certainly succeed.

Shortly after Eisenhower took ill, the journalist and historian Theodore H. White boarded a plane for California in the belief that "all four leading Republican candidates to succeed [Ike] were Californians."[46] The result of his trip was an article for *Collier's* magazine. The outcome of the national political struggle in 1956, he wrote, would depend primarily on "what the California Republicans do to one another." The central element in the struggle, said White, was the Nixon-Knight feud, which neither man would discuss in public but which aides had described in "unrestrained detail."[47]

With Warren insisting he was out of contention, the press focused primarily on the actions and statements of Knight, Knowland and Nixon. "The situation in California is muddled by the rivalries of these men," *U.S. News and World Report* said in early October. The "fight to the finish" over convention delegates, as Knight had characterized it the year before, now promised to be exactly that.

Eisenhower's heart attack placed each of the rivals in a difficult spot. Treacherous obstacles littered all of their paths. Nixon had to remain calm and presidential during the crisis and avoid seeming too eager to step in for Ike. Knowland and Knight had to make a judgment about whether and when to pursue a spot on the Republican ticket, and then be ready at a moment's notice to abandon all their plans and fall in line behind whatever the extremely popular president wanted. Any missteps could be fatal.

## *Nixon Copes with the Crisis*

The news that Ike had been stricken took Nixon completely by surprise. He later described the shock of being told—"it was like a great physical weight holding me down in the chair."[48]

Officially, Nixon was the number-two man in the government and would be expected to assert leadership, but he knew that any appearance of grasping for power would confirm the suspicions of his political opponents and damage his future prospects for the presidency. As he later wrote, "Many eyes would be watching to see whether I became brash or timid in meeting the emergency. My job was to be neither."[49]

Ike's closest advisers, most of whom did not see Nixon as a suitable successor to their chief, moved to minimize his role. They decided that Ike's chief of staff, Sherman Adams, would handle liaison with the president at his bedside in Denver, while Nixon and the cabinet would keep the government running in Washington. Among the cabinet officials, Secretary of State Dulles emerged as the most powerful voice, while Adams represented the president's views from Denver. In general, Nixon was limited to presiding over cabinet and National Security Council meetings.

But he was satisfied with — or at least reconciled to — serving as part of a collective leadership. As he pointed out later, Eisenhower's senior officials were a smoothly running team, which allowed business to be conducted with minimal disruption, even in difficult circumstances. "Contrary to my usual instincts, I knew that the correct course in this crisis was ... to lean with the wind," he later recalled. "As long as the president was seriously ill, this would necessarily be a period of inaction, a period in which I could not act decisively."[50]

In general, he struck the good balance he sought between excessive timidity and trying to control everything. During his public appearances, he was a calm and reassuring presence. He acted confident but not cocky. On most policy matters, he readily deferred to Ike's senior staff. Eisenhower intimate Emmet John Hughes lauded his poise and restraint during the crisis. Altogether, said Hughes, it was his "finest official hour."[51]

As Raymond Moley noted in *Time*, he emerged from the experience with increased prestige and with the concerns of many about his lack of maturity laid to rest. But he was so careful not to overreach that he drew criticism from his conservative backers. "You are the constitutional second-in-command and you ought to assume the leadership," wired one friendly senator. "Don't let the White House clique take command."[52]

Nixon later emphasized that the emergency created by Eisenhower's illness was no time for politics as usual. None of the president's senior counselors thought of "jockeying for the nomination," he recalled. "It would have been in poor taste, ill advised, and, as some who tried it a short while later, political suicide. My concern was how to keep politics out of the picture."[53]

For a man whose main political liability was a reputation for opportunism, taking the high road was arguably the best option. He sent word to Republican state chairmen around the country that he would "do nothing that could possibly be construed as political as long as we had a president who conceivably could run for a second term."[54]

Of course, much that Nixon did and said during this period had political overtones. For example, he moved almost immediately to soften his image as a hard-edged Republican, perhaps in order to be seen as a "credible heir to the general's politics of moderation" and to reduce opposition to his eventual candidacy from Eisenhower loyalists.[55] In a major foreign policy speech in October, he struck a moderate and bipartisan tone and even thanked two Democratic leaders for their support of the administration's objectives.

Nixon may have sought to "keep politics out of the picture," but the national media would not allow it. The crisis restarted a national debate about his suitability for higher office. By virtue of his position, he became the assumed front-runner for president. The overwhelming opinion, reported the *New York Times* on the very day of Ike's heart attack and *The New Republic* soon thereafter, was that Nixon would be nominated if, "as seems almost certain," Eisenhower retires.

But the magazine also pointed to the existence of several stop-Nixon groups, including one led by Ike staffers who were said to "loathe" the vice president. Attacks on his apparent insincerity and aggressive campaign style continued to appear in the national media. An article in *The New Republic*, for example, blasted Nixon as the representative of a "rigidly conformist, suburban America in which all values are translated into salability, all techniques have become devices for persuasion, and persuasion itself is indistinguishable from a hidden bludgeon."[56] Many Republicans feared that a repetition of his slashing attacks in the 1954 campaign would alienate independents and pro–Eisenhower Democrats in 1956.

Whether or not Ike chose to run in 1956, his opinion of Nixon was the key to the vice president's immediate political future. If Ike withdrew, his endorsement would be a highly-sought-after commodity among all Republicans interested in becoming president. Asking Nixon to run with him again would immediately scuttle any attempt by Knight or Knowland to replace him.

Eisenhower's medical problems raised the stakes. In 1952, as in most previous years, choosing a running mate had been a geographic and demographic balancing exercise. Nixon had been selected because he brought youth, campaign experience, and conservative credentials to the ticket that Eisenhower lacked. But the real possibility of Ike's dying in office meant that the person selected in 1956 would need above all the ability to perform the duties of the presidency. On that score, Ike's doubts about Nixon were clear. He had "watched Dick a long time," he told his speechwriter Emmet Hughes, "and he just hasn't grown. So I just haven't honestly been able to believe that he is presidential timber."[57]

As Eisenhower's health improved and his doctors proclaimed him physically capable of a second term, Ike seemed to be searching for a way to get Nixon off the ticket. He made his view known through indirection, in a way that must have been painful for Nixon to experience.

Most bizarrely, he had several private conversations with Nixon in which he expressed the view that the vice president might be better off in a different job. In the first of these sessions in late December, he told Nixon how disappointed he was that he had not become more popular around the country.

"We might have to initiate a crash program for building you up," Ike said.[58] He suggested further that it might be best for Nixon to take a cabinet post during the next term — not attorney general or secretary of state, mind you, but one of the lesser ones.

While Nixon was absorbing this idea, Ike went on to voice his regret at Earl Warren's announcement that he would not leave the Supreme Court to be a candidate for president or vice president. After all, Ike noted, a recent Gallup Poll of likely Republican voters showed Warren with a lead over Nixon for president in the event Ike dropped out. Another poll showed Nixon substantially behind Adlai Stevenson. "I just cannot understand how any sane-minded person could choose Stevenson over you," Eisenhower added.

In his book *Six Crises*, Nixon described this conversation matter-of-factly, claiming that he dismissed Ike's musings as a trial balloon — a typical

Nixon, on a fishing trip with Eisenhower, listens as the president describes the one that got away. Despite Nixon's tireless efforts on behalf of the party and its candidates and general acclaim for his performance as vice president, Ike did not consider him presidential timber and tried to remove him from the 1956 ticket (Richard Nixon Presidential Library/National Archives and Records Administration).

instance of his thinking out loud rather than an expression of his true feelings. But it is more likely that Nixon was shocked, even enraged, by what he heard. He had worked tirelessly for three years on Ike's behalf, had received good reviews for the quality of his service, and handled Ike's health crisis with tact and skill. Now he was being reminded that Earl Warren, of all people, outpolled him for president!

Ike returned to this subject in several subsequent conversations, each time asking Nixon what he thought about taking a cabinet position. Nixon replied that if Ike thought he would be better served with him off the ticket, he would withdraw. But the president insisted that it was up to Nixon to do what he thought was best for him. Nixon later contended that this was typical of Eisenhower's decision-making style — he preferred to ratify decisions made by subordinates rather than make them himself.

Seen from this remove, Ike's message to Nixon seems unambiguous. An idea repeated on several occasions could no longer be considered a trial balloon. During this same period, Dulles also suggested to Nixon that he move to a cabinet post, though Nixon pretended not to know if the president had raised the subject with him. Eisenhower, whether through his own observations or by listening to the anti–Nixon views of those closest to him, had concluded that Nixon could not be counted upon to continue the president's policies and effectively lead the country. He wanted Nixon off the ticket and hoped Nixon would figure this out for himself.

The conversations with Ike understandably threw Nixon into a period of agonizing indecision. Not allowing himself to believe Ike wanted him out, he assumed that the president was reflecting the views of his advisers, some of whom "made little secret of their personal antipathy toward me and wanted to dump me in '56 as they had in '52."[59]

He considered briefly the possibility of a cabinet job but, in the end, it did not matter to him whether his long-term career interests might be best served by doing so, as Ike had argued. He decided it would simply be too humiliating. "I could not switch jobs," he later said, "without the disastrous appearance that 'Nixon had been dumped.'"[60]

In late February 1956, a few days after his doctors proclaimed him healthy enough to serve another term, Eisenhower announced his candidacy for reelection. But he continued to be noncommittal about his choice for the vice presidency — as he reminded the press unconvincingly, he had not been formally nominated yet.

At his next news conference, he was confronted with questions about whether it was true that he had urged Nixon to accept a cabinet post. "The only thing I have asked him to do," replied Ike, "is to chart his own course and tell me what he would like to do. I have never gone beyond that."[61] It might have been hard to judge which was more humiliating for Nixon — to be "dumped" from the ticket or to be reminded almost daily of Ike's lack of confidence in him. Ike's insistence that Nixon "chart his own course" made him seriously consider leaving public life.[62]

Finally, Nixon decided to call Ike's bluff. On April 26 he went to the Oval Office and said he wanted to run for reelection as vice president, if the president would have him. Ike immediately said he was delighted with Nixon's decision, and an announcement was made that very afternoon. For the time being, the 1956 ticket looked settled.

But when Eisenhower expressed his delight at Nixon's decision to run, wordsmiths around the country noted that he still had not endorsed the vice president. In the mid–1950s, it was not unusual for a presidential nominee to distance himself from the choice of a running mate.[63] The result of Ike's failure to fully embrace Nixon was continued activity by the still active "dump Nixon" movement. Eisenhower left the impression right up until the convention that if the party decided someone besides Nixon should join him on the ticket, he would go along. "There should be no doubt about my satisfaction with him as a running mate," he told the press as late as August 1, but he also upheld "the right of the delegates to the convention to nominate whom they choose."[63]

## Knight Resumes the Attack

Even during the national leadership crisis of late 1955, Knight seemed to relish slighting Nixon. In a meeting with the press shortly after Ike's heart attack, he volunteered the names of several Republicans who he felt were qualified to be president — among them Bill Knowland, Secretary of State John Foster Dulles, and Senators Henry Cabot Lodge and Everett Dirksen. Later, speaking to different reporters, he omitted Dirksen and added some others, but not the vice president. When asked why not Nixon, he acted as if the idea had never occurred to him. "Oh, sure," Knight said, "he should be on it."[64]

Knight was the first of the three rivals to go public with his political intentions. In October 1955, less than two weeks after Eisenhower's heart attack, he repeated his earlier statement that he planned to lead the California delegation to the 1956 Republican convention as a favorite son and that he was for Ike "first and foremost." If Eisenhower ran, his delegation would be pledged to his reelection. "We are going all the way, regardless of what Mr. Nixon does," he also declared.[65]

A few days later, interviewed on the news program *Meet the Press*, Knight was coy about whether he was pursuing either the presidency or vice presidency. "I would be less than honest with you," he told the panelists, "if I did not state to you that in my judgment every Republican governor, every Republican senator, and a good sprinkling of Republicans in government would be interested, and I would be one of them. I wouldn't mislead you for a moment. But that doesn't mean I'm running." Quizzed about Earl Warren's professed non-candidacy for president, Knight was eager to take it at face value. "I know he is not a casual or careless speaker," he pointed out. "I am sure that he made that statement after great and careful thought."

Most of the discussion on the program was focused on Knight's alleged feud with Nixon. The governor described the events of the previous year in California as part of a "lively political contest" with Nixon proxies. His goal now, he declared, was simply to keep the delegation "free and open so that in the event some other candidate [for vice president] whom the delegates would prefer should rise upon the scene, they would not be committed."[66]

Knight's high profile comments on the upcoming election, at a time when Eisenhower was still recovering, were seen by many as, at best, premature and, at worst, inappropriate. The author of a *U.S. News and World Report* article believed they could damage his chances for higher office. It would be better, said the piece, for Nixon and Knight to come to an agreement about which Californian would be the national candidate in the 1956 race so as to unify the delegation and maximize its potential effectiveness as a kingmaker.[67]

According to the *Washington Post*, Knight's announcement of his convention plans was a "scarcely veiled attack on the vice president," who sensibly, it pointed out, had not responded. "Knight's performance," continued the *Post*, "at a time when Mr. Nixon is handling affairs for President Eisenhower in a becoming fashion, has set a low mark to shoot at." The newspaper feared that the actions of the rivals could "throw the convention into pandemonium."[68]

*Time* printed an even more negative view of Knight's "blatant" move to the front of the pack. It quoted California congressman (and Nixon ally) Carl Hinshaw, who condemned Knight's "amazing antics" and "fantastic pretensions." "Except in the ambitious dreams of Mr. Knight, he is something of a political joke in national politics," said Hinshaw. "It will prove most unfortunate ... if this unseemly and almost indecent haste to exploit the unfortunate illness of President Eisenhower should result in creating a false impression of his real standing."[69]

An article in the journal *Fortnight* opined that Knight, an "adequately able governor," was in a good position relative to his rivals, if only because Nixon—"the most ardently liked and disliked man in recent political history"—was such a polarizing force. But the piece expressed concern that Knight's overeagerness, both past and present, highlighted his lack of gravitas. In his "long, tireless, and frankly ambitious efforts to become governor of California," it lamented, "he failed to cloak himself in the aura of dignity so necessary" to be a candidate for president.[70]

Knight sometimes claimed to be performing a public service by attempting to block Nixon's candidacy for national office. He pointed to the hundreds of letters in his files from people around the state begging him to contest a Nixon nomination. The truth was that Knight received at least as many— and perhaps more—letters from California Republicans who were angry because he would not support the vice president. "Please remember," wrote one voter, "that you are supposed to be the governor of California, and there are a lot of us who think that Dick Nixon is a wonderful vice president and a fine American."[71] The political reality was that Nixon loyalists had the upper hand in the state Republican committee. A newspaper poll showed that 61 percent of its members backed a Nixon slate and only 22 percent supported the governor.

Knight's attempt to assert control of the California Republican Party while Nixon's responsibilities obliged him to restrain himself infuriated Nixon's men in the state. Roy Day wrote caustically of the "twisted baloney" being tossed about. "I realize that the smart thing to do is shut up and let them hang themselves, and one governor has done an excellent job of hanging himself already." He took particular exception to a Knight public display of bruised feelings over Nixon's undermining of Warren in 1952. "It makes my blood boil," Day said.[72] Knight's aggressive moves convinced Frank Jorgensen that it was not too early to plan a strategy for 1956. "Ike won't run again, I think, and you are the front-runner," he wrote Nixon, "but as long as our *friend* is in Sacramento, we cannot be sure of anything."[73]

Some pundits argued that "the exuberant and defiantly ambitious" Knight could not be dismissed so easily. In October, *U.S. News* reminded its readers that Knight was widely known and immensely popular at home, with a large, devoted following. As the most politically moderate of the three California Republicans, the journal believed, he would be an attractive option as either president or vice president.

With Eisenhower's decision about his candidacy imminent, writer Hale Champion expressed the belief that Knight held the "balance of Republican power," as his February 1956 article in *The Reporter* was subtitled. Champion considered Knight the man to watch—a dark-horse presidential candidate committed to Ike-style moderation but also "perfectly content with the lesser voltage that accompanies the vice presidential nomination." The journal cited several off-the-record conversations in which Knight had bragged that

Knight plants himself firmly between Nixon (left) and Knowland on a sofa in front of several lesser California politicians. Knight had an uncanny ability to get himself "smack-dab" in the middle of any photo that was being taken. "He was an artist at it, he really was," marveled a Nixon campaign worker (Richard Nixon Presidential Library/National Archives and Records Administration).

he was just the man to stop Nixon, to whom he again referred in unprintable language.[74]

All the while, consultants Whitaker and Baxter worked behind the scenes to keep Knight's name before the public. In a letter to *The New Yorker* magazine's editorial department appraising West Coast political developments, they noted that Knight's skill as a campaigner "would help in capturing national attention and public acceptance in a short period of time" if Ike should announce his unavailability. It concluded with an appeal not to make the letter public, because "it would be exceedingly embarrassing if it were made to appear that we were trying to promote Knight's candidacy, which we are not." In a note to his client, Clem Whitaker said he hoped "you will feel that we handled this matter with adequate delicacy."[75]

Mrs. Knight's recollections of this period portrayed a governor buoyed by laudatory media coverage and increasingly convinced of his viability for national office. Whitaker and Baxter sent him newspaper articles suggesting that moderate candidates like him were in tune with the times and that it was not too early to begin campaigning.[76] His feelings about Nixon aside, Knight seemed to reason that he was the strongest Republican governor who might be in the running for president or vice president. His appeal had been tested at the polls, where he had won by almost 600,000 votes. The winning margin of New York's popular Governor Averill Harriman, by contrast, had been only 100,000 votes.

Virginia Knight judged her husband's goal of being a favorite son candidate for president "not unrealistic — he had all the qualifications."[77] Moreover, the couple found all the attention exciting. Unlike Pat Nixon, who disliked campaigning and often urged the vice president to retire from politics, Mrs. Knight seems to have enjoyed the limelight as much as the governor did. She probably encouraged his political ambitions.

Knight decided to take a trip back east in order to test his national appeal. As he had in California, he eagerly sought the endorsement of labor officials. The consensus was that he made a good impression everywhere, and he came away believing that labor considered him an acceptable Republican. In an interview years later, Virginia Knight quoted extensively from enthusiastic newspaper accounts of her husband's trip, one of which noted that he gave "talks that were as refreshing as the fog that blows into San Francisco from the sea."[78]

To his associates, Knight often seemed more interested in discussing politics than the policy issues that crossed his desk each day. "I would go in to talk to him about the budget," recalled Assemblyman Tom Caldecott, "and the first thing he'd say was, 'I understand you just got back from Washington.' I'd say yes, so he'd ask me a number of questions about what was happening in the party and ... that sort of thing."[79] Pat Brown had the same experience: "When I'd go in to talk with him, all he'd do was talk politics; he wouldn't talk government at all."[80]

In his article in *The Reporter*, Hale Champion found that Knight's essence was hard to pin down. Was he only an "amiable, lightweight political hack" with a flair for campaigning, as he sometimes seemed to be? Was he a conservative who was simply acting moderate to get votes, or had his outlook broadened since becoming governor, much as Earl Warren's did? Was he a political technician "more interested in the mechanics, trappings and drama of political life than in the hard work and serious thinking to which he should be dedicated?"[81] The reader was left to draw his own conclusions.

## Knowland's Calculations

Eisenhower's heart attack also forced the third rival, Bill Knowland, to reconsider his options. A wide-open convention, with both ends of the ticket undecided, would present him with the opportunity he had failed to grasp in 1952. For this reason, he was not happy to hear of Governor Knight's intention to bring the California Republicans into line behind his favorite son candidacy. But, like Nixon, he did not want to move with unseemly haste while Ike was recovering.

Even before Ike's future became uncertain, Knowland was being touted as a presidential candidate. A *Los Angeles Times* journalist, writing in July 1954, pronounced him a mature and seasoned politician. "The inner fires of unorthodox, unpopular convictions have done the tempering," he noted. "Now you couldn't hold a meeting in a telephone booth of competent critics who still think Knowland hasn't arrived as a political leader in his own right and as a major force in the national and world events of our time."[82]

The Knowland buzz intensified after Eisenhower's heart attack. Some conservatives viewed him as the ideological successor to his late mentor, Robert Taft of Ohio. James Wick, writing in *Human Events*, noted the deep respect in which he was held in the Senate, his independence from the Eisenhower White House, and his popularity in California, as shown by his landslide victory there four years before. He predicted that Knowland would become president "if conservatives ... will work as hard for [him] in 1956 as Ohio conservatives worked for Taft in 1950."[83] An article in the *New Republic* in February by William S. White praised Knowland as "a man of the highest personal integrity, a man embodying the best rather than the mediocrity or the worst of [the Republican] movement, and, above all, a man so placed as to protect and forward [the party's] truly fundamental design."[84]

Some of these writers saw Knowland as stronger than Nixon in his home state. A profile in *Look* magazine recalled how the senator "flexed his political muscles" when he joined Knight in 1954 to ensure the election of Howard Ahmanson in California. "If Knowland ever decided to get rid of Nixon, he could murder him," a political insider told *Look*. "One sound defeat could ruin Nixon in the state, but Knowland and the *[Oakland] Tribune* will be around for a long time. And the Republicans know it. In a showdown, they'll go along with Knowland."[85] The truth of that questionable judgment was never to be tested.

Rumors had been circulating for some time that Knowland was positioning himself to take advantage of any change in the 1956 Republican ticket. In June 1955, James Reston of the *New York Times* had reported that the senator had his eye on the vice presidency and was working with Knight to take Nixon out of play at the convention. The *Sacramento Bee* echoed this account. "Mr. Knowland's supporters hope that Mr. Knight will not agree to cast the state's delegates for Nixon in the vice presidential balloting," the paper said. "They also hope they will be able to persuade the President that he should not insist on Mr. Nixon as his running mate if Mr. Nixon cannot even get the support of his own state delegation."[86]

Still, Nixon appeared to be the Republican front-runner in the event of Eisenhower's withdrawal, and Knowland was no doubt calculating his chances of overtaking Nixon's lead. Shortly after Ike was taken ill, he bristled when he heard speculation about Nixon succeeding Ike. Without mentioning the vice president's name, he allegedly said: "I do not consider a Pepsodent smile, a ready quip and an actor's perfection with lines, nor an ability to avoid issues, as qualifications for high office."[87]

This startling quote, so much at variance with Knowland's usual caution and lack of rancor in his public remarks, appeared without attribution in a book about Nixon by William Costello. The author considered the comment an outright repudiation of Nixon and evidence of Knowland's lingering bitterness from the 1952 convention. He also believed that it reflected a number of policy disputes between Knowland and the vice president. The quote, if genuine, and if Nixon was the intended target, spoke volumes about the resentment he had been nursing.

As 1955 drew to a close, with no decision from the White House on Eisenhower's candidacy, Knowland's patience grew thin. If he was going to run himself, he would have to put together a campaign in a big hurry. In October, he suggested publicly that Ike announce his plans soon. Then he let it be known that he would be available for the presidential nomination if Eisenhower dropped out.

At the same time, he raised his visibility, giving a number of speeches and prompting speculation about his intentions. Asked on the television show *Face the Nation* about a Nixon comment that the party could win only if Ike ran, Knowland disagreed. "I don't believe in the doctrine of the indispensable man," he emphasized. "I have found no defeatist attitude on the part of the Republicans, and I have spoken in about thirty states of the union."[88]

Back in California, Joe Knowland was busy promoting his son's interests. He met with Knight and campaign consultants Whitaker and Baxter in January 1956. According to Knowland's biographers, Knight tried to strike a deal with the Knowlands to divide up the 70-member California delegation to the 1956 convention and cut Nixon out.[89] He apparently continued to push for a meeting on the subject with Bill Knowland himself. But if the senator had any thoughts about an alliance of convenience with Knight, the governor's hasty declaration of his favorite-son candidacy after Ike's heart attack probably pushed them aside.

Despite his activities in California, Joe Knowland had misgivings about his son's involvement in the struggle to succeed the president. He thought it was a high-stakes gamble with a significant downside. Nixon, he felt, would have Eisenhower's backing and thus a big advantage over the others. Calling his son's chances "a long shot at best," the elder Knowland warned him that "if you lose out in the primary, it would be a tremendous humiliation, in my judgment."[90]

But the senator continued to lay the groundwork for a possible candidacy. To cement his relations with the party's right wing, he accepted an offer from the prominent conservative William Buckley to write an article for the first issue of Buckley's journal, the *National Review*, in which he criticized the administration for negotiating with the Soviet Union. The magazine praised the senator as the titular standard bearer of the conservative movement. For a time, Buckley urged him to run for president.

Knowland's higher profile drew the ire of Eisenhower and the men around him. Even if he were going to withdraw from the race, the president did not consider the California senator electable. In January 1956, Knowland declared publicly that he would not join a draft–Eisenhower movement. Ike exploded. "In his case," he wrote in his diary, "there seems to be no final answer to the question, 'How stupid can you get?' Why he has to talk about such things I wouldn't know unless he's determined to destroy the Republican party."[91] Looking at the field of Republican presidential contenders, Ike began to feel that the party's success in 1956 depended on him alone.

One of Eisenhower's staffers came up with a scheme to delay the announcement of his decision long enough so that, if withdrawal was the president's choice, Knowland would not have time to mobilize for a campaign. But Knowland thwarted that idea by issuing a sort of ultimatum — if Ike had not announced by the end of January, he would enter presidential primaries in several states, including Oregon and Wisconsin. He hoped that signaling an intention to run would create a groundswell of enthusiasm for his candidacy.

## *Jockeying for Position*

At the beginning of 1956, then, it seemed possible that all three California rivals might be running against each other in the state's Republican presidential primary. Such an event threatened to leave a badly split party in its wake.

In fact, the fourth rival may have been revisiting his decision not to run. In a curious January diary entry, President Eisenhower reported being told by an aide that Chief Justice Warren was upset because Ike had publicly endorsed Warren's earlier statement that the Supreme Court and politics should not be mixed. As Ike confided to his journal, if Warren wanted to reverse his previous refusal to run for president, he was free to do so, and such a decision "would be a great relief to me." But he had a duty, in Ike's view, to resign from the Supreme Court "the first time he indicated himself as receptive to the nomination."[92]

Reassured by an encouraging medical prognosis, Eisenhower sent all possible candidates back to the drawing board by announcing his candidacy for reelection on February 29. Knowland, Nixon and Warren no longer had to think about their chances of being nominated for president in 1956.

Knowland may have resolved instead to urge upon Ike a more conservative running mate than Nixon. The *New York Times* reported a few days later that the senator had lobbied the president to consolidate the party by selecting a Taft Republican to run with him. Could he have been referring to himself? He told his daughter Emelyn that Eisenhower called him into the Oval Office and raised the possibility of him being the nominee. "If my president asks me to stand," her father told her, "obviously I would do so" even though he claimed to view it "more or less like being put out to pasture."[93] It is unlikely that Ike considered this option seriously, in view of his strongly negative feelings about the senator and their rocky working relationship throughout his first term.

With the Republican National Convention looming, many party officials, as well as Kyle Palmer of the *Los Angeles Times*, began to urge the remaining rivals to come to an agreement on apportioning California's delegates among them. Knight had long clung to the position that the state's representatives should be unified under his leadership, rather than "split up like a Chinese puzzle into groups of satellite, captive delegates — so many for Knight, so many for Knowland ... so many for Nixon."[94] In response, Chotiner wrote to Nixon: "Who does he think he is kidding?"[95]

By early 1956, Knight realized that he did not have the political strength to lead a favorite son delegation — even one committed to Eisenhower — and understood that the state party's three major factions would have to be represented. The only question was how many delegates each major player would get.

In February, Knight invited representatives of Nixon and Knowland to Sacramento to try to work out a deal. Nixon responded enthusiastically to Knight's proclaimed goal of presenting a harmonious and united front to the convention. "I will be glad to join with you and Senator Knowland in selecting a delegation which will serve that objective," he wrote.[96] Each of the big three designated two loyalists to meet and work out a compromise.

The solution they devised was equitable, though it could not have pleased the governor, in view of his long-held expectations of controlling the delegation. The California contingent would consist of three groups of twenty-three delegates, each headed by one of the rivals. The seventieth and final delegate would be the state's junior senator, Tom Kuchel, who had good relations with all sides. According to California assemblyman Tom Caldecott and others, the representatives of Nixon and Knowland joined forces to impose this agreement on Knight.[97]

In June, the question of Eisenhower's candidacy again looked unsettled after the president underwent surgery for an inflamed lower intestine. As Nixon wrote later, "doubt [about Eisenhower running] rekindled presidential aspirations in some Republican breasts."[98] But Ike recovered quickly and saw no reason to alter his plans.

Even so, he met in July with the Republican leadership in Congress to smoke out any second thoughts about his candidacy. Bill Knowland again put aside any hopes of his own by being the first to speak up and declare congressional Republicans united behind the president. Mindful of Knowland's refusal to endorse a draft–Eisenhower movement earlier in the year, Ike asked the senator if he would mind conveying that message to the media. "Fine," he said, "I think that would be delightful."[99] Knowland's comments to the press were in the same enthusiastic spirit: "He and we are looking forward to a vigorous and active campaign under his leadership."[100]

That same month, Minnesota's Harold Stassen launched a last-minute effort to gather support for the view that Nixon would be a drag on the ticket. Stassen's challenge, coupled with the second Ike health crisis, focused renewed attention on the possibility that the president might die in office during a second term and created what Nixon called a "dangerously fluid situation"—one that jeopardized his nomination. As he noted in his memoirs, several vice presidential candidates were "eagerly waiting in the wings."[101] But Stassen's gambit antagonized so many Republicans that party regulars ran to the beleaguered vice president's defense.

In view of the continued lack of a categorical statement from the president that Nixon was his choice, Sherman Adams suggested that the White House might release a list of acceptable candidates, with Nixon's name first. Congressional Republicans were furious. Nixon must have recognized the proposal as a thinly disguised effort to get people thinking about other possibilities. Fortunately for him, the consensus among the White House staff was that a list of candidates would be extremely difficult to draw up—it would either be so large as to be meaningless or omit people who would be offended.

Governor Knight may have had contacts with those inside the administration who were working to derail a Nixon candidacy. According to aide Doug Barrett, the governor "was encouraged to, at least, let his name be used as a focal point from inside the White House" on opposing Nixon's ambitions and had "considerable communication" with Ike's chief of staff, Sherman Adams. The nature of their talks or the extent of their joint planning, if any, is not known.[102]

With the top of the ticket settled, Bill Knowland's loyalty to the larger cause of Republican electoral success helped Nixon cement his status as Ike's running mate. The senator decided that victory in November could best be assured if the party came together behind the two incumbents. He recognized Goodwin Knight's campaign to split the California delegation and oppose the vice president as the personal vendetta that it mostly was.

Knight's declaration in August that he was available for the vice presidency galvanized Knowland into action. "It was at this point," he later recalled, "that I called Vice President Nixon and told him that, as far as I was concerned, I intended to support him for reelection."[103] This decision took away Knight's leverage over his own delegation. Knowland and Nixon between them would control two-thirds of the state's Republicans at the convention.

## *The 1956 Convention*

The well organized Republican convention that opened in mid–August in San Francisco featured giant Ike-Nixon posters and a don't-rock-the-boat atmosphere. The only lingering uncertainty was provided by Eisenhower's unwillingness to select a vice presidential candidate, which kept Stassen and Knight hoping for the success of their "rearguard action"[104] against Nixon. Upon Ike's arrival in San Francisco, Knight delivered a welcoming speech praising the president but omitting all mention of Nixon. He professed to be concerned solely with party harmony and denied having any interest in the vice presidency himself.

The uncertainty and bad feeling among the California delegates before the convention chilled the atmosphere in San Francisco when the event finally began. "Some of those people couldn't even speak to each other," remembered Assembly Speaker Luther Lincoln. "It was uncomfortable to the point where I recall ... meetings in the morning where we would just identify ourselves, answer the roll, and say goodbye, and nothing would happen."[105]

Nixon seemed confident upon his arrival in San Francisco. He told the press that the convention's most important job was to renominate the "man of the century" and that "personal careers and considerations of anyone are insignificant in comparison. I include myself in that respect." He endorsed the idea of a free and open nomination process. "I have constantly opposed any move to close the convention as far as the vice presidential nomination is concerned."[106] As long as Eisenhower continued not to endorse any other candidate, Nixon apparently felt that he had little to fear. Just to make sure, he made calls on the delegations and outlined his projected role in the campaign to come.

With Nixon now on the scene, the three California heavyweights held an hour-and-a-half meeting to discuss procedural issues. Photographs showed them looking glumly serious at the head table. "We just had three strong leaders who couldn't agree on anything at all," recalled Lincoln.[107]

Knowland, as a Nixon supporter, seemed prepared to serve as the vice president's floor manager in the event that a serious fight over his nomination erupted. In their gratitude, the Nixon forces proposed him as chairman of the California delegation, a role that Knight had long assumed was his. According to a blow-by-blow description in the *San Francisco Chronicle* the next day, Knowland also proposed that the delegation formally endorse Nixon for vice president. Knight "angrily opposed" this motion, and tempers flared.

After a recess, Knight protested that he had been double-crossed on the matter of who would head the state delegation. He resisted Knowland's nomination to that job, fearing a further loss of face and the usurpation of another of his prerogatives. The tenor of his remarks, according to Nixon aide Frank Jorgensen, was: "Don't do this. Don't take me out of this picture. As governor of the state, I ... and so forth and so forth." Jorgensen later insisted that Nixon did his best to accommodate Knight and to try to smooth over relations with him. The two men "weren't seeing eye to eye by any means," he admitted, but Nixon intervened, saying, "Let's don't do this. Let's try to create some harmony if we can, and please don't push it."[108]

The Nixon-Knowland forces then used their superior leverage to propose that, in return for being allowed to head the delegation, Knight agree that the California contingent would vote as a unit. With Knight allies in the minority, unit voting guaranteed that Nixon would receive all seventy votes in the vice presidential balloting. "I'll be damned if I'll be bound by this bunch of phonies," the governor was heard saying. "If the price of my being chairman is that I must yield to steamroller pressure in violation of the president's expressed desire for an open convention ... then the price is too high."[109] Knowland responded that it would be a "disgrace" if Nixon's home state delegation did not endorse him. Knight, in turn, redirected his "disappointment, if not resentment" at Knowland for siding with his enemy.[110]

## 9 — The Rivals and the 1956 Convention

The governor wanted badly to be chairman of the California delegation — a role he had "coveted" and "long anticipated," according to the *San Francisco Chronicle*. So he accepted the deal, bowing to superior numbers, and the unit rule took effect. The Nixon and Knowland people had "pushed Knight out of the way, which I hated to see," confessed one Republican official. "It was a very unhappy situation."[111] When the time came to cast votes for vice president in the California caucus, Knight and his delegates abstained — an act Nixon would not forget.

Amid this squabbling, the rivals, as Californians, were expected to act as hosts in welcoming Republicans from all over the country to San Francisco. These duties must have produced a considerable amount of awkwardness, but it was not apparent from their written exchanges. Prior to the opening of the convention, Nixon wrote to Knight accepting an invitation to join the governor and his wife, Virginia, in receiving the delegates. In a postscript, Nixon asked if Virginia could let Pat know whether women in the reception line would be wearing short or long formals. Later in the week, Nixon again wrote to Knight, saying how much he and Pat had enjoyed their party a few days before and calling it one of the highlights of his San Francisco visit.[112]

Eisenhower's pained and awkward ambivalence about Nixon continued right up until a few hours before his nomination. Asked a final time for his thoughts about choosing a vice president, he responded: "There are many people that could be brought up, and there would be many questions that I would have to take into mind, if I were in that position. But — so I am not going to express an opinion one way or another. I think Dick Nixon knows what I think. I think you know what I think of Dick Nixon."[113]

At a press conference on August 22, the president finally ended the vice presidential drama by accepting Stassen's withdrawal and intention to second Nixon's nomination. As his delegation's chairman, Knight found himself casting California's unanimous vote for the man he hoped to replace and then introducing him to the convention. A later note from Hannah Nixon thanking him for "your fine introduction of Richard" undoubtedly did not ease Knight's pain.[114]

Knight aide Doug Barrett minimized Knight's investment in the stop–Nixon movement. It was true that he had made a "real college try" to control the California delegation in opposition to the vice president. But when that attempt failed, he did not seem concerned with not getting the vice presidential nod himself. He was a realist, Barrett claimed, and he probably did not expect his efforts to succeed.[115]

Nixon extended an olive branch to Knight during the fall campaign. Twice in September, he expressed his gratitude in writing for personal and professional courtesies. Nixon's father had died immediately after the convention, and the vice president thanked Knight on the 17th for wiring his condolences. He added a personal touch by noting that his mother had devoted the last two years of her life to caring for his father and confessed that the past few weeks had been trying ones.[116] Two days later, Nixon thanked Knight for his "sparkling" introduction at a California rally the night before. His only regret, he continued, was the lack of time to get together with him and Virginia. He urged Knight to visit other states in the campaign, where he could give a "great boost to the ticket."[117]

It is not clear whether these friendly notes from Nixon were reciprocated or how much genuine feeling they contained, but they were consistent with his previous efforts to take the high road in their relationship. As the winner, moreover, he could afford to be magnanimous, and the Republican ticket needed Knight's help in the campaign. Nixon's restraint was probably part of a calculated strategy to flatter Knight back into the fold.

In November, Eisenhower and Nixon swept to victory in the national elections. Because he was Chief Justice of the United States, Warren would ordinarily be expected to swear in both the president and vice president at their inauguration in 1957. But when the big day arrived, Warren swore in Eisenhower, while Senate Minority Leader William Knowland swore in Nixon.

## *Nixon's Resilience*

During his travails throughout this period, Nixon showed that he was developing a capacity for resilience in the face of rejection — a capacity he would draw on many times in the years to come. He suffered greatly and demonstrated his vulnerability, yet his self-confidence, coolness under fire, and logical mind brought him through in the end.

The damage to Nixon's psyche from Eisenhower's continued refusal to accept him as a full-fledged partner in his administration was substantial. "No one in public life may have done more to seal Richard Nixon's sense of personal isolation than Dwight Eisenhower," wrote Emmet Hughes. In a telling image, Hughes saw Ike acting as a "political father" to Nixon "with roughly the enthusiasm that most men show in situations of wholly unplanned paternity."[118]

An anecdote provides a glimpse of Nixon's state of mind during the prolonged uncertainty about his vice presidential candidacy. Once the question was finally resolved, a disconsolate Nixon arrived alone one evening for drinks and dinner at Knowland's California home. As related by Knowland's daughter Estelle, he seemed disheartened, almost as if, "Yes, I'm being kept on the ticket, but nobody means it."[119] This anecdote, though impressionistic in nature, provided a small window into the pain he was undoubtedly feeling. It also showed that he felt close enough to Knowland to share his distress.

Yet years later, Nixon wrote dispassionately about the events of 1955–1956, with a view that the obstacles to his renomination were trivial and that a positive outcome was inevitable. Though he certainly was less dispassionate as these events were unfolding, he had an ability — shown time and again throughout his career — to coolly assess the political balance of forces in a given situation before deciding what to do. He knew that he brought important strengths to Eisenhower's presidency, including the allegiance of most Republican Party professionals and a growing record of accomplishment. He would not panic in the face of challenges from Knight or Knowland. "Considering all the practical political aspects," he later said, "I ... concluded that all this was largely a tempest in a teapot. If the president decided to run, I would almost certainly be his running mate."[120]

# 10

## *The Big Switch of 1958 and the End of the Rivalry*

The so-called Big Switch was the perfect denouement to the rivalry of the California Republicans. In an unexpected and bizarre way, it provided a useful public service. It revealed the emptiness of Knowland's and Knight's pretensions to national leadership and the reality of their limitations as politicians. And it was fitting that Richard Nixon should play a role in the event that ended the political careers of his long-time antagonists and left him virtually unopposed for the 1960 Republican presidential nomination.

Republicans had a sense of gloom and foreboding about the elections of 1958. California and the nation were in a recession, and Americans were known to base their votes primarily on economic concerns. At the same time, the success of the Soviet space program, highlighted by the shocking news in 1957 that a Russian satellite was orbiting the earth, led to concerns that the Eisenhower administration was not spending enough on defense and space programs. Both domestic and foreign policy issues, in other words, favored the Democrats.

In California, moreover, the advantage provided to Republicans over the previous forty years by the institution of cross-filing was being eroded. Though cross-filing had not yet been abolished (that would come a few years later), the party affiliations of candidates were required to appear on the ballot in 1958. This change allowed Democrats to exploit more fully their vast superiority in numbers. The California Democratic Party had learned the lesson of its long period in the wilderness — it was better organized than ever before and united behind its candidates for state and federal office.

It was also the first election year in which the political influence of California's newspapers, with their strong pro-Republican bias, was seriously challenged by television and other media. Kyle Palmer seemed to recognize that the golden age of newspapers was drawing to a close when he wrote in frustration that a "lying, deliberately confusing, mischievous billboard, a passion-breeding, deceiving radio announcement or its twin on television has an impact which is almost impossible to correct."[1]

## Knowland Makes a Move

By themselves, these developments might not have spelled disaster for the California Republican Party in 1958. It took a decision by one man — Bill Knowland — to make that happen. One day in December 1956, he articulated an idea that had been taking shape in his mind for some time. He stunned two of his aides by asking: "What would you boys think if I ran for governor instead of senator in 1958?" A month later, during a television interview, he announced matter-of-factly that he did not intend to stand for reelection to the Senate.

The news reached California as Goodwin Knight was delivering his annual State of the State address. When he finished speaking, he was bombarded with questions about Knowland's decision. He admitted he was as shocked and surprised as everyone else. When Vice President Nixon was told, he commented dryly that he hoped the senator "will return to public service in the future."[2]

The reason Knowland gave for quitting the Senate — to spend more time with his family — was unconvincing. He noted that his father, the *Oakland Tribune* publisher, was getting on in years and needed help running the newspaper. The elder Knowland did tell the *New York Times* that he would be glad to have Bill closer, but in private he was adamantly opposed to the move. With his son at the height of his influence as a leader of the Senate, he believed it would be foolish for Bill to give up his position, and he thought Bill had little chance of being elected governor. Emelyn Knowland told an interviewer years later that she still remembered her grandfather's anger.[3]

The real reasons for Knowland's move were both personal and political. His relationship with his wife, Helen, had deteriorated in the aftermath of their extramarital affairs and Blair Moody's death. He was apparently continuing to see Ruth Moody, and Helen wanted Bill out of the Washington "candy shop." She was "tired of it," recalled Knight aide Doug Barrett, referring to social life in the capital.[4] Their daughter Emelyn confirmed that living in Washington was "very tough on mother."[5] A family friend observed that "they weren't the happiest two people."[6] According to credible rumor, Helen gave her husband an ultimatum: they would move back to California as a couple or she would leave him in Washington.

Saving his marriage, then, was an important consideration, but it was not the only one. Knowland wanted to run for president in 1960. A review of recent U.S. history reminded him that eight governors, but only one senator, had been nominated for that office in the twentieth century. Governors, as chief executives of their states, were regarded as natural heirs to the Oval Office.

As governor, Knowland also believed that he could better differentiate himself as an alternative to Nixon. In the capital, he was in the vice president's shadow. He would have more freedom in Sacramento than he had as a Republican senator in Washington to decide when and how to oppose administration policies. Returning to California, with its surging conservative movement, would give him a chance for a fresh start. According to a journalist who knew him well, Knowland felt that "things were not falling his way fast enough."[7] A move of this magnitude, argued a prominent state Republican official, could only be motivated by power. "I think that's all he really recognized and wanted."[8]

Knowland was making a virtue out of necessity. If he believed that a divorce or separation would adversely affect — or even end — his life in politics, then he had to return to California. If he could then succeed in becoming governor, he would be in a better position to control the state delegation to the Republican Party convention in 1960. Though he knew little and cared less about state government, he believed his decision had the potential to repair his broken marriage and, perhaps, to advance his political career as well.

Knowland's tendency to keep his own counsel — termed "Potomac myopia" by many of his critics — isolated him from other points of view that might have been useful. Some contemporary observers believed that Nixon somehow urged him to return to California, but the choice seems to have been his alone. A Nixon staff memo vigorously denied that the vice president was involved in any way.[9] Neither had Earl Warren been consulted — he told a colleague that Knowland had not talked to him for several months about politics.[10] Stranger still, given his domestic problems, he apparently did not even take his wife into his confidence. In a note to her mother, Helen Knowland wrote of being able to "read the signs" that her husband was going to run for governor.[11]

Though Knowland had not yet announced any plans to do so, Knight viewed his withdrawal from the 1958 Senate race as a serious threat. Pat Brown, the eventual Democratic candidate for governor, believed that it "threw him into a panic he never recovered from."[12] During the next few weeks, Knight did everything he could to head off a Knowland challenge. He appealed to his fellow California Republicans to unite behind him in the face of recent Democratic gains, and predicted that the party would lose if split. He watched nervously as Knowland announced that he would make a fact-finding trip to California later in the year.

In fact, little doubt remained about Knowland's intentions. Word soon leaked that he had told a group of congressmen he planned to oppose Knight in the Republican primary.

Knight was both dismayed and incredulous. Looking ahead to 1958, he had been reasonably confident of reelection, despite rumblings of discontent from the right and Democratic gains. Now he had to deal with a challenge from within his own party that he viewed as wholly unnecessary — a manifestation of Knowland's ego.

In late August, Knight decided to fire a shot across his rival's bow. He and Knowland were sitting three seats apart at a breakfast meeting of state Republican Party officials. Departing from the text of a speech he was giving that morning, Knight said:

> I have no inside information as to [Bill Knowland's] plans, but if he should decide to run, I take this occasion to assure him and all of you that I intend to wage a very vigorous campaign, but a fair and clean-cut campaign, conducted on principles, not personalities.... If there is a contest, it is bound to be a hard contest, because Bill and I are both determined men, but I hope and believe it can be fought in good spirit.... Welcome home, Bill. I hope you have a happy homecoming and I wish you success in all your endeavors with the one exception which I am sure you will understand — your possible candidacy for the office which I now hold.[13]

Knowland laughed politely, but he was irritated by the pointed warning. He later told the media that he had "no comment on any politics the governor might have injected into the meeting."

The impending confrontation set off alarm bells in the offices of the *Los Angeles Times*. Political editor Kyle Palmer was badly shaken by Knowland's decision to quit the Senate, which he seemed to take personally. An East Coast journalist walked into his office after the announcement and found him "absolutely white, stunned, muttering: 'How could he do it, how could he do it to me?'" For years, he had written favorably of the senator, but in private, he now called him "stupid and pig-headed and a considerable political liability."[14] In the *Times*, he expressed his disapproval in less personal terms. "Few could safely argue that a Knowland-Knight contest would not represent a truly shattering experience for the Republican party in this state," Palmer wrote.

Determined to defend his hard-won turf, Knight announced in August that he would run for reelection. "It was his way of saying, regardless of what you're going to do, Bill Knowland, I'm going to run again for governor," recalled Virginia Knight. "It's my job. I have done a good job — I have *earned* the right to finish that job."[15]

Undeterred, Knowland ended any suspense by officially entering the California Republican gubernatorial primary in early October. Knight then released the fury that had been building in him for weeks. He bitterly denounced his opponent's "hydra-headed bid for the presidency" and added that, even though Knowland was a native Californian, he was still a carpetbagger.[16] The two Republican giants seemed poised to go head to head in 1958.

To what extent was Knowland's decision a negative judgment on the Knight administration? "By coming in here and running for governor," Knight said after the election, he "was halfway implying my administration hadn't been good enough."[17] Emelyn Knowland believed that her father would not have entered the race if he did not feel that the governor was doing a poor job.[18]

Knowland certainly considered Knight's middle-of-the-road orientation and pro-labor bent out of touch with the shifting mainstream of the Republican Party, but it is unlikely that he was familiar with the details of the Knight administration's policies and programs. It is more correct to say that Knight was simply in Knowland's way. He seemed to have little personal respect for the governor and little concern about his inevitable negative reaction to Knowland's primary challenge. As *Time* magazine put it, "Bill Knowland has no known pangs of conscience."[19] His daughter Estelle was struck by her father's apparent inability to understand the governor's feelings about his candidacy.

Over the next few weeks, Knight fought back as best he could. "It is not one of my characteristics to retreat," he said in November, and he promised that "this will be no pantywaist campaign."[20] His main weapon was the charge that his adversary was really running for president, but he also portrayed Knowland's well-known conservatism and hawkish foreign policy as a bad fit with the California electorate. "No man with a reputation for belligerence either in international affairs or domestic affairs, no matter how high principled he may be, is a safe man for executive office in the Federal Government," Knight warned. "And he is equally unsafe to be entrusted with the governorship of California."[21]

But Knight had to be nervous about the prospect that two of the three major newspapers in the state would oppose him. The *Oakland Tribune*, of course, was owned by the Knowland family. The *Los Angeles Times* had become distinctly unenthusiastic about Knight's administration long before Knowland announced his intentions. His determination not to offend labor leaders had led the *Times* to rage in mid–1955 that "the spectacle of a Republican governor of California kowtowing to labor union officials is a shameful one."[22] In late January 1957, it reported on a recent meeting of national-level Republicans, at which "the consensus ... seemed to be that Knowland or some other strong candidate ... would be preferable to the present governor."[23]

Political editor Kyle Palmer saw a difference between Earl Warren's ability to earn the support of the working class and Knight's outright alliance with union leaders. The governor's actions, Palmer continued, are "losing the respect of many who formerly believed in him." The columnist concluded darkly that the "road of the political opportunist is a dead-end street."[24]

The *Times* had not wanted Knight and Knowland to compete in the primary, but the senator's formal entrance into the race actually eased its dilemma. If the paper was forced to make a choice between the two rivals, it would back Bill Knowland. Though Knight had been close to the Chandlers, Knowland was more in tune with the *Times* ideology and was known affectionately in the family as "our Willie."[25] Soon the *Times* was mocking Knight for suggesting that the Republican Party would suffer if Knowland ran for governor, despite the fact that Palmer had taken that same position a few months earlier.

## *Nixon's Quandary*

In Washington, the dramatic turn of events presented Richard Nixon with both a problem and an opportunity. As the highest ranking California Republican, he could not stand idly by and watch his state party descend into self-destructive bickering. In a bitter primary struggle, Republicans would be attacking each other instead of Democrats, and the usual result of such intra-party strife was a general election defeat.

He also sensed that nervous Republicans would welcome his intervention. "More and more people are looking to RN to straighten this thing out," said California republican Bob Finch. Nixon resolved to help arbitrate the matter but in as low-key a way as possible. The "problem is to try to keep RN's name out of this thing," wrote his secretary Rose Marie Woods. "Obviously, he has to be protected."[26] This goal proved unachievable.

With Knight and Knowland at loggerheads, which way would Nixon tilt? Twice since Earl Warren bowed out of the rivalry in 1953, two of the remaining rivals had teamed up to foil the plans of the third. Knight and Knowland came together in 1954 to keep Nixon from placing an ally in a critical position on the state Republican committee. Two years later, Knowland switched sides and backed Nixon for the vice presidency at the party convention, thus ending Knight's challenge.

Nixon's actions were certain to be influenced by his assessment of the relative strength of the California candidates. "There is no question now, of course," he wrote to Jorgensen in August 1957, "but that Knowland will run and that unless some unforeseen development occurs, he will win." He also thought "it would be well for some of our other friends to get in on the ground floor of the Knowland campaign."[27]

A few weeks later, he apparently decided on a more detached posture. He ordered that "under no circumstances should [Nixon allies] make any commitments to Knowland at this time." His California forces were told via staff memo that "naturally, his [Nixon's] personal preference will be Knowland but he cannot announce and no one is going to know."[28] Still later, he urged his people to vote in the gubernatorial primary based solely on their perceptions of the abilities of the candidates and not on how it might affect Nixon's chances in 1960.[29]

Knight could not have been cheered at the prospect of Nixon's involvement. He suspected that the vice president was looking for an opportunity to punish him for his participation in the "dump Nixon" campaign of 1956. Aide Doug Barrett later claimed that Nixon's allies earlier had approached nearly every qualified California Republican in an effort to find someone to compete against Knight in the 1958 primary.[30] It was "perfectly clear" to Virginia Knight that Nixon wanted to "get rid of" her husband, because he was a threat to his ambitions.[31]

After Knowland decided to quit the Senate, however, Knight seemed to be issuing "circuitous invitations" to the vice president to support his reelection bid.[32] In March, he told the *Los Angeles Examiner* that he had "spent some time with [Nixon allies] Pat Hillings, Ray Arbuthnot, Jack Drown.... We hadn't always seen eye to eye. Arbuthnot and Drown said they'd never met my wife and I'd never met theirs. That was accomplished." He and Hillings then "reviewed some of our differences and found they weren't too fundamental."[33] Two months later, he sent Nixon a hand-written note thanking him for some positive comments he had made about Knight to a California state official. "These expressions are very helpful and I appreciate very much your good will."[34]

Nixon could ill afford to see either of his rivals strengthened in the 1958 elections. Ultimately, he decided that the biggest danger lay in a primary battle between them. Whichever man won would emerge with increased power and prestige. Besides, in such a contest, it would be hard for Nixon to avoid taking sides. If he had to support one over the other, it would undermine years of diligent work building bridges to both wings of the party. He was both a leading member of a moderate Republican administration and a favorite of the growing southern California conservative movement. He would need both moderates and conservatives in his camp if he wanted the 1960 Republican nomination. How could this train wreck be avoided?

One thing was clear: the Knowland train had already left the station. It was far too late to persuade the stubborn and determined senator to turn back. He had staked everything on this bold gambit. Early signs pointed to his being a stronger candidate for governor than Knight. Polls taken immediately after he entered the race showed him opening a big lead over the incumbent. The major media organs would certainly endorse Knowland as well, and he had the resources of his family's *Oakland Tribune* to fall back on.

In contrast, Goodie Knight's toughness and perseverance were open to question. He had quit before under similar circumstances. He flirted publicly for weeks with a challenge to Earl Warren in the 1950 Republican gubernatorial primary, only to drop the idea after concluding that he did not have sufficient financial backing or rank-and-file support. Six years before that, he was easily persuaded not to run for the Senate after having declared his candidacy.

Maybe he could be sold on the idea of running for Knowland's vacant Senate job, Nixon thought, instead of for reelection as governor. In that case, Republicans could close ranks behind both men, and a disastrous party split would be avoided. Knight often seemed more interested in the trappings of high office than in the nitty-gritty of public policy anyhow, so perhaps it did not matter to him which of the two jobs he held. The Knights were a social — even glamorous — couple and might thrive on the excitement of life in the nation's capital. Still, Nixon suspected that Knight would not easily walk away from a job to which he had aspired most of his life. Somehow he had to be convinced that, as in 1950, he stood little chance of winning.

In putting forward a plan that could smooth Knowland's path to the governorship, Nixon knew he was taking a risk. A convincing Knowland victory could propel him to the front ranks of serious presidential candidates in 1960. But Nixon thought this outcome was unlikely. He had worked side by side with Knowland for years, knew his weaknesses, and suspected that the senator overestimated his political appeal. By taking on Goodie Knight, Knowland would make many enemies. As David Halberstam later wrote, Nixon probably believed that Knowland would be "so awkward and ham-handed he would no doubt alienate diverse elements in the state and become a very vulnerable figure."[35]

Nixon also thought that Knowland was positioning himself too far outside of the Republican mainstream. The senator's hard-line foreign policy had already been a source of irritation to the administration, and he was preparing to run for governor on an anti-union, right-to-work platform that Nixon viewed as politically unwise. Unlike Knowland, the vice president did not regard the conservative movement as the wave of the future. With Republicans already in a minority in California, Knowland had no chance of a decisive victory if he alienated Knight's moderate supporters.

A successful Knight campaign for the Senate worried Nixon even less. It was unlikely that Knight would be a thorn in Nixon's side as a junior senator with no seniority and little influence in California politics, especially compared to the damage he could do as a reelected governor.

## *Goodie Under Pressure*

Nixon's hope that Knight would react positively to the idea of running for the Senate was a forlorn one. "I have no other interests, no other work" than being governor, Knight had often told the press. And he had recently made a public promise not to give up without a fight. Running for the Senate was "ridiculous," Virginia Knight said dismissively years later. "The Knowlands, settled in Washington, moving to Sacramento. The Knights, settled in Sacramento, moving to Washington. I repeat — ridiculous."[36]

But Nixon had powerful help in his effort to get Knight to change his mind — the Chandlers and Kyle Palmer. Knight began to receive such persistent calls from Norman Chandler and his wife, Buffy, that they almost seemed orchestrated. They urged him to quit the race for governor and sweetened the pot by promising him the support of the *Times* if he would run for the Senate. The implied warning, Knight recognized, was that if he did not switch, the *Times* would oppose him. According to Halberstam, Palmer even threatened to reveal a bad appointment Knight had made because of his wife's involvement—"he hated to print it, but he had all the facts."[37] It must have been hard to hear these messages, because they came from people he thought were his friends.

The weapons at the *Times*' disposal were not limited to informal pressure and the withholding of an endorsement. According to a study of the *Times*' role in California politics, Kyle Palmer finally "used his ultimate power." He warned Knight that if he did not end his reelection campaign, his sources of financial backing would dry up. If he were to shift to the Senate campaign, money would again become available.[38] The threat hardly seemed credible, but Knight made his own calls to southern California money men, and they confirmed what Palmer had told him.

The ability to get wealthy people to stop contributing to a sitting governor's campaign vividly illustrated the outsized influence Palmer and the

Chandlers wielded during the 1950s. Some of Nixon's correspondence with the state Republican finance chairman during this period indicates that he supported the *Times*' efforts to deny funding to Knight.[39] Of all the obstacles to his reelection, Knight considered a lack of financing to be the most serious. "I never made a political race in my life without having the money in the bank before I started," he told his administrative aide, "and I'm not about to do it now."[40]

The first few days of November 1957 were especially stressful for Knight, as he received conflicting counsel from all sides. Polls showing Knowland with a strong early lead depressed him. Friends and aides, angry at the bullying tactics of the *Times*, reminded him that he still had the advantages of incumbency and urged him not to give up. "I think the people of this state will rise as one man if you have the courage to stand up and defy them [the *Times*] and say: 'I am the titular head of this party. I am the governor. I am seeking reelection, and I demand to have that prerogative honored,'" one Republican legislator told him.[41]

Supporters dismissed his concerns about funding. Some believed that many people would be willing to bankroll him—people who were beyond the reach of the mighty *Times*. Some pointed out that he could use the expense-free facilities of his office. Friends of the Knights approached the couple during this period and pledged a few dollars to the cause.

Clem Whitaker and his partner, Leone Baxter, believed Knight could adopt the role of underdog and campaign against the kind of "bossism" that had tried to drive him out of the race. "We told him we were convinced he could win it. He was not so convinced." According to journalist Stewart Alsop, Whitaker and Baxter would have him "primed for battle, but then Buffy of the *Times* would call and his resolution would crumble."[42] "We worked as strenuously as we knew how to keep Goodwin in the race," Whitaker recalled years later.[43]

Knight also had Richard Nixon to deal with. The vice president, possibly in league with the Chandlers, sent word to Knight in Sacramento, promising White House support if he would only switch to the Senate race. Then Nixon dispatched an intermediary to the governor's mansion in Sacramento—Clint Mosher, the political columnist of the *San Francisco Examiner*—who was a good friend of both men.

Virginia Knight remembered the Mosher visit well.

> I can still see Clint in his trench coat…. The three of us sat in the living room, where many other important decisions had [been made] throughout the mansion's history. Clint said: "Governor, there's no way. If you stay in the race for governor, Dick Nixon will campaign in every county against you." After he left, we talked for a long time. For weeks he debated in his heart: What was the

best thing for him to do? Those were the long nights he paced the floor of the governor's mansion. It was such an unhappy time for us."[44]

Along with the mental anguish involved in deciding how to meet Knowland's challenge, Knight had recently caught the flu and was suffering from one of his periodic bouts with ulcers. His appointments secretary recalled that he did not look or feel good during this period. She remembered that he and a staffer who also had ulcers were continually drinking a "horrible" homemade concoction, made from cabbage and sauerkraut. She believed that Knight's various ailments reduced his will to fight.[45] Doug Barrett remembered that his boss "tend[ed] to physically feel tremendous emotional stress" when under pressure.[46]

In early November, the governor suddenly dropped out of sight. It was soon learned that he, his wife, a few close aides, and Clem Whitaker and Leone Baxter had slipped away to a friend's estate in Phoenix, where he was refusing to take phone calls. According to Virginia, Knight was leaning toward giving up the race before leaving Sacramento and was going to Arizona to recover from the flu. But things were "still nebulous in his mind and heart."[47]

In Arizona, he apparently continued to swing back and forth. Halberstam described a sequence of events in which one minute he would tell Whitaker and Baxter: "I will run, the hell with them." Then Palmer would call with threats and pressure and "he would lie down on the couch in a fetal position, a man broken." Then by dinner his confidence would return. Then Buffy Chandler would call and tell him how wonderful it was to live in Washington, D.C., and he would fold again.[48] Referring to Mrs. Chandler, Pat Brown later expressed the view that getting Knight out of the race was "the work of one woman."[49]

## *Capitulation*

After Arizona, Knight made his way to Washington and a meeting with Eisenhower and Nixon — a last opportunity to plead his case. The governor met first with Ike, but that turned out to be a mere formality, as he refused to be drawn into the affair. "I leave these California matters in Dick Nixon's hands," he told Knight and the press.[50]

Then Knight had a brief audience with Nixon. "We were still hoping against hope that something might happen to change it all around," Virginia Knight recalled. But, as Knight told the press later, the vice president "urged me to take a course of action which would be in the best interest of the party."[51] In other words, as a Knight aide phrased it, Nixon "turned thumbs down on him."⁵² Resigned now to the inevitable, Knight announced on the last day of October that he would run for the Senate after all. He later argued that he "had no other choice. I was like a man in the middle of the ocean, standing on the deck of a burning ship."⁵³

Knight's reversal and the apparent involvement of the White House in his decision caused a furor around the state. Letters to newspapers all over California expressed voter incredulity and outrage. A political cartoonist depicted Nixon as a puppeteer with Knowland and Knight dancing on strings below him. Former President Truman, always an outspoken critic of Nixon, called for an investigation of a possible conspiracy to force Knight out. "There is a bug under the chips somewhere," he said.

The episode provided California's Democrats with months of campaign material. The *San Francisco Chronicle* echoed many other newspapers in calling the Knight-Knowland switch "the solution Nixon has been working behind the scenes to obtain."⁵⁴ Democrats charged that a deal had been made and that political bosses had deprived the voters of their right to choose. Nixon was running Knowland and Knight "in tandem," quipped Democratic Senate candidate Claire Engle.⁵⁵ The "big switch," as it was promptly named, so alienated voters that Engle and Democratic gubernatorial candidate Pat Brown led in polls from that day forward.

Some newspapers reported that Nixon, in exchange for his backing of Knowland for governor, had extracted a promise from the senator not to run in any presidential primaries outside of California in 1960. Drew Pearson clearly believed this story. In a column, he ribbed the "honest but pachydermic" Knowland for allowing Nixon to steal a march on the 1960 presidential campaign and pull off the "most brilliant coup of this generation."⁵⁶ Knowland denied that he had made any such promise.

It was a measure of Knowland's self-confidence that he was not at all pleased by Knight's withdrawal — even though it guaranteed him a primary victory. According to his confidant Paul Manolis and others, he was spoiling for a showdown with Knight, believing that it would resolve once and for all the question of what the California Republican Party stood for. If he won in a fair fight, it would unify the party behind him. Helen Knowland felt that Knight had "pulled the rug from under Billy" by withdrawing and that unfounded charges of a deal damaged her husband's reputation for integrity.⁵⁷ Knowland also blamed Nixon for upsetting his plans. "I think probably the vice president played a part in this," he later told an interviewer."⁵⁸

"Who forced the switch? Who talked Goodie into this?" asked Manolis rhetorically. "I have no doubt in my mind. It was the Nixon crowd and the *Los Angeles Times*, pointing out to Goodie the unmistakable signs of defeat that lie ahead for him. This weak man caved in and refused to face the fire

Nixon (left) jokes with Knight and his wife, Virginia, at a conference in San Francisco in 1957. Nixon never publicly acknowledged Knight's hostility and political opposition. A few weeks later he pressured Knight not to run for reelection as governor, leaving him "like a man in the middle of the ocean, standing on the deck of a burning ship" (Nat Farbman/Time Life Pictures/Getty Images).

of battle."[59] Clem Whitaker believed Knight decided that, ultimately, he could not fight the *Times*. "His concern was that the *Times* would kill him, they would destroy him as a political figure."[60]

Knight's lack of resolution disappointed his supporters. Labor advisor Harry Finks believed he would have won "hands down" and that he listened to the wrong people. "I thought it was the weakest thing I had ever seen a man do," said Finks.[61] Paul Mason, a legislative aide, and many other friends also believed he could have won, despite the opposition of major newspapers and a lack of money. Mason argued that he could have switched parties and won as a Democrat. Knight was a good administrator and a good human being, Clem Whitaker noted, but he added: "In the crunch, I wish that he had been stronger."[62] Somewhat less charitably, conservative Republican Vernon Cristina called Knight "the most gutless candidate we ever had."[63]

When Knight confided to his friend Milton Polland that a lack of money was the main issue, Polland erupted: "Goodwin, I don't care if you haven't got a nickel, we'll go out elsewhere for it. You've got to stay in this race and you've got to beat Knowland in the primaries.... At least you'll be fighting for a cause." He felt Knight should be making a case against the "shenanigans of the Republican party and the architect of the whole thing — being Richard Nixon."[64]

Virginia Knight rejected these criticisms of her husband. "When everything is pulled away from you and your money's pulled away from you, that doesn't make you weak as far as your character is concerned — or your ability," she insisted. "He just became weak monetarily."[65] The Knights concluded that registering as a Democrat, running as an independent, or hoping that money would somehow materialize were all impractical options.

## A Long and Bitter Fall

Though his switch to the Senate race was supposed to eliminate intraparty conflict, Knight immediately found himself embroiled in a public spat with San Francisco's Republican mayor, George Christopher, who had announced for the Senate himself. Christopher had not wanted to run against Knight and had asked the governor earlier if he was going to be a candidate. Assured several times that he was not, Christopher then entered the race, only to learn that Knight had reversed himself. Believing it was too late to make a dignified exit, Christopher was livid, and he accused the governor of breaking his "sacred word." The episode made for a dispiriting beginning to the Knight campaign.

The campaign itself was marked by poor preparation and a lack of enthusiasm. "He didn't have the heart for the Senate race," Virginia Knight admitted, but "he didn't want to leave the profession he dearly loved."[66] His vague answers to questions posed by an interviewer early in 1958 showed that he knew little about Knowland's Senate record or the views of his Democratic opponent. When a top aide urged him to stay on the sidelines that year and wait for a more promising opportunity, he responded that he wanted to prove that he could get more votes for his candidacy than Knowland. He knew, he said, that he was not going to be elected to anything.[67]

Whitaker and Baxter also advised Knight not to run for the Senate. "We had the feeling that Goodwin didn't want to be a US senator, that he would hurt himself by making the run," said Clem Whitaker years later. "We just did not believe that it was a good campaign for him.... It was unlikely that he was going to prevail."[68] The couple stuck with him through the primaries, but then they parted company.

Knight's bitterness knew no bounds. Knowland naively hoped that the two men could mount a unified campaign, and he publicly endorsed Knight for the Senate, but Knight did not return the favor. As George Christopher observed, the two men "weren't even talking to each other. They were this far apart."⁶⁹ Pat Brown, the Democratic candidate for governor, said incredulously: "I'd see Mrs. Knight at meetings and she'd say, 'I'm going to vote for you.'"⁷⁰

In June 1958, during an unguarded moment at a political event, Knight abandoned all pretense and excoriated his Republican rival:

> Senator Bill Knowland is an ambitious man. He wants to be President. In order to beat out Dick Nixon for the nomination in 1960 he decided to come back here and run for governor. If he could beat out a popular governor and then lick the most popular man the Democrats could put up, he figured he'd be almost invincible as a candidate for the presidential nomination.⁷¹

While Knight stewed, Knowland remained confident. He reminded himself that he had the support of the major state newspapers, and his allies, the Chandlers, had made sure he had access to sufficient funds. Perhaps most important, he viewed himself as a proven vote-getter and national leader. He had been the subject of flattering portraits in both *Time* and *Newsweek*. Knowland did not even consider it necessary to spend more than two weeks in California prior to the June 1958 primary.

The *Los Angeles Times* made up for his absence by giving positive coverage to his every move and statement. According to Whitaker, "Kyle [Palmer] figured that if he could elect Knowland, then the governor would be more responsive to him." In a typical commentary, the paper called Knowland "a hard but always fair and honorable fighter" and predicted that "our attorney general [Pat Brown] will learn some of these facts himself as the campaign progresses." The *Times* also warned that Brown, as governor, would inevitably become a tool of the labor bosses. An aide to Clair Engle, the Democratic candidate for the Senate, likened the *Times'* enthusiasm for Knowland to official campaign propaganda. "It's like sending out a leaflet every day," he said.⁷²

Nixon lieutenant Frank Jorgensen was also impressed with the Knowland campaign's early efforts. "The immediate reaction to the Knight shift," he wrote Nixon in November, "has been to build Knowland's stature in the state as a king-maker and the bully boy of the party." Jorgensen warned the vice president that he "may take the bit in his teeth and be a very hard individual to do business with, particularly if he is elected governor, as far as our hopes for 1960 are concerned."⁷³

Even before Knowland entered the race for governor, however, there were signs of trouble. In contrast to Jorgensen's upbeat assessment, Nixon received several gloomy reports from California on Knowland's progress and prospects. The senator's fact-finding trip to the state in the fall of 1957 had apparently stirred up little enthusiasm among the voters. "Audiences listened politely to a dull speech day after day, and applauded very politely at the end," reported journalist Clint Mosher in a phone call to the vice president. "[But] at no stage of the game did anyone jump and yell 'Please run, Bill.'"[74]

Knowland's most fateful decision was to make the right-to-work issue central to his campaign. In the late 1950s, the growing power of labor was worrying conservatives. In heavily unionized cities like San Francisco, new employees were often required to join unions — this was called the closed shop. But in southern California, open-shop sentiment was prevalent. The *Los Angeles Times*, in particular, was rabidly anti-union. The issue was hard to avoid in any case, because a right-to-work initiative was on the California ballot that fall. Knowland tried to keep his campaign separate from that of the initiative's supporters, but he stated his belief that "no person should have to pay tribute [to a union] before he can have a job."[75]

Many Republicans were nervous about this strategy, which seemed certain to unite the labor movement behind Democratic candidate Pat Brown. It did not help that neither of the leaders of the national Republican Party — Eisenhower and Nixon — had endorsed right-to-work. Goodwin Knight, who considered himself a friend of labor, lost no time in attacking Knowland's stand. "No politician can successfully turn the clock back in labor-management relations any more than he can reverse the trend of our rapidly expanding economy," he told an audience.[76]

Knight knew that California's demographics had changed in the years since Knowland's reelection to the Senate. The largest cities were becoming industrial centers, and over a million workers belonged to California unions. These unions now proved capable of mobilizing their resources. Whenever Knowland expressed support for the right to work, money from labor poured into Brown's camp. Knowland's belief in a deep reservoir of anti-union sentiment showed that it was he, rather than Knight, who was out of touch with the changing dynamics of his home state.

Despite his optimism, Knowland's gubernatorial campaign was a disaster from beginning to end. In March 1958, he was still trailing Brown in the polls, and Jorgensen reversed his earlier view that Knowland was a sure winner. Both Republican candidates, he said, were spending "too blessed much time tearing down [each] other" rather than going after Democrats. He saw a defeatist attitude in the party and considerable worry about the economy, both of which were translating into Democratic inroads.

If Californians had not noticed or been concerned with Knowland's awkwardness and lack of rapport with voters in 1952, his "mixture of haste and bluster"[77] at rallies made him few converts in 1958. "He was so pompous in his style," recalled a journalist, "that it would seem demeaning for him to make this approach toward little country newspaper people and to go into hick towns."[78] To the despair of his aides, he wore his formal suit and tie even to barbecues and farmer's markets. Historian Gladwin Hill quipped that Knowland lost two thousand votes a day by campaigning.[79]

Instead of showing an interest in critical state issues, such as water resources and growth management, Knowland often concluded his speeches with references to Hungarian freedom fighters. When he demanded that Pat Brown state his position on Red China, the Democratic candidate recommended that the senator "do his homework so that he does not have to try to divert public attention elsewhere."[80] In this and other ways, Knowland seemed "off kilter," as though campaigning for a job he had not thought much about.

Pat Brown, California's long-time attorney general and the only Democrat among major state office holders, had little respect for Knowland as a serious candidate for governor. "I knew the state backwards and forwards," Brown said. "Knowland had been back in Washington for twenty years. He didn't know the problems of the state; he was the senator from Formosa. He was more interested in protecting Formosa than he was in helping California."[81] Clem Whitaker agreed with Brown. Knowland was a believable senator who might have been a believable candidate for president. But, in Whitaker's view, he was not a believable candidate for governor of California.[82]

In the June primaries, Brown and Knowland won their respective party primaries, but Brown received over a half million more votes than his adversary. He was understandably buoyed by these results, which he saw as a defeat for all three of the California rivals. He said:

> Governor Knight withdrew. That was one little Indian down. Now I have defeated Knowland. The second little Indian was down. As for Vice President Nixon, we will wait to see what happens to the third little Indian.[83]

## *Lukewarm Support from Washington*

Nixon's prestige may have been tarnished by Knowland's poor showing in the primary, but he was not prepared to do much actual campaigning for him. "Nixon's participation in Dad's campaign was nil, which says a great deal," Estelle Knowland recalled bitterly.[84] The vice president regarded Knowland's primary campaign issue as a serious tactical error and did not wish to be identified as anti-labor himself. When asked whether he supported the right to work, he refused to say. "Obviously, I am not going to take a position," Nixon later told a confidant. "If I say I am against it, they will say I am against Knowland."[85]

## 10— The Big Switch of 1958 and the End of the Rivalry

The vice president made fitful, if trivial, attempts to aid the Knight campaign. He tried, with little success, to persuade Knight to endorse Knowland, believing that doing so would help both candidates. He wrote Knight to recommend that he use his status as a veteran as a selling point against opponent Clair Engle, who had no military experience.[86] Knight seemed appreciative. He wrote Nixon in February 1958 that he was looking forward to seeing him in southern California during an upcoming appearance, and he called the vice president's office while passing through Washington in March. He told a Nixon aide that he had nothing important to raise but just wanted to say hello and pass along his warm regards.[87]

Nixon did take two trips to California, where he made several public appearances with both Republicans. Knowland showed his gratitude by declaring him the "leading contender and the only major candidate" for the Republican presidential nomination in 1960. But Nixon sensed it was a futile effort. "In the last few weeks of the campaign," he recalled in his memoirs, "I labored under a feeling of total hopelessness."[88]

President Eisenhower sent a letter supporting Knowland's candidacy to California Republican fund-raisers in August, but even his endorsement could not hide his serious misgivings:

> I know that he has been called stubborn, a bit of a lone wolf, and likely to follow his own conclusions and decisions, disregarding the opinions and convictions of able people who would like to be his friends. In other words, he is considered by some to be a bit of a bull in a china shop. But ... Bill Knowland is impeccably honest, courageous, studious and serious.... Regardless of any blunders that he may or may not have made, these attributes are not to be lightly dismissed.[89]

Ike visited the state as well, meeting with the Republican candidates and calling for an end to "family bickering," but his trip only underlined the tension. As Totten J. Anderson reported, Knowland and Knight "acted as characters in a comic opera, jockeying for position in reception lines, showing resentment when one received a slightly larger audience with the President than the other, and generally accentuating their differences in public exhibitions."[90]

Knowland continued to think that a public declaration of party unity might turn things around, so he pressed the reluctant Knight for a meeting and finally succeeded in arranging one in June. The two rivals met for a little more than an hour, after which Knight's press secretary issued a one-sentence summary of their talks and concluded by saying that "they have nothing further to say regarding their meeting at this time." If Knowland expected a joint resolution to cooperate, he went away disappointed.

Because Knowland had decided to spend much of the campaign at his desk in Washington, his wife, Helen, and their daughters often made public appearances in California on his behalf. Helen's prominence led to errors caused by excessive zeal. In mid–September, she mailed to hundreds of state Republicans a virulent tract attacking United Auto Workers president Walter Reuther, written by a man widely regarded as a fascist and anti–Semite. Bad publicity from the incident did irreparable damage. Soon afterwards, the Hearst newspapers endorsed Pat Brown.

In October, Helen Knowland referred to Knight in a letter as a man with a "macaroni spine," which the press and public viewed as a low blow. Knowland defended his wife's "great assistance," but, according to Paul Manolis, he shouted, "You've blown the election already!" at her in front of several campaign workers.[91]

As Knowland's campaign began to disintegrate — "shedding pieces of itself like a cheap boat in a storm," in the words of his biographers — observers wondered not if he would win but how badly he would lose. In October, with his own candidacy in tatters, Knight decided to kick his rival while he was down. He took his earlier non-endorsement one step further, announcing flatly that he could not support Knowland for governor because of his right-to-work views.

The fratricidal struggle eroded the ideological solidarity of California's leading newspapers. While the *Times* struggled to keep Knowland's candidacy alive, the *San Francisco Chronicle* notified its readers that it could no longer unqualifiedly urge Knowland's election and suggested that its readers vote for the candidate of their choice. The newspaper did endorse Knight, however.

In the final days of the campaign, even the *Times* damaged the Republican cause by highlighting rather than downplaying the Knight-Knowland feud, calling it a "scandal and an invitation to disaster."[92] Its endorsement of Knight was tepid — he is a "calculable quantity," it wrote. "The people who vote for him know pretty well what they will get from him." But it also published a series of editorials, under the heading "It's Got to be Knowland," which called the senator "the only man with the nerves and staying power to prevent the catastrophe."[93]

The two men limped to the finish line. The Democrats, aided by organized labor's drive to defeat the right-to-work initiative, had mounted a massive voter registration drive, and with interest in the elections high, they now had 1.1 million more enfranchised Californians than the Republicans. Had Knowland not made his fateful decision to abandon the Senate, he might have cruised to reelection, but instead he lost the governorship to Brown by over a million votes. Without Knowland's interference, Knight might have been returned to the office he loved, but instead he lost the Senate race to Engle by 700,000. The disaster was complete.

Anyone would be forgiven for feeling bitter after such a loss, but Knowland proved to be a graceful loser. A day after the election, a Sacramento correspondent saw him at the airport welcoming his aide Paul Manolis. Pat Brown happened to be on the same plane. A member of the press corps observed that Knowland "just clawed his way over to get to Pat Brown, and shook his hand, and embraced him."[94] Their bond as politicians trumped the reality that one was the winner and the other the loser.

Another winner was Richard Nixon. His two main competitors in California had been eliminated. Norman Chandler of the *Times* was asked what he made of the election debacle. He replied that it was not so bad, since the great hope for the Republican Party was really Nixon.[95] Robert Kenny, the veteran Democratic politician, offered his own pithy summary of the 1958 campaign: "Nixon, Knight and Knowland played a game of musical chairs. And when the music finally stopped, it appeared that Nixon was occupying all three chairs."[96]

Nixon (second from left), with wife Pat, waits to give a campaign speech on behalf of Knight (left) and Knowland (right) in October 1958, but all three men appear discouraged by their prospects. "I labored under a feeling of total hopelessness," Nixon later recalled (Ralph Crane/Time Life Pictures/Getty Images).

## Sifting Through the Wreckage

The 1958 elections effectively ended the rivalry of the California Republicans. The political careers of Knight and Knowland, which only a year earlier were full of promise, now seemed to be over. They were relatively young men in their prime, who had recently believed that their greatest successes were ahead of them. But in November 1958 they found themselves out of office and on the sidelines, with no immediate prospect of recovery. Knowland, at least, could rejoin his family and help run the *Oakland Tribune*—and he did. Knight declared that his defeat was "no reason why I should get out of politics,"[97] but Norman Chandler disagreed. "He's through," Chandler said — and he was.[98]

After the election, a chastened Kyle Palmer offered his views on how the personalities of the two men had undermined their chances. Knight, he wrote, "is highly emotional and apt to indulge in impulsive utterance," while Knowland "has shown no willingness to compromise when a modicum of adjustment in position or point of view might accomplish results." Palmer dismissed them both as future leaders of the party and suggested that Republicans "forget old quarrels and look to new inspirations."[99]

It was now clear that the flaws of Knight and Knowland as candidates and public officials had long been disguised by superior Republican organization and by the party's stranglehold on the state media. Knowland, in particular, had proved his complete unsuitability as a political leader. He had no ability to compromise or consider different points of view, his political judgment was faulty, his foreign policy views were bellicose and often reckless, and he made little effort to understand the problems of ordinary voters. He had few of the necessary tools for high office in a democracy.

Most Californians had considered Knight a decent governor, and he might have continued to be one. But he was not a strong or decisive leader, and he allowed his personal feelings to affect his political judgment. He was replaced by a man who, ideology aside, was far more interested in the policy issues a governor must face and better prepared to find solutions to the state's problems.

# *Epilogue*

Though the direct competition of the California rivals for power and influence came to an end in 1958, it was not the end of their relationship. They continued to watch each other carefully as the years went by, and Warren and Knight nursed their resentment of Nixon well into old age,

## *Knight: Not Ready to Give Up*

During November 1958, Goodwin Knight went from being one of the country's most promising political figures to sifting through job offers from banks and insurance companies at his home in Los Angeles. He soon took a position as president of Cosmopolitan Underwriters and helped organize a southern California bank, on whose board of directors he served for the rest of his life. Playing to his strength, he also worked as a news commentator and took part in a television show called *Judge for Yourself*, which explained complex legal issues to the viewers.

A few months later, he was still bitter about Bill Knowland. "It's a basic rule of politics that you always support your party's administrations," he told the media in April 1959. "Neither Mr. Knowland nor Mr. Nixon gave my administration the backing it deserved."[1]

Whether out of genuine ambivalence or a calculated strategy, Knight seemed to be trying to maintain a cordial relationship with Nixon both during and after the disastrous 1958 campaign. Even as he sensed that his bid for the Senate was lost, the governor took the time to send a wire to the vice president following his trip to South America, where he and Pat had been threatened by a hostile mob. Events, he said, have "earned you even greater respect from your fellow countrymen for the courageous, proud and distinguished way in which you represented and defended the nation."[2] After Knight's defeat, Nixon wrote to thank him for the "gallant fight you made."[3]

When Nixon ran for president against John Kennedy in 1960, Knight publicly endorsed the Republican ticket and even served as a member of Nixon's delegation to the 1960 convention. Nixon wrote to Knight in April 1960 thanking him for the "friendship and support you have shown me over the past years ... particularly ... your desire to be counted in my corner [at the Republican convention] in Chicago.[4] After his loss to Kennedy, Knight commiserated with him. "I hope you will complete all of your duties in Washington in every proper way," he wrote graciously, "and then we shall be glad to welcome you back to southern California."[5]

These amicable exchanges showed how the sharp edges of the rivalry were often blurred and softened by a shared identity as Californians and Republicans. But Knight may have had another reason to support Nixon in 1960 and to stay on good terms with him. He had not given up the possibility of making another run for public office in his home state, and a repudiation of the Republican standard bearer would have been politically short-sighted. In other words, his endorsement of Nixon was not an effort at personal reconciliation.

Knight's cheerleading role in the 1960 campaign revived his competitive spirit and made him consider plans to regain the office he had once held. Typically, he was of two minds. "What do I need with it? Why do I need the aggravation?" he said on one occasion. "I've already had my picture painted."[6] As the 1962 election approached, however, he sounded prepared to run and confident of success. "You might say I temporarily mislaid my key to the governor's office," he told *Newsweek* magazine with a smile.[7]

Knight's appetite for battle was whetted by the strong possibility that Nixon would begin a political comeback by entering the California gubernatorial primary. Here was an opportunity not only to return to public life but also to settle a score. Early in 1961, a series of letters to his confidant Paul Mason showed him following Nixon's decision-making process with great interest. "Of course, if he [runs for governor and] loses, he is through," Knight wrote in February.[8] Two months later, Knight edged closer to throwing his hat in the ring. "If both Nixon and I ran in the primary, he would have much to lose — me — nothing!" he wrote Mason.[9] In September, he decided to take the plunge. Two weeks later, Nixon too entered the race.

That fall, the big political story in California was a report that Nixon had attempted to buy Knight's withdrawal from the primary. In a scenario reminiscent of Clint Mosher's visit to Knight at Nixon's behest in 1957, Knight claimed that Nixon had sent an emissary with the message that, if Nixon ran unopposed by Knight and won, he was prepared to offer the former governor any state government position he wanted. A Knight ally speculated that Nixon purposely used the words "prepared to offer" so that he could not be accused of actually making an offer. Both Nixon and the alleged emissary denied making any approach to Knight.

The episode seemed to provide Knight with potent ammunition against Nixon in the Republican primary, and he prepared to mount an aggressive campaign. In November 1961, he challenged Nixon to a debate on state government issues. "He was a star debater at Whittier College and last year debated before eighty million people," Knight told an interviewer, "so he ought not to be afraid of me."[10]

But suddenly the former governor's health gave way. He had not been feeling well for some time, and he learned in November that he had contracted infectious hepatitis. It was apparent to his doctors that he could not continue, and he was obliged to end his candidacy in January 1962. Nixon wrote that it was "not easy for such an active and tireless campaigner as you are to have to abide by the edict of your doctor, and I sympathize fully with the feeling of disappointment I know is yours."[11]

Sidelined once again, Knight watched Nixon's campaign against Pat Brown, who was seeking reelection. "I think Brown will win ... and Nixon will be relegated to the political oblivion he has always merited," he confided to Mason in early November 1962. "It couldn't happen to a nicer guy!"[12] As he predicted, Nixon did lose, and Knight was one of many Americans who believed his political career was over. "Nixon was so greedy for power and his little gang so hungry they risked everything," he wrote to Mason.[13]

Knight recovered his health and returned to his business pursuits, but his remaining years were not happy ones. "He's not getting along too well," Virginia wrote to a friend, "but he's getting by in a way."[14] He kept one eye on the world of politics and briefly considered running again for governor in 1966, but by then the era of successful moderate Republicans had passed and the Ronald Reagan era had dawned. One of his daughters committed suicide in 1970; after that, according to his good friend Milton Polland, he lost much of his spirit. He died in May of that year.

Unfortunately for his mental state, he survived to see his nemesis Nixon elected president but not long enough to witness his disgrace and resignation. Through the illnesses and disappointments of his later years, according to Polland, "one thing he kept uppermost in his mind ... was the distrust and dislike that he had for Richard Nixon — that was prevalent until the last day of his life."[15]

## *Knowland: Descent into Darkness*

Bill Knowland's 1958 defeat — his first real failure in politics — had severely shaken his self-confidence. Emelyn Knowland later said it left an emotional scar on her father that never healed.[16] Not only had he let his father down but had ignored his sound advice not to quit the Senate. After concluding his term of office and moving his belongings out of Washington, he exercised his only real option. He returned to the family business, the *Oakland Tribune*, and his father named him assistant publisher.

Poor relations with family members continued to plague him in the years that followed. His brother Russ was general manager of the newspaper, but the two men rarely spoke. Russ began drinking heavily and died of a heart attack in 1961. Bill's son Joe also worked at the *Tribune* and was hoping to assume more responsibility, but Knowland declined to promote Joe and instead appointed Paul Manolis, the son he always wished he had had, to the post of executive editor.

Along with handling administrative duties, Knowland wrote the *Tribune*'s editorials and personally covered the party conventions of 1960. He was credited by many with convincing his old friend and political adversary, Lyndon Johnson, to accept the vice presidential nomination if John Kennedy offered it to him. Like Goodwin Knight, he remained publicly loyal to national Republican candidates and supported Nixon against Kennedy in 1960 and against Pat Brown in 1962.

But no one would mistake Knowland for a friend of Nixon. The former vice president made an obligatory visit to the *Tribune* during his campaign for governor in 1962. Knowland kept him waiting for twenty minutes in the lobby. When Nixon asked permission to walk around and shake hands with the employees in his offices, Knowland asked a receptionist to act as escort and then left him to fend for himself. The *Tribune* did its Republican duty and endorsed Nixon, but after the election Knowland was observed walking around the building with a broad smile on his face.[17]

Nixon's two defeats prompted speculation in 1963 that Knowland might attempt a comeback by running again for the Senate. Goodwin Knight, in a letter to his friend Mason, observed that he was "running around the state making noises like a candidate,"[18] but Knowland decided to channel his energies into Barry Goldwater's campaign for president in 1964. Following Goldwater's nomination by a badly divided Republican Party, Knowland hit the road in support of the candidate and made speeches in sixteen states. It would prove to be his last active national political effort, though he continued to supply advice to Republican candidates into the 1970s and remained involved in civic activities in Oakland.

The last few years of his life were defined by failed relationships and gambling problems. He had an affair in 1964 with a woman who went public with his indiscretion, to the embarrassment of his family. In 1966, he endured the death at age 92 of his father and mentor, and then succeeded him as publisher of the *Tribune*.

While gambling in Las Vegas in 1974, he met Ann Dickson, a divorced actress in television commercials. She was volatile, extravagant and unpredictable, but Knowland was infatuated and soon found himself asking Helen for a divorce, which she reluctantly granted. Over time, the new marriage became ever more tempestuous, while gambling debts became a constant drain on Knowland's funds. His unsuccessful efforts to secure another divorce in 1972 and 1973 consumed time, money and emotional energy. He considered selling the *Tribune* to raise money to pay debts.

In early 1974 Knowland's associates thought he appeared fatigued, stressed and disengaged, and they urged him to get medical attention. On February 21, Governor Ronald Reagan appeared at a gala luncheon at the *Tribune* building to help Knowland and his staff celebrate the paper's 100th anniversary. Throughout the luncheon, Knowland's eyes were glazed and he appeared oblivious to his surroundings.

Two days later, he drove alone to a family compound on the Russian River north of the Bay Area and shot himself. On February 25, under a headline that read "There Were Giants in Congress," the newspaper his family had turned into a major force in the state reported his death at the age of 65.

## *Warren: Nursing His Grudge*

Earl Warren spent eleven more years as chief justice of the United States after 1958. The distance from California, his busy life, and perhaps his embarrassment at the personal and professional decline of Bill Knowland minimized any contact with his old friend. He apparently dropped by the *Oakland Tribune* building on occasion to chat, but the two men did not have an active relationship.

Warren continued to speak dismissively of his former lieutenant governor, Goodwin Knight, whose antics in the 1940s had convinced him that he was a lightweight and not a serious prospect for national office. In order to get a reaction from Warren, aide Merrell Small in later years articulated his own negative view of Knight. "No," agreed the governor, "he didn't know much."[19]

Richard Nixon expressed disapproval of the Warren court's judicial activism during the 1950s, which did not help his relationship with the former governor. He seemed to believe, as he wrote in his memoirs, that the justices had "too often us[ed] their interpretation of the law to remake American society according to their own social, political and ideological precepts,"[20] but he may have also been responding to a deluge of critical mail he received from Republicans while he was vice president about the court's liberal direction.

In the late 1950s, two well reported episodes seemed to reconfirm Warren's lasting bitterness toward Nixon. In the first, Warren made it known that he would not accept an invitation to a convention of the American Bar Association in London in 1957 after he heard that Nixon had also been invited. He contended that Nixon's presence would give the event a political rather than legal thrust and denied in his memoirs that personal animosity had anything to do with his attitude. When Nixon then decided not to attend, Warren was reported to have told a friend: "Was he sore!"[21]

Two years later, Warren ran into Nixon biographer Earl Mazo at a social event. The *Minneapolis Tribune* reported that he confronted Mazo about his "dishonest account" of Warren's view of Nixon's tactics in the election of 1950 and said: "I don't like it when you use me, when you use this book to step on my head — to go over my body to promote Nixon."[22] He denied the claims of onlookers that he called Mazo a "damned liar," saying that he had been "taught better manners than that."[23]

Of Nixon's California rivals, only Warren remained in the national spotlight through the 1960s and into Nixon's presidential administration. While chief justice, he periodically made known his strong feelings about the man he often called "Tricky." Nixon was a "bad man," he reminded aide Merrell Small, and he mentioned to a biographer that he voted for Kennedy for president in 1960.

Nixon did not succumb to the temptation to strike back at Warren, even in the aftermath of his disappointing loss to Kennedy. A few months after the election, he responded to calls from conservatives for Warren's impeachment with an eloquent defense of the chief justice. "I regard him unreservedly as a devoted and loyal public servant and a man of unimpeachable character," he told an interviewer. "I do not always agree with his opinions — this, it seems to me, is inevitable when complex policy questions are at issue — but that they are sincere and carefully formulated I have no doubt at all. Thus I am disturbed by these current suggestions that he somehow be 'removed' from office."[24]

Unimpressed by this statement of support, Warren became so aroused by Nixon's decision to run for governor of California in 1962 against Pat Brown that he found it impossible to maintain the dignified neutrality his position on the court required. He made a point of dropping in on Brown, with whom he was good friends, during the campaign and posing smilingly for press photographs. A Brown publicist called it a "very conscious show."

As November drew near, Warren told an interviewer: "I think [Brown is] going to beat the hell out of Nixon! I can just feel it. I can't get involved, of course. But Nixon has to be stopped."[25] Three days after the election, columnist Mary McGrory saw Warren and John Kennedy "chortling" about Nixon's defeat. "It would have been hard to say, watching their faces, who enjoyed the downfall more, the Chief Justice or the President," McGrory reported. The two of them were "laughing like schoolboys."[26]

Nixon's election as president in 1968 must have come as a severe blow to Warren. As chief justice, he was obliged to swear in Nixon before a national audience. Administering the oath, Warren's open wound throbbed. He told an interviewer later that he could not help thinking: "But for Nixon, that might have been me taking the oath of office in 1953. I might have won."[27]

Warren was reticent about discussing his relationship with Nixon for the record. The head of the University of California's regional oral history project noted that the only time Warren became irritable during her interview with him was when she raised that subject. When he showed Merrell Small his memoirs in draft, Small commented: "Have you not treated Richard Nixon with too kindly a touch?... I have had the understanding that you believed [he] was ... prepared to cut your political throat."[28]

Warren resigned from the court in 1969. In an act of generosity toward an old foe, Nixon became the first sitting president to address the court and paid warm tribute to Warren's many years of public service. "It is great to be great," he quoted Will Rogers as saying, but "it is greater to be human."[29]

Warren survived into the Watergate era and was able to follow the daily revelation of excesses that brought the president down in August 1974. He did not live to see Nixon's resignation, however — he died only a month before, on July 9. As the scandal reached its height, Warren, in a summing up of his animus, branded Nixon "perhaps the most despicable president this nation has ever had. He was a cheat, a liar, and a crook, and he brought my country, which I love, into disrepute. Even worse than abusing the office, he abused the American people."[30]

## Nixon: The Weakened Survivor

Nixon may have eliminated his California rivals as competitors in 1958 and emerged as the frontrunner for the 1960 Republican nomination, but he had genuine concerns about the future. Nineteen fifty-eight had been a bad year for Republicans, and the Eisenhower administration had clearly lost its earlier momentum.

Still, Nixon had come a long way. Without question, he had become a skilled and sophisticated political operator. The self-righteousness and moral fuzziness that would blemish his later career were not yet in full bloom. It would take the two traumatic defeats — at the hands of Kennedy in 1960 and Brown in 1962 — to bring his negative qualities, as well as his impressive resilience, more fully into play. Some of those close to him noticed, however, that he seemed more angry and insecure as the 1950s wore on. He had more periods of black despair and became less accessible and more resentful of the press. A critic said he was no longer the "reasonably approachable young man" of his earlier years.[31]

Those who were inclined to dislike Nixon were further alienated by his 1962 memoir, *Six Crises*, which struck them as transparently self-promoting. President Kennedy, who had congratulated Nixon for his victory over Helen Douglas twelve years before, read the book and said: "It makes me sick. He's a cheap bastard, that's all there is to it."[32] Arthur Schlesinger echoed the views of liberals everywhere when he wrote: "Nixon's self-absorption, his obsessive concern with the impression he is making on others, his lack of taste and lack of style — all these things are given overwhelming documentation in *Six Crises*."[33] Nixon's so-called "last press conference," following his defeat for governor of California later that same year, showed him at his least sympathetic, raging at the press and wallowing in self-pity.

His three California rivals were not as liberal as Kennedy or Schlesinger, but their views of Nixon were similar. His ideology was not the issue. He had been a Republican like them, but they could neither get past their dislike of Nixon the man nor forget that he had frustrated their career objectives. None of them rejoiced when he was elected president in 1968.

## *The Rivalry in Retrospect*

Even as the California rivals denied being in competition with each other between 1946 and 1958, the facts on the ground argued otherwise. *Look* magazine was correct in 1955 when it declared that they could deny a split among them "until hell freezes over" but "anything else wouldn't be natural." All four men were from the same state. They all belonged to the same political party. They all expressed an interest in being part of a presidential ticket. The political realities of candidate selection dictated that only one of them could succeed. Under these circumstances, it would have been impossible for them to avoid conflict.

Their common ambition was coupled with a common conviction — each man believed that he was better qualified than the others for national office. Warren saw himself as pragmatic and incorruptible with a proven record of administrative success. Knight believed his leadership skills and his ability to connect with people were demonstrably superior to any of his rivals. Knowland was convinced by a lifetime of electoral successes that he had an enlightened vision of the national interest and the steadiest of nerves. Nixon considered himself the only professional politician in a field of amateurs and the only Republican already steeped in nationwide battle against the Democrats.

Except for the early bond between Knowland and Warren, the four men did not have a high comfort level with each other. Warren, Nixon and Knowland were political lone wolves with few close friendships, let alone with the other rivals. From the beginning of his association with them, Warren was disdainful of both Knight and Nixon. Knight was a personable man with many friends, but his sensitivity and status consciousness poisoned his relations with his cool and aloof competitors. Knowland's self-regard and social ineptitude isolated him from nearly everyone. Most pictures of the four men together showed them tense, serious and glum.

The conflict of interest of the California rivals, magnified by their confinement to the same small political stage, guaranteed frustration and anger. It is no wonder that Pat Brown came to the conclusion that "there was awful hatred in that [state] Republican party. Everybody hated everybody else."[34] The inability of Warren and Knight to keep their feelings in check certainly suggested that they were indeed "good haters," as intimates called them. Nixon was more in control of himself—he was the one, after all, who felt that anger should only be staged. But his personal story revealed a deep well of resentment, which was expressed in his aggressive and tireless campaigning, his distrust of the media, and his obsession with winning.

And yet they exchanged warm and friendly correspondence, even as their competition heated up. They were careful to observe important occasions in each other's lives; conveyed their appreciation for support, real or imagined; asked after the health and welfare of each other's families; and joked about media caricatures of their relationships. They managed to remain civil and to cooperate in support of the national Republican ticket. Warren and Knowland — and even Knight — put aside their resentment of Nixon to campaign for Eisenhower and Nixon in 1952. Knowland and Knight did so again in 1956.

On some level, in other words, their enforced association over many years turned them into reluctant friends as well as rivals. As their wives and children became acquainted and they undertook the common cause of winning elections, it was difficult not to feel a kind of bond. Knowland, in particular, took pains not to let his competitiveness become personal. "The senator was not one to talk about people, he never gossiped," recalled Paul Manolis. "As close as I was to Knowland, he never said unkind things."[35]

Nixon's correspondence and behavior always presumed a shared identity as Californians and Republican politicians. He seemed the most interested of the four in maintaining the good opinion of the others. His sincerity in this effort has been doubted, because he simultaneously worked to undermine their influence.

But even when he had abundant evidence of a rival's ill will, he consistently refused to acknowledge anything resembling a feud. He thanked Knight repeatedly for his tepid political support and either convinced himself, or made believe, that Knowland was "proud and happy" to nominate him as vice president in 1952. Despite years of hostility from Earl Warren, Nixon continued to praise him in public and seemed genuinely respectful of his political success. Perhaps reflecting his Quaker upbringing, Nixon remained resolutely non-confrontational — a quality that disarmed many of his contemporary critics and blunted the hostility of his California rivals, even as it tried the patience of his more combative allies.

## *Nixon's Central Role*

Richard Nixon was, of course, the focal point of the rivalry. The attitudes of Nixon's competitors were driven by a belief that he was both far less prepared for high office than they were and far more prepared to say anything to get there. Warren and Knowland, in particular, had toiled in the state Republican Party organizations and had held responsible positions in state politics before Nixon even had a law practice. In 1952 they were genuine national figures, yet they had to adjust to the startling success of a younger man who they considered manipulative and dishonorable. Nixon appeared to his rivals as he appeared to most Democrats in the 1950s — as a political opportunist concerned first and foremost with moving his career forward.

His training and skill as a debater were part of his problem. Good debaters must be prepared to argue either side of an issue with equal persuasiveness. Their goal is to present a better argument than their opponent and thus win the debate, regardless of what they actually believe. Nixon seemed to view politics as another debating venue, and this outlook made him more interested in tactics and strategy than in policy.

Eisenhower adviser Emmet Hughes, who knew Nixon well, believed that his focus on tactics was due to a "want of resolution — a chronic personal incapacity for commitment." According to Hughes, Nixon always feared that if he took a strong position on any of the great issues of the moment, the voters would "hoard their dissents until election day." Thus, he developed an acute sensitivity to public opinion. For example, he rejected the conservative wing of his party partly because he knew that the middle of the political spectrum was where most of the votes were.

Hughes was struck by Nixon's confidence that he was a true professional in an arena cluttered with amateurs. This confidence served him well in his relations with Warren, Knight and Knowland. To Hughes, however, Nixon was not professional at all. As a close associate pointed out: "He does not even handle people intelligently — or carefully.... No real 'professional' could be as willful and self-centered and withdrawn as he was." His mastery of technique, Hughes concludes, never compensated for his uncertainty in matters of substance. He was always the pupil who "heard the music yet missed the tune."[36]

A major issue with Democrats, as well as Nixon's rivals, Warren in particular, was Nixon's election rhetoric, which often seemed to them like character assassination. Nixon freely admitted that he harshly criticized his opponents during campaigns. He even quoted some of that rhetoric in his memoirs, as if to argue that its use was justified by the circumstances.

For example, he conceded telling audiences during his 1950 Senate campaign that the choice between him and Helen Douglas was "between freedom and state socialism," and in the presidential election of 1952 that he would rather have a "khaki-clad president than one clothed in State Department pinks." He owned up to the comment that Truman and Acheson were "traitors to the high principles in which many of the nation's Democrats believe." He seemed not to understand why Truman and Acheson took offense at his use of the word "traitor." If they had read the statement more carefully, he convinced himself, they would have understood his more limited meaning.[37]

He confessed that some of his attacks had been "very rough." Perhaps, he said, he had been unconsciously overreacting to the things said about him during and after the fund crisis. Perhaps he had been carried away by the partisan role Eisenhower had assigned him. But, as he pointed out in his memoirs, someone had to "fire up the faithful."

Eisenhower's refusal to shoulder his responsibilities as a politician and Republican spokesman during election seasons made the vice president the party's most visible and partisan campaigner and a lightning rod for Democratic attacks. Under a more partisan and less popular president, Nixon might not have attracted so much unfavorable publicity and hostility. His relationship with Ike not only scarred him on a personal level, but the role Ike assigned to him set back his political career as well.

As he himself pointed out, many of the burdens Nixon bore were thrust upon him by circumstances. In the 1940s, he won his first election by boldly challenging the legitimacy of the New Deal and the legacy of Franklin Roosevelt, a man regarded as a god in liberal circles. In bringing down Alger Hiss and crusading against internal subversion, he ended up questioning the loyalty of leaders who had led the nation to victory in World War II. These were explosive and divisive issues, and talking about them as bluntly as he did was certain to evoke a highly emotional response from Democrats.

Yet we should not feel too sorry for Nixon. He understood on a gut level that aggressive, often negative campaigning was both necessary and effective. As described earlier, Eisenhower needed Nixon's strongly partisan attacks, yet was uncomfortable with them. Believing that the negative tone of the 1954 campaign had alienated many American voters from Republican candidates, the president urged him prior to the 1956 campaign to "work in a smile or two."[38] Instead of "give 'em hell," Ike advised, Nixon should "give 'em heaven."[39]

Nixon tried this for a while, but the experiment left his audiences deflated and the press corps "stupefied." In the meantime, Democratic candidate Adlai Stevenson became more shrill. One day, Nixon decided that he had to go back on the attack. Late that night, according to his memoirs, "suddenly I felt as if a great weight had been lifted from me. I had not realized how frustrating it had been to suppress the normal partisan instincts and campaign with one arm tied behind my back."[40] At that moment, though everyone around him was asleep, he went to the piano and happily began playing Brahms' *Rhapsody in G Minor*. From that moment, he wrote, the campaign caught fire and audiences were delighted. He later summarized the lesson he learned from this experience: "I don't believe in adopting a strictly defensive attitude.... You always lose in the end."[41]

Many journalists of the period reported that Nixon never appeared as malign or devious in person as the forces he set in motion. He may have chosen his words primarily for their emotional impact rather than their literal meaning, but his supporters often believed he meant exactly what he said. His California mafia, with Murray Chotiner playing the leading role, time and again displayed a willingness to go to any lengths to see their candidate succeed.

During his presidency, Nixon avoided personal conflict by ordering subordinates to perform tasks he did not have the stomach for. He may well have done the same in the 1950s, and his ultimate responsibility for the actions of his supporters cannot be denied. But whatever his specific instructions were, they often seemed to have unintended consequences. It was Nixon's representatives, rather than Nixon himself, who annoyed Warren by demanding his assent to a joint campaign in 1950. It was Nixon's zealous allies on the campaign train in 1952 who demanded that Nixon begin "cutting up" Warren rather than accommodating him. It was Chotiner and others who implemented the attempt to steal the state committee election from Knight in 1954. His committed backers helped him organize and campaign effectively but often left a trail of bruised feelings in their wake. They certainly did not help his relations with Knight, Warren and Knowland.

Earl Mazo, one of Nixon's earliest biographers, recognized that the unusual dedication of his supporters was sometimes counterproductive and tarnished his reputation. Mazo contended that it was impossible for a Nixon devotee "to halt, even for a moment, regardless of the circumstances, the drive to achieve his or her ambition for the leader. Their aim is the presidency.... Leaders of the California Nixon faction point out that party faithful are devoted to him because of his campaigning for everyone."[42] To them, the middle course he habitually steered was evidence not of an exquisite sensitivity to poll data but of his role as a natural peacemaker within the Republican Party, whose fortunes were uppermost in his mind.

Whatever excesses of zeal or rhetoric could be associated with Nixon, by 1958 he had met every challenge thrown his way by the other California Republicans. He won election to the House and Senate without Warren's help, outmaneuvered the governor in 1952, coopted Knowland and beat back a Knight challenge in 1956, and talked Knight into running for the Senate in 1958.

Nixon triumphed in part because he had the element of surprise going for him before 1952 and a superior power position afterwards. He came to believe that none of the other rivals had the skills, the political appeal, or the capacity for work that would enable them to successfully compete with him on a national level — and it was probably true. Earl Warren struck him as a holier-than-thou politician lacking in tactical flexibility. He had worked closely with Bill Knowland and surely sensed that the plodding, awkward senator could be out-maneuvered and out-campaigned.

Of the three, Nixon seems to have had the least regard for Knight. The volatile California governor was his antithesis in many ways — imprudent, impetuous, easily rattled, more of a show horse than a work horse. He also had several qualities — warmth, likeability and humor among them — that Nixon could only envy. Reading about Knight's tirades against him, he probably alternated between anger and amusement. In several hundred pages of political reminiscences covering his long career, he never once mentioned Knight.

Though Knight and Knowland did not survive the 1958 disaster, it would be a mistake to think that Nixon was not hurt by it as well. Californians across the political spectrum were enraged by the Big Switch, and the unintended result of Nixon's mediation in the affair was that he received most of the blame for it. The perception that he was pulling the strings behind the scenes sharply diminished his prestige in California. It dealt him a severe blow from which he did not recover for a decade. The fallout from Republican defeats in 1958 contributed to his inability to beat John Kennedy in 1960 and played an even stronger role in his humiliating defeat in his race for governor in 1962 at the hands of Pat Brown.

## *Personality and Political Behavior*

The story of the California rivals makes an excellent case for the often decisive impact of personality on political behavior. It also demonstrates the strong motivating forces of animosity and friendship. Each of the rivals based career-changing decisions on their dislike of, or loyalty to, one another. Each of them was undone by shortcomings of temperament or style.

For example, Earl Warren admitted that he ran for a third term as governor partly to spite Knight. He was never in a position to retaliate directly for his humiliation at the hands of Nixon at the 1952 Republican convention, but he undoubtedly did his best behind the scenes to discredit Nixon with others.

Bill Knowland labored willingly for his benefactor, Earl Warren, but when he finally decided in 1953 that his debt was paid off, he found that he had lost ground to Nixon. At both Republican conventions in the 1950s, he deferred his own political goals in the interest of being a team player, yet he had "ambition and self-assurance bordering on feelings of divine right." Nixon's problems gaining Eisenhower's confidence offered Knowland a golden opportunity to displace his rival on the 1956 Republican ticket, but the senator's obstreperousness guaranteed that Ike would find him an even less suitable political partner than Nixon. In 1957 Knowland calculated that he could not escape Nixon's shadow while serving in the Senate, so he made his calamitous decision to return to California.

The rivalry of the California Republicans had its greatest impact on Knight. Everywhere he turned, one of them was standing in his way. He chafed under Earl Warren's domination of California and could not advance to the governorship until Warren finally moved on. He envisioned his primary role at the 1956 convention as standing bravely against Richard Nixon's ambitions, only to be muscled out of the way by his former ally Bill Knowland, acting in concert with Nixon. Finally, Knowland ruined Knight's chances for reelection in 1958 by making a shockingly insensitive and ill-advised decision. Knight's entire political career reflected his opposition to the other three men.

Knight's differences with Warren and Nixon were personal, not ideological. Knight acted like a conservative in the late 1940s but only to attract conservative backing for a challenge of the governor. Then, once in office, his administration continued Warren's nonpartisan and pragmatic approach. Knight did not even bother to cook up a policy-based rationale for his hatred of Nixon.

He could not avoid policy issues in his fight against Knowland in 1957. The senator identified himself with the California Republican Party's growing conservative movement — in particular, its anti-unionism. By then Knight had decided that only a moderate could win a gubernatorial election in California. He believed labor opposition would be fatal to his reelection prospects, which were predicated on attracting Democratic votes. But his campaign against Knowland also was bitterly personal — he could not contain his rage over the senator's incomprehensible challenge of a sitting Republican governor.

Did Nixon reciprocate the negative feelings of the others? He left little direct evidence of how he regarded Warren, Knowland and Knight. He was the most prudent and judicious of the four. His critical remarks about them were usually set in political contexts that were hard to take personally. He might have "set out to destroy these three men — to destroy their credibility," as Knight aide Milton Polland believed, because he feared them and believed they could deny him the presidential nomination.[43] But he was never careless enough to say so.

The twelve-year contest of California's four giants was an absorbing human drama with a colorful cast of characters. In no other era of American history was one state's impact on national political life so great. A time will probably never again come when a journalist can board a plane, as Teddy White did in late 1955, and fly to a place that is the home of all four leading candidates for president or vice president of a major political party.

# Notes

## Introduction

1. Royce Delmatier, Clarence F. McIntosh and Earl G. Waters, *The Rumble of California Politics, 1848–1970* (New York: Wiley and Sons, 1970), p. 308.
2. Robert Gottlieb and Irene Wolt, *Thinking Big: The Story of the Los Angeles Times, Its Publishers, and Their Influence on Southern California* (New York: G.P. Putnam's Sons, 1977), p. 273.
3. Gottlieb and Wolt, *Thinking Big*, p. 271.
4. David Halberstam, *The Powers That Be* (New York: Knopf, 1979), p. 119.
5. Melvin Harry Bernstein, "Political Leadership in California: A Study of Four Governors," Ph.D. diss., University of California at Los Angeles, 1970, pp. 47, 55.
6. Garry Wills, *Nixon Agonistes: The Crisis of the Self-Made Man* (Boston: Houghton Mifflin, 1970), p. 76.
7. Gladwin Hill, *Dancing Bear: An Inside Look at California Politics* (New York: Wiley, 1970), p. 162.
8. Theodore H. White, "The Gentlemen from California," *Collier's*, February 3, 1956.
9. Herbert L. Phillips, *Big Wayward Girl: An Informal Political History of California* (Garden City, NY: Doubleday, 1968), p. 163.

## Chapter 1

1. *Time*, January 31, 1944.
2. Roger Morris, *Richard Milhous Nixon: The Rise of An American Politician* (New York: Holt, 1990), p. 269.
3. Kevin Starr, *Embattled Dreams: California in War and Peace* (New York: Oxford University Press, 2002), p. 247.
4. Cited in Jim Newton, *Justice for All: Earl Warren and the Nation He Made* (New York: Riverhead Books, 2006), p. 164.
5. Oral History Interview with Clement Sherman Whitaker, Jr., California State Archives, State Government Oral History Program, Sacramento, CA, 1988–1989, p. 48.
6. Leo Katcher, *Earl Warren: A Political Biography* (New York: McGraw-Hill, 1967), p. 212.
7. Thomas J. Cunningham, "Southern California Campaign Chairman for Earl Warren, 1946," *Earl Warren's Campaigns*, Vol. I, Regional Oral History Office, University of California, Berkeley, 1976, p. 8.
8. Starr, *Embattled Dreams*, p. 266.
9. Katcher, *Warren*, p. 80.
10. Edmund Brown, Jr., "The Governor's Lawyer," *Earl Warren: Fellow Constitutional Officers*, Earl Warren Oral History Project, Regional Oral History Office, University of California, Berkeley, 1979, p. 29.
11. Katcher, *Warren*, p. 217.
12. Gladwin Hill, cited in Bernstein, "Political Leadership in California," p. 129.
13. Katcher, *Warren*, p. 216.
14. Ibid.
15. Paul Mason, "Covering the Legislature for Governor Goodwin J. Knight," The Governor's Office Under Goodwin Knight, *The Goodwin Knight and Edmund G. Brown Eras in California, 1953–1966*, Regional Oral History Office, University of California, Berkeley, p. 17.
16. Earl C. Behrens, "Gubernatorial Campaigns and Party Issues: A Political Reporter's View, 1948–1966," *Reporting from Sacramento*,

Regional Oral History Office, University of California, Berkeley, 1981, p. 15.

17. Brown, "The Governor's Lawyer," p. 28.

18. Oral History Interview with Hon. Gardiner Johnson, State Government Oral History Program, California State Archives, 1973, 1983, p. 127.

19. Cited in Newton, *Justice for All*, p. 155.

20. Merrell Small, Introduction to the Earl Warren Papers, California State Archives Website.

21. *Newsweek*, August 20, 1947.

22. Cited in Bernstein, "Political Leadership in California," p. 115.

23. Brown, "The Governor's Lawyer," pp. 8–9.

24. Florence Clifton, "California Democrats, 1934–1950," *California Democrats in the Earl Warren Era*, Regional Oral History Office, University of California, Berkeley, 1976, p. 14.

25. Katcher, *Warren*, p. 309.

26. Warren to Knowland, October 26, 1934, Subseries K, Earl Warren Papers, California State Archives, Sacramento.

27. Warren to Dewey, December 8, 1939, Republican Organizations, Earl Warren Papers, California State Archives, Sacramento.

28. Earl Warren, *The Memoirs of Earl Warren* (Garden City, NY: Doubleday, 1977), p. 122.

29. Cited in Gottlieb and Wolt, *Thinking Big*, p. 275.

30. Joseph Holt to Warren, August 24, 1949, Warren Personal Papers, Republican Organizations, California State Archives, Sacramento.

31. Bernstein, "Political Leadership in California," pp. 126, 128.

32. Both Kenny and McWilliams cited in Lloyd Ray Henderson, "Earl Warren and California Politics," Ph.D. diss., University of California, Berkeley, 1965, pp. 404, 406.

33. Ethan Rarick, *California Rising: The Life and Times of Pat Brown* (Berkeley: University of California Press, 2005), p. 59.

34. Gottlieb and Wolt, *Thinking Big*, p. 276.

35. Merrell Farnham Small, "The Office of the Governor Under Earl Warren," The Earl Warren Era in California, 1925–1953, Regional Oral History Office, University of California, Berkeley, 1972, p. 153.

36. Hill, *Dancing Bear*, p. 100.

## Chapter 2

1. Geraldine McConnell, "Governor Warren, the Knowlands and Columbia State Park," *Earl Warren: Views and Episodes*, Regional Oral History Office, University of California, Berkeley, 1976, p. 13.

2. Phillips, *Big Wayward Girl*, p. 177.

3. Warren, *Memoirs*, pp. 68–69.

4. Warren letter to California Republican Party, August 26, 1932, Earl Warren Papers, California State Archives, Sacramento.

5. Warren to Joe Knowland, February 6, 1936, Earl Warren Papers, California State Archives, Sacramento.

6. Bill Knowland to Warren, undated, Earl Warren Papers, California State Archives, Sacramento.

7. Oscar J. Jahnsen, "Enforcing the Law Against Gambling, Bootlegging, Graft, Fraud, and Subversion, 1922–1942," *The Earl Warren Era in California*, Regional Oral History Office, University of California, Berkeley, 1976, p. 32.

8. Knowland to Warren, September 26, 1941, Sub-series K, Earl Warren Papers, California State Archives, Sacramento.

9. Knowland to Warren, October 17, 1941, Sub-series K, Earl Warren Papers, California State Archives, Sacramento.

10. Gayle B. Montgomery and James W. Johnson, *One Step from the White House: The Rise and Fall of Senator William F. Knowland* (Berkeley: University of California Press, 1998) p. 26.

11. Joe Knowland to Warren, undated, with the two articles, also undated. In Warren Papers, Sub-series K, California State Archives, Sacramento.

12. *California Independent Review*, February 26, 1942.

13. Bill Knowland to Warren, October 11, 1942, Earl Warren Papers, California State Archives, Sacramento.

14. Knowland to Warren, November 4, 1942, Earl Warren Papers, California State Archives, Sacramento.

15. Montgomery and Johnson, *One Step*, p. 31.

16. Knowland to Warren, December 21, 1943, Earl Warren Papers, California State Archives, Sacramento.

17. Warren's secretary to Knowland, April 29, 1944, Sub-series K, Earl Warren Papers, California State Archives, Sacramento.

18. Starr, *Embattled Dreams*, p. 189.

19. Cited in Ray Leon Clark, "The 1958 Gubernatorial Election: How Republican Infighting Affected the Outcome," master's thesis, California State University, Long Beach, 1999, p. 31.
20. Mary Ellen Leary, "A Journalist's Perspective: Government and Politics in California and the Bay Area," *Goodwin Knight and Edmund G. Brown Eras in California, 1953–1966*, Regional Oral History Office, University of California, Berkeley, 1981, p. 30.
21. Thomas C. Lynch, "A Career in Politics and the Attorney General's Office," *Goodwin Knight and Edmund G. Brown Eras in California, 1953–1966*, Regional Oral History Office, University of California, Berkeley, 1982, p. 132–133.
22. Ronald A. Button, "California Republican Party Official and State Treasurer of California, 1956–1958," California Constitutional Officers, *Goodwin Knight and Edmund G. Brown Eras in California, 1953–1966*, Regional Oral History Office, University of California, Berkeley, 1980, p. 22.
23. Leary, "A Journalist's Perspective," p. 30.
24. Edmund G. Brown, "Years of Growth, 1939–1966: Law Enforcement, Politics and the Governor's Office," *Goodwin Knight and Edmund G. Brown Eras in California, 1953–1966*, Regional Oral History Office, University of California, Berkeley, 1982, p. 245.
25. Douglas Cater, "Knowland: The Man Who Wants to Be Taft," *The Reporter*, March 8, 1956, p. 35.
26. Fletcher Knebel and Dan Fowler, "He Would Rather Be Right and President," *Look*, April 5, 1955, p. 53.
27. Delmatier, *The Rumble of California Politics*, p. 311.
28. Montgomery and Johnson, *One Step*, p. 62.
29. Ibid., p. 61.
30. Paul Bullock, *Jerry Voorhis: The Idealist as Politician* (New York: Vantage Press, 1978), p. 259.

4. Ernest Haveman, "California's Excellency Excels at Jokes as Well as Politics," *Life*, March 29, 1954.
5. Ibid.
6. Hale Champion, "California's Governor Knight: Balance of Republican Power?" *The Reporter*, February 23, 1956, p. 22.
7. The account of this event in Frank J. Taylor, "How to Run for Office," *Saturday Evening Post*, October 29, 1955, is one of many.
8. Small, "The Governor's Office Under Earl Warren," p. 90.
9. Stuart Alsop, "The Great California Drama," *Saturday Evening Post*, October 18, 1958, p. 102.
10. Milton R. Polland, "Political and Personal Friend of Earl Warren, Goodwin Knight and Hubert Humphrey," *Goodwin Knight: Aides, Advisors and Appointees*, Regional Oral History Office, University of California, Berkeley, 1977–79, p. 16.
11. Friedman, "The Gay Beaver," p. 10.
12. Ibid., p. 11.
13. "Don Juan In Heaven."
14. Ibid.
15. Ibid.
16. Haveman, "California's Excellency."
17. "Don Juan in Heaven."
18. Kurt Schuparra, *The Triumph of the Right: The Rise of the California Conservative Movement* (Armonk, NY: Sharpe, 1998), p. 23.
19. Los Angeles *Sunday News*, April 10, 1938.
20. *Los Angeles Eagle*, July 3, 1936.
21. "Don Juan in Heaven."
22. Taylor, "How to Run for Office," p. 82.
23. Ibid.
24. Ed Cray, *Chief Justice: A Biography of Earl Warren* (New York: Simon & Schuster, 1997), p. 175.
25. Stanley P. Isaacs, "Knight Over California," *The Nation*, May 29, 1954, p. 462.

## Chapter 3

1. White, "The Gentlemen from California."
2. "Don Juan in Heaven," *Time*, May 30, 1955.
3. Ralph Friedman, "The Gay Beaver," *Frontier*, June 1958, p, 15.

## Chapter 4

1. Arthur Woodstone, *Nixon's Head* (New York: St. Martin's Press, 1972), p. 34.
2. Morris, *Nixon*, p. 47.
3. Wills, *Nixon Agonistes*, p. 31.
4. Vamik Volkan, Norman Itzkowitz and Andrew D. Dod, *Richard Nixon: A Psychobi-*

*ography* (New York: Columbia University Press, 1997), p. 35. Nixon publicly denied that his father was abusive. "I would not recognize my father from the grotesque caricatures that have appeared in some of the media," he later wrote. "I would simply say that there was never a day I was not proud of him." [Richard Nixon, *In the Arena: A Memoir of Victory, Defeat and Renewal* (New York: Simon and Schuster, 1990), p. 79.].

5. Stewart Alsop, *Nixon and Rockefeller: A Double Portrait* (Garden City, NY: Doubleday, 1960), p. 134.

6. Richard M. Nixon, *RN: The Memoirs of Richard Nixon* (New York: Grosset and Dunlap, 1978), p. 10.

7. Morris, *Nixon*, p. 147.

8. Alsop, *Nixon and Rockefeller*, p. 129.

9. Kenneth Clawson, "A Loyalist's Memoir," *The Washington Post*, August 9, 1979, cited in Greg Mitchell, *Tricky Dick and the Pink Lady: Richard Nixon vs. Helen Gahagan Douglas — Sexual Politics and the Red Scare, 1950* (New York: Random House, 1998), p. 40.

10. William Costello, *The Facts About Nixon: An Unauthorized Biography* (New York: The Viking Press, 1960), p. 7.

11. Volkan, Itzkowitz and Dod, *Nixon: A Psychobiography*, pp. 48–50.

12. Bruce Mazlish, *In Search of Nixon: A Psychohistorical Inquiry* (New York: Basic Books, 1972), p. 51.

13. William A. Arnold, *Back When It All Began: The Early Nixon Years* (New York: Vantage Press, 1975), p. 21.

14. *Fortnight*, May 26, 1950, p. 8.

15. George Christopher, "Mayor of San Francisco and Republican Party Candidate" in San Francisco Republicans, *Goodwin Knight and Edmund G. Brown Eras in California, 1953–1966*, Regional Oral History Office, University of California, Berkeley, 1980, pp. 9, 32.

16. Caspar Weinberger, "California Assembly, Republican State Central Committee, and Elections, 1953–1966," San Francisco Republicans, *Goodwin Knight and Edmund G. Brown Eras in California, 1953–1966*, Regional Oral History Office, University of California, Berkeley, 1980, p. 70.

17. Volkan, Itzkowitz and Dod, *Nixon: A Psychobiography*, p. 90.

18. David Abrahamsen, *Nixon vs. Nixon: An Emotional Tragedy* (New York: Farrar, Straus and Giroux, 1976), pp. 55, 139–140.

19. Bela Kornitzer, *The Real Nixon: An Intimate Biography* (New York: Rand McNally, 1960), pp. 222, 53.

20. Halberstam, *The Powers That Be*, p. 259.

21. Volkan, Itzkowitz and Dod, *Nixon: A Psychobiography*, p. 99.

22. Wills, *Nixon Agonistes*, p, 32.

23. Bullock, *Jerry Voorhis*, p. 243.

24. Stephen E. Ambrose, *Nixon: The Education of a Politician, 1913–1962* (New York: Simon and Schuster, 1987), p. 123.

25. Ambrose, *Nixon*, pp. 123–124.

26. Ibid., p. 131.

27. Bullock, *Voorhis*, p. 241.

28. Ibid., pp. 112, 272.

29. Starr, *Embattled Dreams*, p. 283.

30. Irwin F. Gellman, *The Contender: Richard Nixon, The Congress Years, 1946–1952* (New York: The Free Press, 1999), p. 73.

31. Cited in Ambrose, *Nixon*, p. 121.

32. Ambrose, *Nixon*, p. 124.

33. Morris, *Nixon*, p. 323.

34. Starr, *Embattled Dreams*, p. 277.

35. Newton, *Justice for All*, p. 199.

36. Starr, *Embattled Dreams*, pp. 277–278.

37. Mitchell, *Tricky Dick and the Pink Lady*, p. 50.

38. Edmund G. Brown, "The Governor's Lawyer," p. 28.

39. Cited in Morris, *Nixon*, p, 324.

40. Katcher, *Earl Warren*, p. 203.

41. Mitchell, *Tricky Dick and the Pink Lady*, p. 50.

42. *U.S. News and World Report*, July 13, 1959.

43. Biographer Jack Harrison Pollack believes that Warren strongly favored Voorhis. [Jack Harrison Pollack, *Earl Warren: The Judge Who Changed America* (Englewood Cliffs, NJ: Prentice-Hall, 1979), p. 103.].

44. Arnold, *Back When It All Began*, p. 30.

45. Ibid., pp. 31–32.

46. Newton, *Justice for All*, p. 201.

## Chapter 5

1. Cited in Delmatier, *The Rumble of California Politics*, p. 312.

2. Katcher, *Warren*, p. 238.

3. Earl Warren, "Conversations with Earl Warren on California Government," *The Earl Warren Era in California*, Regional Oral History Office, University of California, Berkeley, 1981, pp. 166–167.

4. Haveman, "California's Excellency," p. 119.
5. Friedman, "The Gay Beaver," p. 14.
6. Champion, "California's Governor Knight."
7. H. Brett Melendy and Benjamin F. Gilbert, *The Governors of California: Peter H. Burnett to Edmund G. Brown* (Georgetown, CA: Talisman Press, 1965), p. 428.
8. "Don Juan in Heaven."
9. "Goodwin Knight: Will He Run?" *Fortnight*, January 6, 1950, p. 9.
10. The history of the state, and the country, might have been very different if Knight had run for the Senate in 1950 and won. Instead, Richard Nixon was the Republican nominee and ultimate victor.
11. "Don Juan in Heaven."
12. San Francisco *Call-Bulletin*, January 17, 1947.
13. Small, "Office of the Governor Under Warren," p. 48.
14. Earl Adams, "Financing Richard Nixon's Campaigns from 1946 to 1960," *Richard M. Nixon in the Warren Era*, Regional Oral History Office, University of California, Berkeley, 1975, p. 30.
15. Gellman, *The Contender*, p. 189.
16. According to Earl Warren's administrative secretary, Knight's vigorous celebration caused a perforation of his duodenal ulcer, which required emergency surgery. (Small, "Office of the Governor," p. 90.).
17. Katcher, *Earl Warren*, p. 229.
18. Booth Mooney, *The Politicians: 1945–1960* (Philadelphia: Lippincott, 1970), p. 79.
19. Taylor, "How to Run for Office," p. 82.
20. Raymond Scheussler, "An Eagle to Watch," *Eagle*, June 1955.
21. Katcher, *Warren*, p. 236.
22. Ibid., p. 246.
23. Behrens, "Gubernatorial Campaigns and Party Issues," p. 15.
24. Earl Warren, Jr., "California Politics," *The Governor's Family*, Regional Oral History Office, University of California, Berkeley, 1980, p. 28.
25. Warren, *Memoirs*, p. 264.
26. Earl Warren, Jr., "California Politics," p. 27.
27. Small, "Office of the Governor," p. 92.
28. *Los Angeles Times*, December 25, 1949.
29. *Los Angeles Herald-Express*, November 14, 1949.
30. *Corona Daily Independent*, November 22, 1949.
31. *Fortnight*, September 30, 1949.
32. Gottlieb and Wolt, *Thinking Big*, p. 282.
33. *Life*, June 8, 1953.
34. John Weaver, *Warren: The Man, The Court, The Era* (Boston: Little, Brown, 1967), p. 159.
35. "Goodwin Knight: Will He Run?" *Fortnight*.
36. Warren, *Memoirs*, p. 201.
37. Thomas J. Mellon, "Republican Campaigns of 1950 and 1952," *Earl Warren's Campaigns*, Vol. 2, Regional Oral History Office, University of California, Berkeley, 1977, p. 13.
38. Christopher, "Mayor of San Francisco and Republican Party Candidate," p. 2.
39. Warren, *Memoirs*, p. 201.
40. Champion, "California's Governor Knight," p. 22.

## Chapter 6

1. Cited in Ambrose, *Nixon*, p. 147.
2. *Fortnight*, December 31, 1948.
3. Gellman, *The Contender*, p. 183.
4. Nixon to Day, April 21, 1948, Roy Day correspondence, Richard Nixon Pre-Presidential Papers, Nixon Library, Yorba Linda.
5. Arnold, *Back When It All Began*, p. 34.
6. Gellman, *The Contender*, p. 190.
7. William Manchester, *The Glory and the Dream: A Narrative History of America, 1932–1972* (Boston: Little, Brown, 1973), p. 510.
8. Gellman, *The Contender*, p. 261.
9. Arnold, *Back When It All Began*, p. 36.
10. Ibid.
11. All citations in this paragraph from Gellman, *The Contender*, pp. 241, 272.
12. Alsop, *Nixon and Rockefeller*, p. 187.
13. Morris, *Nixon*, p. 524.
14. Arnold, *Back When It All Began*, preface.
15. Nixon to Day, March 2, 1949, Roy Day correspondence, Nixon Pre-Presidential Papers.
16. Cited in Gellman, *The Contender*, p. 277.
17. Jorgensen to Nixon, February 16, 1949, Nixon Pre-Presidential Papers.
18. Nixon to Jorgensen, June 10, 1949, Nixon Pre-Presidential Papers.
19. Jorgensen to Nixon, June 6, 1949, Nixon Pre-Presidential Papers.

20. Cited in Gellman, *The Contender*, p. 281.
21. Perry to Nixon, June 17, 1949, Nixon Pre-Presidential Papers (emphasis in original).
22. Nixon to Jorgensen, July 28, 1949, Nixon Pre-Presidential Papers.
23. Nixon to Perry, June 21, 1949, Nixon Pre-Presidential Papers.
24. Hillings to Nixon, July 20, 1949, Nixon Pre-Presidential Papers.
25. Jorgensen to Nixon, July 21, 1949, Nixon Pre-Presidential Papers.
26. Ibid.
27. Hillings to Nixon, July 20, 1949, Nixon Pre-Presidential Papers.
28. Day to Nixon, July 7, 1949, Nixon Pre-Presidential Papers.
29. Hillings to Nixon, no date, Nixon Pre-Presidential Papers.
30. Jorgensen to Nixon, July 21, 1949, Nixon Pre-Presidential Papers.
31. Day to Nixon, August 2, 1949, Nixon Pre-Presidential Papers.
32. *Los Angeles Times*, August 5, 1949.
33. Jorgensen to Nixon, August 5, 1949, Nixon Pre-Presidential Papers.
34. Jorgensen to Nixon, September 26, 1949, Nixon Pre-Presidential Papers.
35. Nixon, *Memoirs*, p. 72.
36. Helen Gahagan Douglas, *A Full Life* (Garden City, NY: Doubleday, 1982), p. 301.
37. Arnold, *Back When It All Began*, p. 13.
38. Cited in Douglas, *A Full Life*, p. 311.
39. Edmund G. Brown, "Years of Growth," p. 177.
40. Nixon, *Memoirs*, p. 76.
41. Wolt, *Thinking Big*, p. 278.
42. Herbert Parmet, *Richard Nixon: An American Enigma* (New York: Pearson and Longman, 2008), p. 30.
43. Cited in Pollack, *Earl Warren*, p. 120.
44. Cited in Mitchell, *Tricky Dick and the Pink Lady*, p. 211.
45. Arnold, *Back When It All Began*, p. 12.
46. Nixon, *Memoirs*, p. 74.
47. William Lee Miller, "The Debating Career of Richard M. Nixon," *The Reporter*, April 19, 1956, p. 14.
48. Ibid., p. 15.
49. Woodstone, *Nixon's Head*, p. 11.
50. Nixon allegedly justified his campaign style by saying: "I had to win. That's the thing you don't understand. The important thing is to win." (Mitchell, *Tricky Dick and the Pink Lady*, p. 43).
51. Katcher, *Warren*, p. 260.
52. M.F. Small, "The Country Editor," unpublished manuscript, Bancroft Library, Berkeley, CA, cited in Morris, *Nixon*, pp. 609–610.
53. Keith McCormac, "The Conservative Republicans of 1952," *Earl Warren's Campaigns, Vol. III*, Regional Oral History Office, University of California, Berkeley, 1978, p. 193.
54. Earl Warren, Jr., "California Politics," p. 60.
55. Pollack, *Earl Warren*, pp. 119–120.
56. Ibid., p. 119.
57. Earl Warren, Jr., "California Politics," p. 59.
58. Cited in Cray, *Chief Justice*, p. 244.
59. Katcher, *Warren*, p. 261.
60. Earl Warren, Jr., "California Politics," p. 60.
61. Arnold, *Back When It All Began*, p. 40.
62. Mitchell, *Tricky Dick and the Pink Lady*, p. 249.
63. Ambrose, *Nixon*, p. 219.
64. Mitchell, *Tricky Dick and the Pink Lady*, p. 255.
65. Douglas, *A Full Life*, p. 340.
66. Mitchell, *Tricky Dick and the Pink Lady*, p. 256.
67. Fawn M. Brodie, *Richard Nixon: The Shaping of His Character* (New York: Norton, 1981), p. 244.
68. Douglas, *A Full Life*, pp. 303–304.
69. Carey McWilliams, "Bungling in California," *The Nation*, November 4, 1950.
70. Mitchell, *Tricky Dick and the Pink Lady*, p. 108.
71. Morris, *Nixon*, p. 564.
72. Cited in Douglas, *A Full Life*, p. 328.
73. Mitchell, *Tricky Dick and the Pink Lady*, p. 257.
74. Phillips, *Big Wayward Girl*, p. 150.
75. Nixon, *In the Arena*, p. 195.

## Chapter 7

1. *Time*, March 10, 1947.
2. McIntyre Faries, "California Republicans, 1934–1953," *Earl Warren's Campaigns*, Vol. 2, Regional Oral History Office, University of California, Berkeley, 1973, pp. 30, 38.
3. Cited in Montgomery and Johnson, *One Step*, p. 88.
4. Ibid., p. 86.
5. Delmatier, *The Rumble of California Politics*, p. 335.

## Notes — Chapter 7

6. Montgomery and Johnson, *One Step*, p. 220.
7. Knebel and Fowler, "He Would Rather Be Right and President."
8. All quotes from Alsop, "The Great California Drama," p. 35.
9. Rarick, *California Rising*, p. 89.
10. Clifford Case Oral History, Lyndon Baines Johnson Library, Austin, Texas.
11. Thomas H. Kuchel, "California State Controller," *Earl Warren: Fellow Constitutional Officers*, Regional Oral History Office, University of California, Berkeley, 1979, p. 6.
12. Knebel and Fowler, "He Would Rather Be Right and President."
13. Brown, "Years of Growth," p. 238.
14. Montgomery and Johnson, *One Step*, p. 139.
15. *U.S. News and World Report*, January 13, 1950.
16. Gellman, *The Contender*, p. 353.
17. Letters cited in Ambrose, *Nixon*, p. 233.
18. Gellman, *The Contender*, p. 399.
19. Montgomery and Johnson, *One Step*, p. 104.
20. *Washington Star*, March 28, 1958.
21. Montgomery and Johnson, *One Step*, p. 105.
22. Warren, *Memoirs*, pp. 249–251.
23. Five-term San Francisco mayor James Rolph probably sought the governorship in 1930 for the same reason. See James Worthen, *Governor James Rolph and the Great Depression in California* (Jefferson, NC: McFarland, 2006).
24. Starr, *Embattled Dreams*, p. 276.
25. Cray, *Warren*, p. 225.
26. Isaacs, "Knight Over California."
27. Cited in Henderson, "Earl Warren and California Politics," p. 357.
28. Phillips, *Big Wayward Girl*, pp. 144–146.
29. In this era, favorite-son delegations, like Warren's, often complicated and delayed the task of selecting a presidential nominee. Governors without much of a national following could tie up enough votes to keep any of the legitimate front runners from clinching their party's nomination.
30. Cray, *Warren*, p. 226.
31. Arnold, *Back When It All Began*, p. 44.
32. Gelman, *The Contender*, p. 393.
33. Nixon to Warren, January 17, 1952, Cushman Files, Nixon Pre-Presidential Papers.
34. Mazo, *Warren*, p. 88.
35. Katcher, *Warren*, p. 283.
36. Nixon, *Memoirs*, p. 82.
37. Gelman, *The Contender*, p. 392.
38. Nixon, *Memoirs*, pp. 376–77.
39. Arnold, *Back When It All Began*, pp. 40–41.
40. Perry to Nixon, July 7, 1952, Nixon Pre-Presidential Papers.
41. Perry to Bernard Brennan, May 12, 1952, Nixon Pre-Presidential Papers.
42. Perry to Brennan, March 10, 1952, Nixon Pre-Presidential Papers.
43. Gellman, *The Contender*, p. 407.
44. Cray, *Warren*, p. 228.
45. Warren, *Memoirs*, p. 251.
46. Montgomery and Johnson, *One Step*, p. 108.
47. Perry to Nixon, May 28, 1952, Nixon Pre-Presidential Papers.
48. *San Francisco Call Bulletin*, August 3, 1951.
49. *Los Angeles Times*, November 14–15, 1951.
50. Morris, *Nixon*, p. 677.
51. Perry to Nixon, November 26, 1951, Herman Perry file, Nixon Pre-Presidential Papers.
52. Warren, "Conversations," p. 279.
53. Katcher, *Warren*, p. 283.
54. Gellman, in arguing that Nixon remained loyal to Warren throughout the pre-convention period, maintains that Nixon controlled only 10 percent of the delegates and alternates.
55. Gellman, *The Contender*, p. 405.
56. Faries, "California Republicans," p. 94.
57. Ibid., p. 18.
58. Cited in Ambrose, Nixon, p. 252.
59. Herbert Parmet, *Eisenhower and the American Crusades* (New York: Macmillan, 1972), p. 92.
60. Parmet, *Eisenhower and the American Crusades*, p. 101.
61. Cray, *Chief Justice*, p. 231.
62. Morris, *Nixon*, p. 689.
63. Gellman, *The Contender*, p. 423.
64. Nixon to Perry, June 6, 1952, Nixon Pre-Presidential Papers.
65. Richard Nixon, *Six Crises* (Garden City, NY: Doubleday, 1962), p. 75.
66. Cited in Katcher, *Warren*, p. 286.
67. *Portland Oregonian*, May 17, 1952.
68. Harold J. Powers, "On Prominent Issues, the Republican Party, and Political Campaigns: A Veteran Republican Views the

Goodwin Knight Era," *California Constitutional Officers*, Regional Oral History Office, University of California, Berkeley, 1980, p. 34.
69. Montgomery and Johnson, *One Step*, p. 116.
70. Jewett, "My Father's Political Philosophy and Colleagues," p. 2.
71. Montgomery and Johnson, *One Step*, p. 114.
72. Earl Mazo and Stephen Hess, *Nixon: A Political Portrait* (New York: Harper and Row, 1968), p. 84.
73. Cray, *Warren*, p. 235.
74. Newton, *Justice for All*, p. 245.
75. Jewett, "My Father's Political Philosophy and Colleagues," p. 16.
76. According to a source of historian Irwin Gellman, Taft was slightly ahead of Eisenhower in Nixon's poll. If true, and if the results had become more widely known, the poll gambit would have backfired as a way of advancing Ike's candidacy.
77. Gottlieb and Wolt, *Thinking Big*, p. 278.
78. Montgomery, *One Step*, p. 111.
79. Mellon, "Republican Campaigns of 1950 and 1952."
80. Katcher, *Warren*, pp. 288–289.
81. *Los Angeles Times*, June 24, 1952.
82. Pollack, *Warren*, p. 130.
83. Gellman, *The Contender*, p. 433.
84. Powers, "On Prominent Issues, the Republican Party, and Political Campaigns," p. 34.
85. Frank E. Jorgensen, "The Organization of Richard Nixon's Congressional Campaigns, 1946–1952, *Richard M. Nixon in the Warren Era*, Regional Oral History Office, University of California, Berkeley, 1980, p. 70.
86. Patrick Hillings, cited in Cray, *Chief Justice*. p. 233.
87. Weaver, *The Man, The Court, The Era*, p. 182.
88. Ambrose, *Nixon*, p. 259.
89. Cray, *Chief Justice*, p. 234.
90. Morris, *Nixon*, p. 709.
91. Mellon, "Republican Campaigns," p. 9.
92. Ibid.
93. Warren, *Memoirs*, p. 251.
94. Katcher, *Warren*, p. 291.
95. Morris, *Nixon*, p. 712.
96. Victor Hansen, "West Coast Defense During World War II; The California Gubernatorial Campaign of 1960," *Earl Warren's Campaigns*, Vol. 2, Regional Oral History Office, University of California, Berkeley, 1977, p. 89.
97. *New York Times*, July 3, 1952.
98. *Oakland Tribune*, July 6, 1952. Also, Morris, *Nixon*, p. 714.
99. Mellon, "Republican Campaigns," p. 9.
100. Cited in Cray, *Chief Justice*, p. 237.
101. See, for example, Frank C. Hanighen in *Human Events*, January 6, 1958.
102. Morris, *Nixon*, p. 717.
103. Costello, *The Facts About Nixon*, p. 88.
104. "Republican National Convention: Notes of Paul H. Davis," Hoover Institution Archives, Stanford University.
105. See also Warren, *Memoirs*, pp. 252–253.
106. Ibid., p. 253.
107. Ibid., p. 252.
108. Cray, *Chief Justice*, pp. 239–240.
109. Sherman Adams, *Firsthand Report: The Story of the Eisenhower Administration* (New York: Harper and Bros., 1961), p. 26.
110. Drew Pearson, *Diaries* (New York: Holt, Rinehart & Winston, 1974), p. 217.
111. McCormac, "The Conservative Republicans of 1952," p. 111.
112. Cited in Montgomery and Johnson, *One Step*, p. 114.
113. Nixon, *Memoirs*, p. 85.
114. Pearson, *Diaries*, p. 217.
115. Montgomery and Johnson, *One Step*, p. 115.
116. *San Francisco Examiner*, July 13, 1952.
117. Mazo, *Nixon*, pp. 87–88.
118. Ibid.
119. Adams, *Firsthand Report*, p. 26.
120. Warren. *Memoirs*, p. 283.
121. Faries, "California Republicans," p. 24.
122. Warren, *Memoirs*, p. 254.
123. Nixon, *Memoirs*, p. 88.
124. Polland, "Political and Personal Friend," p. 11.
125. Montgomery and Johnson, *One Step*, p. 120.
126. Cited in Katcher, *Earl Warren*, p. 40.
127. Faries, *California Republicans*, p. 93.
128. Cited in Cray, *Chief Justice*, p. 234.
129. Jorgensen, "The Organization of Richard Nixon's Congressional Campaigns," p. 73.
130. Ambrose, *Nixon*, p. 255.
131. Morris, *Nixon*, p. 658.
132. Christopher Matthews, *Kennedy and*

*Nixon: The Rivalry That Shaped Postwar America* (New York: Simon and Schuster, 1996), p. 79.

133. Costello, *Nixon*, p. 7.
134. Pollack, *Earl Warren*, p. 140.
135. Perry to Dorothy Cox, Nixon's secretary, August 4, 1952, Nixon Pre-Presidential Papers.
136. Cited in Cray, *Chief Justice*, p. 241.
137. Cited in Newton, *Justice for All*, p. 250.
138. Brown, "The Governor's Lawyer," p. 28.
139. Brown, "Years of Growth," p. 450.
140. Cited in Peter Lyon, *Eisenhower: Portrait of the Hero* (Boston: Little, Brown, 1974), p. 446.
141. Cited in Wills, *Nixon Agonistes*, p. 94, and Pollack, *Earl Warren*, p. 214.
142. Ivan Hinderaker, "The 1952 Elections in California," *Western Political Quarterly*, March 1953, p. 105.
143. Roger Rapoport, *California Dreaming: The Political Odyssey of Pat and Jerry Brown* (Berkeley, CA: Nolo Press, 1982), p. 45.
144. *Fresno Bee*, October 19, 1962.
145. Knowland to Nixon, July 14, 1952, William Knowland Correspondence, Nixon Pre-Presidential Papers.
146. Montgomery and Johnson, *One Step*, p. 114.
147. Warren, *Memoirs*, p. 254.
148. *Long Beach Press Telegram*, July 29, 1952.
149. *New York Times*, September 22, 1952.
150. Morris, *Nixon*, p. 778.
151. Nixon, *Six Crises*, p. 88.
152. Stassen telegram to Nixon, September 21, 1952, Stassen File, Nixon Pre-Presidential Papers.
153. Nixon, *Six Crises*, p. 98.
154. Ibid., p. 93.
155. Parmet, *Eisenhower and the American Crusades*, p. 136.
156. Gottlieb and Wolt, *Thinking Big*, p. 279.
157. Adams, "Financing Richard Nixon's Campaigns," p. 10.
158. Morris, *Nixon*, p. 845.
159. Nixon, *Six Crises*, p. 124.
160. Montgomery and Johnson, *One Step*, p. 122. Mazo, *Nixon*, p. 121.
161. Nixon, *Memoirs*, p. 108.

## Chapter 8

1. Cray, *Chief Justice*, p. 188.
2. *Los Angeles Times*, January 15, 1952.
3. Cray, *Chief Justice*, p. 229.
4. William Bragg Ewald, *Eisenhower the President: Crucial Days, 1951–1960* (Englewood Cliffs, NJ: Prentice-Hall, 1981), p. 78.
5. Quoted in Weaver, *Warren*, p. 193.
6. Justice William O. Douglas, quoted in Montgomery and Johnson, *One Step*, p. 146.
7. Pollack, *Earl Warren* p. 153.
8. Cray, *Chief Justice*, p. 246n.
9. Estelle Knowland Johnson, "My Father as Senator, Campaigner and Civic Leader," *Remembering William Knowland*, Regional Oral History Office, University of California, Berkeley, p. 13. Despite considerable evidence of Knowland's involvement in the appointment, Warren never publicly credited the senator's role. Knowland aide Paul Manolis later grumbled that "if you read his [memoirs], everything happened to Warren because of Warren." (Paul Manolis, "A Friend and Aide Reminisces," *Remembering William Knowland*, Regional Oral History Office, University of California, Berkeley, p. 15.).
10. David W. Reinhard, *The Republican Right Since 1945* (Lexington, KY: University Press of Kentucky, 1983), pp. 115–116.
11. Barry M. Goldwater, *With No Apologies: The Personal and Political Memoirs of United States Senator Barry M. Goldwater* (New York: Morrow, 1979), p. 68.
12. Cited in Montgomery and Johnson, *One Step*, p. 133.
13. Barry Goldwater Oral History, June 15, 1967, Oral History Office, Butler Library, Columbia University, pp. 42–43.
14. Quote from Sherman Adams, cited in Montgomery and Johnson, *One Step*, p. 205.
15. *Time*, December 13, 1954.
16. Manchester, *The Glory and the Dream*, p. 667.
17. Hedrick Smith, *The Power Game: How Washington Works* (New York: Random House, 1988), p. 453.
18. Eisenhower diary, June 15, 1954, cited in Reinhard, *The Republican Right*, p. 126.
19. Montgomery and Johnson, *One Step*, p. 137.
20. Malcolm E. Jewell, *Senatorial Politics and Foreign Policy* (Lexington, KY: University of Kentucky Press, 1962), p. 64.
21. James C. Hagerty, *The Diary of James*

## Notes — Chapter 8

*C. Hagerty* (Bloomington: Indiana University Press, 1983), p. 165.
22. Montgomery and Johnson, *One Step*, p. 172.
23. Ibid., pp. 147, 150.
24. William Bragg Ewald, *Who Killed Joe McCarthy?* (New York: Simon and Schuster, 1984), p. 261.
25. White, "The Gentlemen from California," p. 70.
26. Cater, "Knowland: The Man Who Wants to Be Taft, p. 33.
27. Montgomery and Johnson, *One Step*, p. 226.
28. Ibid., pp. 226–227.
29. *Frontier*, October 1958.
30. Montgomery and Johnson, *One Step*, p. 260.
31. Nixon, *Memoirs*, p. 143.
32. Jewett, "My Father's Political Philosophy and Colleagues," p. 18.
33. Jewett, "My Father's Political Philosophy and Colleagues," p. 17.
34. Walter P. Jones, "An Editor's Long Friendship With Earl Warren," *Bee Perspectives on the Warren Era*, Regional Oral History Office, University of California, Berkeley, 1976, p. 32.
35. Cited in Pollack, *Earl Warren* p. 99.
36. Thomas Caldecott, "Perspectives on the Republican Party and the Legislature: A Prominent Assemblyman Reviews the Goodwin Knight Era," Regional Oral History Office, University of California, Berkeley, p. 12.
37. "Nixon — The Real Number Two Man," *U.S. News and World Report*, October 2, 1953.
38. "Nixon: A Political Sinecure Becomes a Success Story," *Newsweek*, October 5, 1953.
39. Manchester, *The Glory and the Dream*, p. 619.
40. "Why Do the Democrats Hate Nixon So Much?" *Washington Post*, September 25, 1955.
41. Ibid.
42. Cited in James J. Rawls and Walton Bean, *California — An Interpretive History* (Boston: McGraw Hill, 1998), p. 366.
43. Cited in Costello, *The Facts About Nixon*, p. 154.
44. Miller, "The Debating Career of Richard Nixon," p. 14–15.
45. Ibid. p. 17.
46. *Newsweek*, November 15, 1954.
47. Nixon, *Memoirs*, p. 163.
48. Alsop, *Nixon and Rockefeller*, p. 46.

49. Richard H. Rovere, "Nixon: Most Likely to Succeed," *Harper's Magazine*, September 1955, pp. 57–63.
50. Emmet John Hughes, *The Ordeal of Power: A Political Memoir of the Eisenhower Years* (New York: Atheneum, 1963), p. 319.
51. Alsop, *Nixon and Rockefeller*, pp. 46, 49–50.
52. The father image is consistent with the comment Nixon made during the fund crisis when Ike demanded that Republicans be "clean as a hound's tooth" (see page 115): "It made me feel like a little boy caught with jam on his face." (Nixon, *Six Crises*, p. 93.).
53. Hughes, *Ordeal of Power*, p. 183.
54. Cited in Manchester, *The Glory and the Dream*, p. 649.
55. Abrahamsen, *Nixon vs Nixon*, p. 168.
56. Woodstone, *Nixon's Head*, p. 33.
57. *U.S. News and World Report*, July 16, 1954.
58. Arnold, *Back When It All Began*, p. 39.
59. Joe Knowland to J. Edgar Hoover, September 27, 1950, Hoover Library, West Branch, IA.
60. Nixon, *Memoirs*, p. 89.
61. Montgomery and Johnson, *One Step*, p. 238.
62. Knebel and Fowler, "He Would Rather Be Right and President."
63. Drew Pearson column, August 1956, William Knowland Papers, Bancroft Library, University of California, Berkeley.
64. Hannah Nixon to Knowland, July 23, 1952, and Knowland reply, September 27, 1952, William Knowland Papers, Bancroft Library, University of California, Berkeley. Knowland's final sentence contained a reference to a just-published article by Pat Nixon entitled, "I Say He's A Wonderful Guy" (*Saturday Evening Post*, October 6, 1952).
65. Knowland to Nixon, November 25, 1952, William Knowland Papers, Bancroft Library.
66. Nixon to Knowland, October 19, 1954, William Knowland Papers, Bancroft Library.
67. Nixon to Knowland, July 12, 1956, and Knowland to Nixon, July 16, 1956, William Knowland Papers, Bancroft Library.
68. Nixon to Knowland, August 27, 1956, and Knowland to Nixon, August 29, 1956, William Knowland Papers, Bancroft Library.
69. *Newsweek*, October 5, 1953.
70. Ambrose, *Nixon*, pp. 334–335.
71. Rovere, "Nixon: Most Likely to Succeed," pp. 58–59.

72. Drew Pearson column, August 1956, in William Knowland Papers, Bancroft Library.

## Chapter 9

1. Phillips, *Big Wayward Girl*, p. 175.
2. *San Francisco Call Bulletin*, unidentified issue, Warren Papers, California State Archives.
3. Warren, *Memoirs*, p. 271.
4. Jackson K. Putnam, *Modern California Politics* (San Francisco: Boyd and Fraser, 1984), p. 42.
5. Richard Richards, "South of the Tehachapis: A Southern California Senator Comments on the 1953–1956 Era," California Legislative Leaders, Vol. 1, *The Goodwin Knight and Edmund G. Brown Eras in California, 1953–1966*, Regional Oral History Office, University of California, Berkeley, 1980, p. 67.
6. *Sacramento Bee*, November 1, 1954.
7. Cited in Bernstein, "Political Leadership in California: A Study of Four Governors," p. 173.
8. "Don Juan in Heaven."
9. Luther H. Lincoln, "Young Turk to Speaker of the California Assembly, 1948–1958," California Legislative Leaders, Vol. 2, *The Goodwin Knight and Edmund G. Brown Eras in California, 1953–1966*, Regional Oral History Office, University of California, Berkeley, 1981, p. 47.
10. "Don Juan in Heaven."
11. Weinberger, "California Assembly," pp. 16, 39–40.
12. Christopher, "Mayor of SF and Republican Party Candidate," p. 6.
13. Knight to Nixon, March 9, 1952, Goodwin Knight Correspondence File, Nixon Pre-Presidential Papers.
14. Knight to Nixon, July 16, 1952, Goodwin Knight Correspondence File, Nixon Pre-Presidential Papers.
15. Knight to Nixon, June 30, 1953, Goodwin Knight Correspondence File, Nixon Pre-Presidential Papers.
16. White, "The Gentlemen from California."
17. Jorgensen, "Richard Nixon's Campaigns," p. 101.
18. Polland, "Personal and Political Friend," p. 30.
19. Champion, "California's Governor Knight," p. 24.
20. Ibid.
21. The Knight papers at Stanford contain a copy of a note to Nixon from Knight on November 7, 1952, acknowledging Nixon's "very kind telegram" following the death of his wife, and another from Nixon to Knight during the 1952 campaign (on August 22) thanking Knight for his help and noting "how helpful you have been to me in the past."
22. Nixon Staff Memorandum, February 23, 1956, Knight Correspondence File, Nixon Pre-Presidential Papers.
23. Jorgensen, "Richard Nixon's Campaigns," pp. 100–101.
24. Martin Hall, "A House Divided: California's GOP," *Frontier*, October 1954.
25. *Los Angeles Examiner*, August 1, 1954.
26. Taylor, "How to Run for Office," p. 80.
27. Caldecott, "Perspectives on the Republican Party," pp. 24–25. After winning this donnybrook, it came as a blow to Knight when Ahmanson later suffered a heart attack and had to resign his party posts. The loss of Ahmanson weakened Knight's hand in the run-up to the 1956 Republican convention.
28. Hall, "A House Divided."
29. Jorgensen to Nixon, August 26, 1954, Frank Jorgensen Correspondence File, Nixon Pre-Presidential Papers.
30. Champion, "California's Governor Knight," p. 24.
31. Ibid., p. 28.
32. Caldecott, "Perspectives on the Republican Party," pp. 28–29.
33. Jorgensen to Nixon, August 26, 1954, Jorgensen File, Nixon Pre-Presidential Papers.
34. Rarick, *California Rising* p. 231.
35. "Don Juan in Heaven."
36. Alsop, *Nixon and Rockefeller*, p. 31.
37. Douglas W. Barrett, "Goodwin Knight's Governor's Office, 1953–1958, and the Youth Authority, 1958–1965," *The Governor's Office Under Goodwin Knight*, Regional Oral History Office, University of California, Berkeley, 1980, pp. 47, 49, 52.
38. *Time*, March 28, 1955.
39. Knowland-Nixon correspondence file, Box 261, William Knowland Papers, Bancroft Library, University of California, Berkeley.
40. Chotiner to Nixon, April 11, 1955, Goodwin Knight Correspondence File, Nixon Pre-Presidential Papers.
41. Palmer to Nixon, August 27, 1954,

January 18, 1955, October 19, 1955, July 17, 1956, Nixon Pre-Presidential Papers. Also cited in Clark, "The 1958 Gubernatorial Election," p. 33.
42. *Los Angeles Times*, June 4, 1955.
43. Nixon to Knight, June 3, 1955, Nixon Pre-Presidential Papers.
44. Pollack, *Earl Warren*, p. 7.
45. Ibid., p. 9.
46. Theodore H. White, *America In Search of Itself: The Making of the President, 1956–1980* (New York: Harper and Row, 1982), p. 63.
47. White, "The Gentlemen from California."
48. Nixon, *Six Crises*, p. 133.
49. Ibid., p. 134.
50. Ibid., p. 143.
51. Hughes, *The Ordeal of Power*, p. 317.
52. Parmet, *Eisenhower*, p. 417.
53. Nixon, *Six Crises*, p. 145.
54. Ibid., p. 147.
55. Parmet, *Eisenhower*, p. 422.
56. "Poor Richard Nixon," *The New Republic*, May 7, 1956.
57. Hughes, *The Ordeal of Power*, p. 173.
58. Nixon, *Six Crises*, p. 159.
59. Ibid., p. 161.
60. Ibid., p. 162.
61. Parmet, *Eisenhower*, p. 433.
62. Earl Mazo, *Richard Nixon: A Political and Personal Portrait* (New York: Harper, 1959), pp. 163–166.
63. At the Democratic National Convention that year, Adlai Stevenson himself opened up the issue of the vice presidency, asking the party to decide.
64. *New York Times*, August 2, 1956.
65. *Time*, October 10, 1955.
66. Associated Press wire service report, October 5, 1955.
67. *U.S. News and World Report*, October 21, 1955.
68. *The Washington Post*, October 11, 1955.
69. *Time*, October 17, 1955.
70. *Fortnight*, Vol. 18, no. 13, November 1955.
71. Letter to Knight from Frank Graham, September 28, 1955, Goodwin Knight Papers, Stanford University, Palo Alto.
72. Day to Nixon, October 19, 1955, in Roy Day File, Richard Nixon Pre-Presidential Papers.
73. Jorgensen to Nixon, October 3, 1955, Frank Jorgensen Correspondence File, Nixon Pre-Presidential Papers (emphasis in original).
74. Champion, "California's Governor Knight," p. 20.
75. Letter from Whitaker and Baxter to Bernard Taper, Editorial Department, *The New Yorker*, June 21, 1956, Goodwin Knight Papers, Stanford University, Palo Alto.
76. See, for example, Samuel Lubell in the *Wall Street Journal*, October 25, 1955.
77. Virginia Knight, "California's First Lady, 1954–1958," *The Goodwin Knight and Edmund G. Brown Eras in California, 1953–1966*, Regional Oral History Office, University of California, Berkeley, 1981, p. 22.
78. Virginia Knight, "California's First Lady," p. 24.
79. Caldecott, "Perspectives on the Republican Party," p. 14.
80. Brown, "Years of Growth," p. 190.
81. Champion, "California's Governor Knight," p. 20.
82. Holmes Alexander, "A Statesman's Seasoning," *Los Angeles Times*, July 21, 1954.
83. Montgomery and Johnson, *One Step*, p. 196.
84. William S. White, "What Bill Knowland Stands For," *The New Republic*, February 27, 1956.
85. Knebel and Fowler, "He Would Rather Be Right and President."
86. *Sacramento Bee*, June 8, 1955.
87. Costello, *The Facts About Nixon*, p. 145.
88. "Face the Nation," interview transcript, William Knowland Correspondence File, Nixon Pre-Presidential Papers.
89. Montgomery and Johnson, *One Step*, p. 196.
90. Ibid., pp. 195–196.
91. Dwight Eisenhower, *The Eisenhower Diaries* (New York: Norton and Norton, 1981), p. 291.
92. Ibid., p. 314.
93. Jewett, "My Father's Political Philosophy," p. 15.
94. *Los Angeles Herald Express*, August 17, 1955.
95. Undated note attached to the August 17, 1955, *Herald Express* clipping, Nixon Pre-Presidential Papers.
96. Nixon to Knight, February 23, 1956, Nixon Pre-Presidential Papers.
97. Tom Caldecott, "Perspectives on the Republican Party," p. 27.
98. Nixon, *Memoirs*, p. 173.
99. Montgomery and Johnson, *One Step*, p. 198.

100. *U.S. News and World Report*, July 14, 1956.
101. Nixon, *Memoirs*, p. 174.
102. Adams vigorously denied being involved in any anti–Nixon bloc. There was no reason, he said, to change a winning ticket (Adams, *Firsthand Report*, p. 232.).
103. William Knowland Oral History, Oral History Office, Columbia University, p. 82.
104. Charles A. H. Thompson and Frances M. Shattuck, *The 1956 Presidential Campaign* (Washington, DC: The Brookings Institution, 1960), p. 185. Nixon made no mention of Knight in his memoirs.
105. Lincoln, "Young Turk to Speaker," p. 47.
106. *Washington Star*, August 19, 1956.
107. Lincoln, "Young Turk to Speaker," p. 47.
108. Frank Jorgensen, "Richard Nixon's Campaigns," pp. 100–101.
109. *San Francisco Chronicle*, August 19, 1956.
110. Barrett, "Goodwin Knight's Governor's Office," p, 55.
111. Button, "California Republican Party Official," p. 21.
112. Nixon to Knight, August 23, 1956, Goodwin Knight Papers, Stanford University, Palo Alto.
113. Fletcher Knebel, "Did Ike Really Want Nixon?" *Look*, October 30, 1956.
114. Hannah Nixon to Goodwin Knight, October 9, 1956, Goodwin Knight Papers, Stanford University, Palo Alto.
115. Barrett, "Goodwin Knight's Governor's Office," pp. 49, 53.
116. Nixon to Knight, September 17, 1956, Goodwin Knight Papers, Stanford University, Palo Alto.
117. Nixon to Knight, September 19, 1956, Goodwin Knight Papers, Stanford University, Palo Alto.
118. *New York Times*, April 4, 1971. Cited in Mazlish, *In Search of Nixon*, p. 100.
119. Estelle Knowland Johnson, "My Father as Senator," p. 14.
120. Nixon, *Memoirs*, p. 174.

## Chapter 10

1. *Los Angeles Times*, November 2, 1958.
2. *Sacramento Bee*, January 8, 1957.
3. Jewett, "My Father's Political Philosophy," p. 4.
4. Barrett, "Goodwin Knight's Governor's Office," p. 59.
5. Jewett, "My Father's Political Philosophy," p. 3.
6. Polland, "Political and Personal Friend," p. 31.
7. Leary, "A Journalist's Perspective," p. 30.
8. Schuparra, *The Triumph of the Right*, p. 166.
9. Memo from Nixon aide to journalist Roscoe Drummond, June 25, 1958, Nixon Pre-Presidential Papers.
10. Caldecott, "Perspectives on the Republican Party," p. 30.
11. Montgomery and Johnson, *One Step*, p. 233.
12. Brown, "Years of Growth," p. 237.
13. *San Francisco Examiner*, September 1, 1957.
14. Halberstam, *The Powers That Be*, p. 264.
15. Virginia Knight, "California's First Lady," p. 26.
16. Hill, *Dancing Bear*, p. 146.
17. *Washington Daily News*, April 10, 1959.
18. Jewett, "My Father's Political Philosophy," p. 5.
19. Montgomery and Johnson, *One Step*, p. 234.
20. Cited in Bernstein, *Political Leadership in California*, pp. 186–187.
21. *San Francisco Examiner*, September 17, 1957.
22. Gottlieb and Wolt, *Thinking Big*, p. 282.
23. *Los Angeles Times*, January 20, 1957.
24. Ibid., August 21, 1955.
25. Ronnie Dugger, "Politics in California," *The New Republic*, June 23, 1958, p. 12.
26. Both quotes from Ambrose, *Nixon*, p. 446.
27. Nixon to Jorgensen, August 20, 1957, Frank Jorgensen Correspondence File, Nixon Pre-Presidential Papers.
28. Nixon staff note to field, August 30, 1957, Frank Jorgensen Correspondence File, Nixon Pre-Presidential Papers.
29. Nixon to Jorgensen and others, September 19, 1957, Frank Jorgensen File, Nixon Pre-Presidential Papers.
30. Barrett, "Goodwin Knight's Governor's Office," p. 59.

## Notes — Chapter 10

31. Virginia Knight, "California's First Lady," p. 30.
32. Fulton Lewis, Jr., column, April 14, 1957.
33. *Los Angeles Examiner*, March 27, 1957.
34. Knight to Nixon, May 30, 1957, Goodwin Knight Correspondence File, Nixon Pre-Presidential Papers.
35. Halberstam, *The Powers That Be*, p. 264.
36. Virginia Knight, "California's First Lady," p. 29.
37. Halberstam, *The Powers That Be*, p. 265.
38. Gottlieb and Wolt, *Thinking Big*, p. 284.
39. Clark, "The 1958 Gubernatorial Election," p. 56.
40. Tom M. Bright, "The Governor's Office of Goodwin J. Knight, 1953–1958," The Governor's Office Under Goodwin Knight, *The Goodwin Knight and Edmund G. Brown Eras in California, 1953–1966*, 1980, p. 29.
41. Frank D. Lanterman, "Crusades of a Republican Legislative Leader, 1951–1978: Water, Mental Health, Education, Ways and Means," *California Legislative Leaders*, Vol. 1, Regional Oral History Office, University of California, Berkeley, 1980, p. 57.
42. Alsop, "The Great California Drama," p. 103.
43. Whitaker oral history, California State Archives, p. 52.
44. Virginia Knight, "California's First Lady," pp. 26–27.
45. Maryalice Lemmon, "Working in the Governor's Office, 1950–1959," The Governor's Office Under Goodwin Knight, *The Goodwin Knight and Edmund G. Brown Eras in California, 1953–1966*, Regional Oral History Office, University of California, Berkeley, 1980, p. 31.
46. Barrett, "Goodwin Knight's Governor's Office," p. 68.
47. Virginia Knight, "California's First Lady," p. 27.
48. Halberstam, *The Powers That Be*, pp. 265–266.
49. Dugger, "Politics in California," p. 12.
50. Montgomery and Johnson, *One Step*, p. 243.
51. It will be recalled that Knight had also been advised to act "in the best interest of the party" when he was forced from the 1950 gubernatorial primary against Earl Warren (see p. 58).
52. Bright, "The Governor's Office of Goodwin J. Knight," p. 30.
53. *Christian Science Monitor*, West Coast edition, November 7, 1958.
54. *San Francisco Chronicle*, November 2, 1957.
55. *Los Angeles Herald Express*, November 19, 1958.
56. *San Francisco Chronicle*, November 7, 1957.
57. Helen Knowland undated letter to unnamed journalists, Nixon Pre-Presidential Papers.
58. Montgomery and Johnson, *One Step*, p. 243.
59. Ibid., p. 242.
60. Whitaker oral history, California State Archives, p. 54.
61. Harry Finks, "California Labor and Goodwin Knight, the 1950s," *Goodwin Knight: Aides, Advisers and Appointees*, Regional Oral History Office, University of California, Berkeley, 1981, p. 34.
62. Whitaker oral history, California State Archives, p. 180.
63. Vernon Cristina, "A Northern Californian Views Conservative Politics and Policies, 1963–1970," Republican Campaigns and Party Issues, 1964–1976, *The Ronald Reagan Era in California, 1966–1974*, Regional Oral History Office, University of California, Berkeley, 1986, p. 5.
64. Polland, "Political and Personal Friend," pp. 31–32.
65. Virginia Knight, "California's First Lady," p. 28.
66. Ibid.
67. Barrett, "Goodwin Knight's Governor's Office," pp. 66–67.
68. Whitaker oral history, California State Archives, pp. 52–53.
69. Christopher, "Mayor of San Francisco," p. 5.
70. Brown, "Years of Growth," p. 245.
71. *San Francisco Chronicle*, May 10, 1958.
72. Dugger, "Politics in California."
73. Jorgensen to Nixon, November 12, 1957, Frank Jorgensen Correspondence File, Nixon Pre-Presidential Papers.
74. Phone call from Clint Mosher to Nixon, September 9, 1957, Nixon Pre-Presidential Papers.
75. Montgomery and Johnson, *One Step*, p. 236.
76. Cited in Montgomery and Johnson, *One Step*, p. 239.

77. Montgomery and Johnson, *One Step*, p. 241.
78. Leary, "A Journalist's Perspective," p. 37.
79. Hill, *Dancing Bear*, p. 157.
80. Rarick, *California Rising*. p. 100.
81. Brown, "Years of Growth," p. 250.
82. Whitaker oral history, California State Archives, p. 53.
83. *Sacramento Bee*, June 9, 1958.
84. Estelle Knowland, "My Father as Senator, Campaigner and Civic Leader," p. 9.
85. Ambrose, *Nixon*, p. 447.
86. Nixon to Knight, March 12, 1958, Nixon Pre-Presidential Papers.
87. Knight call to Nixon, March 18, 1958, Nixon Pre-Presidential Papers.
88. Nixon, *Memoirs*, p. 199.
89. Quoted in Montgomery and Johnson, *One Step*, p. 248.
90. Totten J. Anderson, "The 1958 Election in California," *The Western Political Quarterly*, March 1959, p. 288.
91. Montgomery and Johnson, *One Step*, p. 252.
92. *Los Angeles Times*, October 22, 1958.
93. Gottlieb and Wolt, *Thinking Big*, p. 285.
94. Richard Rodda, "From the Capitol Press Room," Bee *Perspectives on the Warren Era*, Regional Oral History Office, University of California, Berkeley, 1976, p. 13.
95. Halberstam, *The Powers That Be*, p. 266.
96. Cited in Hill, *Dancing Bear*, p. 149.
97. *Sacramento Bee*, November 6, 1958.
98. Ibid., November 26, 1958.
99. *Los Angeles Times*, November 9, 1958.

## Epilogue

1. *Washington Daily News*, April 10, 1959.
2. Knight to Nixon, May 15, 1958, Goodwin Knight Papers, Stanford University, Palo Alto.
3. Nixon to Knight, November 7, 1958, Goodwin Knight Papers, Stanford University, Palo Alto.
4. Nixon to Knight, April 21, 1960, Knight Personality Files, Nixon folder, Goodwin Knight Papers, Stanford University, Palo Alto.
5. Knight to Nixon, December 31, 1960, Knight Personality Files, Nixon folder, Goodwin Knight Papers, Stanford University, Palo Alto.
6. Barrett, "The Governor's Office Under Goodwin Knight," p. 71.
7. *Newsweek*, August 7, 1961.
8. Knight to Mason, February 16, 1961, Goodwin Knight Papers, Stanford University, Palo Alto.
9. Knight to Mason, April 28, 1961, Goodwin Knight Papers, Stanford University, Palo Alto.
10. Knight interview on *Kaleidoscope* radio show, KNX, November 3, 1961, Nixon Pre-Presidential Papers.
11. Nixon to Knight, January 17, 1962, Earl Warren Papers, California State Archives, Sacramento.
12. Knight to Mason, November 1, 1962, Goodwin Knight Papers, Stanford University, Palo Alto.
13. Knight to Mason, June 7, 1963, Goodwin Knight Papers, Stanford University, Palo Alto.
14. Mason, "The Governor's Office Under Goodwin Knight," p. 91.
15. Polland, "Goodwin Knight: Aides, Advisors and Appointees," p. 36.
16. Jewett, "My Father's Political Philosophy," p. 12.
17. Montgomery and Johnson, *One Step*, pp. 267–268.
18. Knight to Mason, June 7, 1963, Goodwin Knight Papers, Stanford University, Palo Alto.
19. Small, "The Office of the Governor Under Earl Warren," pp. 92, 202.
20. Nixon, *Memoirs*, p. 418.
21. Cray, *Chief Justice*, p. 340.
22. *Los Angeles Examiner*, June 30, 1959.
23. Warren, *Memoirs*, p. 343.
24. Interview transcript, April 20, 1961, Nixon Pre-Presidential Papers.
25. Cray, *Chief Justice*, p. 215.
26. Ibid., p. 398; Matthews, *Kennedy and Nixon*, p. 218.
27. Cray, *Chief Justice*, p. 505.
28. Newton, *Justice for All*, p. 250.
29. *New York Times*, June 24, 1969.
30. Alden Whitman, "Alden Whitman's Golden Oldies," *Esquire*, April 1975, p. 83.
31. Halberstam, *The Powers That Be*, p. 333.
32. Matthews, *Kennedy and Nixon*, p. 208.
33. Arthur Schlesinger, *Journals: 1952–2000* (New York: Penguin Press, 2007), p. 132.
34. Brown, "Years of Growth," p. 245.

35. Manolis, "A Friend and Aide Reminisces," p. 14.
36. Hughes, *The Ordeal of Power*, pp. 315, 318–319.
37. Nixon, *Memoirs,* pp. 73, 112.
38. Ibid., p. 146.
39. Ibid., p. 177.
40. Ibid., pp. 177–178.
41. Alsop, *Nixon and Rockefeller*, p. 197.
42. Earl Mazo, *New York Herald Tribune*, October 3, 1955.
43. Polland, "Political and Personal Friend," p. 30.

# Bibliography

## Unpublished Sources

### Dissertations and Theses

Bernstein, Melvin Harry. *Political Leadership in California: A Study of Four Governors.* Ph.D. diss., University of California at Los Angeles, 1970.

Clark, Ray Leon. *The 1958 Gubernatorial Election: How Republican Infighting Affected the Outcome.* Master's thesis, California State University, Long Beach, 1999.

Henderson, Lloyd Ray. *Earl Warren and California Politics.* Ph.D. diss., University of California, Berkeley, 1965.

### Oral History Transcripts

Adams, Earl. "Financing Richard Nixon's Campaigns from 1946 to 1960." *Richard M. Nixon in the Warren Era,* Regional Oral History Office, University of California, Berkeley, 1975.

Barrett, Douglas W. "Goodwin Knight's Governor's Office, 1953–1958, and the Youth Authority, 1958–1965." *The Governor's Office Under Goodwin Knight,* Regional Oral History Office, University of California, Berkeley, 1980.

Behrens, Earl C. "Gubernatorial Campaigns and Party Issues: A Political Reporter's View, 1948–1966." *Reporting from Sacramento,* Regional Oral History Office, University of California, Berkeley, 1981.

Bradley, Donald L. "Managing Democratic Campaigns, 1954–1966." *The Goodwin Knight and Edmund G. Brown Eras in California, 1953–1966,* Regional Oral History Office, University of California, Berkeley, 1982.

Bright, Tom M. "The Governor's Office of Goodwin J. Knight, 1953–1958." *The Goodwin Knight and Edmund G. Brown Eras in California, 1953–1966,* Regional Oral History Office, University of California, Berkeley, 1980.

Brown, Edmund G. "The Governor's Lawyer." *Earl Warren: Fellow Constitutional Officers,* Earl Warren Oral History Project, Regional Oral History Office, University of California, Berkeley, 1979.

———. "Years of Growth, 1939–1966: Law Enforcement, Politics and the Governor's Office." *Goodwin Knight and Edmund G. Brown Eras in California, 1953–1966,* Regional Oral History Office, University of California, Berkeley, 1982.

Button, Ronald A. "California Republican Party Official and State Treasurer of California, 1956–1958." *California Constitutional Officers, Goodwin Knight and Edmund G. Brown Eras in California, 1953–1966,* Regional Oral History Office, University of California, Berkeley, 1980.

Caldecott, Thomas. "Perspectives on the Republican Party and the Legislature: A Prominent Assemblyman Reviews the Goodwin Knight Era." Regional Oral History Office, University of California, Berkeley, 1979.

Case, Clifford. Oral History, Lyndon Baines Johnson Library, Austin, Texas.

Christopher, George. "Mayor of San Francisco and Republican Party Candidate." In *San Francisco Republicans, Goodwin Knight and Edmund G. Brown Eras in California, 1953–1966,* Regional Oral History

Office, University of California, Berkeley, 1980.

Clifton, Florence. "California Democrats, 1934–1950." *California Democrats in the Earl Warren Era*, Regional Oral History Office, University of California, Berkeley, 1976.

Cristina, Vernon. "A Northern Californian Views Conservative Politics and Policies, 1963–1970." Republican Campaigns and Party Issues, 1964–1976, *The Ronald Reagan Era in California, 1966–1974*, Regional Oral History Office, University of California, Berkeley, 1986.

Cunningham, Thomas J. "Southern California Campaign Chairman for Earl Warren, 1946." *Earl Warren's Campaigns*, Vol. I, Regional Oral History Office, University of California, Berkeley, 1976.

Dutton, Fred. "Domestic Campaigns and Controversies, 1954–1966." *The Goodwin Knight and Edmund G. Brown Eras in California, 1953–1966*, Regional Oral History Office, University of California, Berkeley, 1981.

Faries, McIntyre. "California Republicans, 1934–1953." *Earl Warren's Campaigns*, Vol. 2, Regional Oral History Office, University of California, Berkeley, 1973.

Finks, Harry. "California Labor and Goodwin Knight, the 1950s." *Goodwin Knight: Aides, Advisers and Appointees*, Regional Oral History Office, University of California, Berkeley, 1981.

Goldwater, Barry. Oral History, June 15, 1967, Oral History Office, Butler Library, Columbia University.

Hansen, Victor. "West Coast Defense During World War II; The California Gubernatorial Campaign of 1960." *Earl Warren's Campaigns*, Vol. II, Regional Oral History Office, University of California, Berkeley, 1977.

Jahnsen, Oscar J. "Enforcing the Law Against Gambling, Bootlegging, Graft, Fraud, and Subversion, 1922–1942." *The Earl Warren Era in California*, Regional Oral History Office, University of California, Berkeley, 1976.

Jewett, Emelyn Knowland. "My Father's Political Philosophy and Colleagues." *Remembering William Knowland*, Regional Oral History Office, University of California, Berkeley, 1981.

Johnson, Hon. Gardiner. Oral History, State Government Oral History Program, California State Archives, 1973, 1983.

Johnson, Estelle Knowland. "My Father as Senator, Campaigner and Civic Leader." *Remembering William Knowland*, Regional Oral History Office, University of California, Berkeley, 1981.

Jones, Walter P. "An Editor's Long Friendship With Earl Warren." *Bee Perspectives on the Warren Era*, Regional Oral History Office, University of California, Berkeley, 1976.

Jorgensen, Frank E. "The Organization of Richard Nixon's Congressional Campaigns, 1946–1952." *Richard M. Nixon in the Warren Era*, Regional Oral History Office, University of California, Berkeley, 1980.

Knight, Virginia. "California's First Lady, 1954–1958." *The Goodwin Knight and Edmund G. Brown Eras in California, 1953–1966*, Regional Oral History Office, University of California, Berkeley, 1981.

Kuchel, Thomas H. "California State Controller." *Earl Warren: Fellow Constitutional Officers*, Regional Oral History Office, University of California, Berkeley, 1979.

Lanterman, Frank D. "Crusades of a Republican Legislative Leader, 1951–1978: Water, Mental Health, Education, Ways and Means." *California Legislative Leaders*, Vol. 1, Regional Oral History Office, University of California, Berkeley, 1980.

Leary, Mary Ellen. "A Journalist's Perspective: Government and Politics in California and the Bay Area." *Goodwin Knight and Edmund G. Brown Eras in California, 1953–1966*, Regional Oral History Office, University of California, Berkeley, 1981.

Lemmon, Maryalice. "Working in the Governor's Office, 1950–1959." The Governor's Office Under Goodwin Knight, *The Goodwin Knight and Edmund G. Brown Eras in California, 1953–1966*, Regional Oral History Office, University of California, Berkeley, 1980.

Lincoln, Luther H. "Young Turk to Speaker of the California Assembly, 1948–1958." California Legislative Leaders, Vol. 2, *The Goodwin Knight and Edmund G. Brown Eras in California, 1953–1966*, Regional Oral History Office, University of California, Berkeley, 1981.

Lynch, Thomas C. "A Career in Politics and the Attorney General's Office." *Goodwin Knight and Edmund G. Brown Eras in California, 1953–1966*, Regional Oral History Office, University of California, Berkeley, 1982.

Manolis, Paul. "A Friend and Aide Reminisces." *Remembering William Knowland*, Regional Oral History Office, University of California, Berkeley, 1981.

Mason, Paul. "Covering the Legislature for Governor Goodwin J. Knight." The Governor's Office Under Goodwin Knight, *The Goodwin Knight and Edmund G. Brown Eras in California, 1953–1966*, Regional Oral History Office, University of California, Berkeley, 1980.

McConnell, Geraldine. "Governor Warren, the Knowlands and Columbia State Park." *Earl Warren: Views and Episodes*, Regional Oral History Office, University of California, Berkeley, 1976.

McCormac, Keith. "The Conservative Republicans of 1952." *Earl Warren's Campaigns*, Vol. III, Regional Oral History Office, University of California, Berkeley, 1978.

Mellon, Thomas J. "Republican Campaigns of 1950 and 1952." *Earl Warren's Campaigns*, Vol. 2, Regional Oral History Office, University of California, Berkeley, 1977.

Polland, Milton R. "Political and Personal Friend of Earl Warren, Goodwin Knight and Hubert Humphrey." *Goodwin Knight: Aides, Advisors and Appointees*, Regional Oral History Office, University of California, Berkeley, 1977–79.

Powers, Harold J. "On Prominent Issues, The Republican Party, and Political Campaigns: A Veteran Republican Views the Goodwin Knight Era." *California Constitutional Officers*, Regional Oral History Office, University of California, Berkeley, 1980.

Richards, Richard. "South of the Tehachapis: A Southern California Senator Comments on the 1953–1956 Era." California Legislative Leaders, Vol. 1, *The Goodwin Knight and Edmund G. Brown Eras in California, 1953–1966*, Regional Oral History Office, University of California, Berkeley, 1980.

Rodda, Richard. "From the Capitol Press Room." *Bee Perspectives on the Warren Era*, Regional Oral History Office, University of California, Berkeley, 1976.

Schulte, Renee, ed. "The Young Nixon: An Oral Inquiry." Richard M. Nixon Project, Oral History Program, California State University, Fullerton, 1978.

Small, Merrell Farnham. "The Office of the Governor Under Earl Warren." *The Earl Warren Era in California, 1925–1953*, Regional Oral History Office, University of California, Berkeley, 1972.

Warren, Earl. "Conversations with Earl Warren on California Government." *The Earl Warren Era in California, 1925–1953*, Regional Oral History Office, University of California, Berkeley, 1981.

Warren, Earl, Jr. "California Politics." *The Governor's Family*, Regional Oral History Office, University of California, Berkeley, 1980.

Weinberger, Caspar. "California Assembly, Republican State Central Committee, and Elections, 1953–1966." San Francisco Republicans, *Goodwin Knight and Edmund G. Brown Eras in California, 1953–1966*, Regional Oral History Office, University of California, Berkeley, 1980.

Whitaker, Clement Sherman, Jr. Oral History, State Government Oral History Program, California State Archives, Sacramento, 1988–1989.

## Archival Papers

"Republican National Convention: Notes of Paul H. Davis." Hoover Institution Archives, Stanford University, Palo Alto.

Goodwin Knight Papers. Green Library, Stanford University, Palo Alto.

William Knowland Papers. Bancroft Library, University of California, Berkeley.

Richard Nixon Pre-Presidential Papers. Richard Nixon Library, Yorba Linda.

Small, Merrell. Introduction to the Earl Warren Papers, California State Archives Website.

Small, M. F. "The Country Editor." Unpublished manuscript, Bancroft Library, Universioty of California Berkeley.

Earl Warren Papers. California State Archives, Sacramento.

## *Published Sources*

### Books

Abrahamsen, David. *Nixon vs. Nixon: An Emotional Tragedy*. New York: Farrar, Straus and Giroux, 1976.

Adams, Sherman. *Firsthand Report: The Story of the Eisenhower Administration*. New York: Harper and Bros., 1961.

Alsop, Stewart, *Nixon and Rockefeller: A Double Portrait*. Garden City, NY: Doubleday, 1960.

# Bibliography

Ambrose, Stephen E. *Nixon: The Education of a Politician, 1913–1962.* New York: Simon and Schuster, 1987.

Arnold, William A. *Back When It All Began: The Early Nixon Years.* New York: Vantage Press, 1975.

Brodie, Fawn M. *Richard Nixon: The Shaping of His Character.* New York: Norton, 1981.

Bullock, Paul. *Jerry Voorhis: The Idealist as Politician.* New York: Vantage Press, 1978.

Costello, William. *The Facts About Nixon: An Unauthorized Biography.* New York: Viking Press, 1960.

Cray, Ed. *Chief Justice: A Biography of Earl Warren.* New York: Simon & Schuster, 1997.

David, Lester. *The Lonely Lady of San Clemente: The Story of Pat Nixon.* New York: Crowell, 1978.

Delmatier, Royce, Clarence F. McIntosh, and Earl G. Waters. *The Rumble of California Politics, 1848–1970.* New York: Wiley and Sons, 1970.

Douglas, Helen Gahagan. *A Full Life.* Garden City, NY: Doubleday, 1982.

Eisenhower, Dwight D. *The Eisenhower Diaries.* New York: Norton and Norton, 1981.

Ewald, William Bragg. *Eisenhower the President: Crucial Days, 1951–1960.* Englewood Cliffs, NJ: Prentice-Hall, 1981.

Ferrell, Robert H., ed. *Off the Record: The Private Papers of Harry S. Truman.* New York: Harper and Row, 1980.

Fowle, Eleanor. *Cranston: The Senator from California.* San Rafael, CA: Presidio Press, 1980.

Gellman, Irwin F. *The Contender: Richard Nixon, The Congress Years, 1946–1952.* New York: The Free Press, 1999.

Goldwater, Barry M. *With No Apologies: The Personal and Political Memoirs of United States Senator Barry M. Goldwater.* New York: Morrow, 1979.

Gottlieb, Robert, and Irene Wolt. *Thinking Big: The Story of the Los Angeles Times, Its Publishers, and Their Influence on Southern California.* New York: G.P. Putnam's Sons, 1977.

Hagerty, James C. *The Diary of James C. Hagerty.* Bloomington: Indiana University Press, 1983.

Halberstam, David. *The Powers That Be.* New York: Knopf, 1979.

Harvey, Richard B. *Earl Warren: Governor of California.* New York: Exposition Press, 1969.

Hill, Gladwin. *Dancing Bear: An Inside Look at California Politics.* New York: Wiley, 1970.

Hoyt, Edwin P. *The Nixons: An American Family.* New York: Random House, 1972.

Hughes, Emmet John. *The Ordeal of Power: A Political Memoir of the Eisenhower Years.* New York: Atheneum, 1963.

Jewell, Malcolm E. *Senatorial Politics and Foreign Policy.* Lexington, KY: University of Kentucky Press, 1962.

Katcher, Leo. *Earl Warren: A Political Biography.* New York: McGraw-Hill, 1967.

Kornitzer, Bela. *The Real Nixon: An Intimate Biography.* New York: Rand McNally, 1960.

Lyon, Peter. *Eisenhower: Portrait of the Hero.* Boston: Little, Brown, 1974.

Manchester, William. *The Glory and the Dream: A Narrative History of America, 1932–1972.* Boston: Little, Brown, 1973.

Mankiewicz, Frank. *Perfectly Clear: Nixon from Whittier to Watergate.* New York: Quadrangle/The New York Times Book Company, 1973.

Matthews, Christopher. *Kennedy and Nixon: The Rivalry That Shaped Postwar America.* New York: Simon and Schuster, 1996.

Mazlish, Bruce. *In Search of Nixon: A Psychohistorical Inquiry.* New York: Basic Books, 1972.

Mazo, Earl. *Richard Nixon: A Political and Personal Portrait.* New York: Harper, 1959.

_____, and Stephen Hess. *Nixon: A Political Portrait.* New York: Harper and Row, 1968.

McWilliams, Carey. *California: The Great Exception.* New York: Wyn, 1949.

Melendy, H. Brett, and Benjamin F. Gilbert. *The Governors of California: Peter H. Burnett to Edmund G. Brown.* Georgetown, CA: Talisman Press, 1965.

Mitchell, Greg. *Tricky Dick and the Pink Lady: Richard Nixon vs. Helen Gahagan Douglas — Sexual Politics and the Red Scare, 1950.* New York: Random House, 1998.

Montgomery, Gayle B., and James W. Johnson. *One Step from the White House: The Rise and Fall of Senator William F. Knowland.* Berkeley: University of California Press, 1998.

Mooney, Booth. *The Politicians: 1945–1960.* Philadelphia: Lippincott, 1970.

Morris, Roger. *Richard Milhous Nixon: The Rise of An American Politician.* New York: Holt, 1990.

Newton, Jim. *Justice for All: Earl Warren and the Nation He Made.* New York: Riverhead Books, 2006.

Nixon, Richard M. *RN: The Memoirs of Richard Nixon.* New York: Grosset and Dunlap, 1978.
———. *Six Crises.* Garden City, NY: Doubleday, 1962.
Parmet, Herbert. *Eisenhower and the American Crusades.* New York: Macmillan, 1972.
———. *Richard Nixon: An American Enigma.* New York: Pearson and Longman, 2008.
Pearson, Drew. *Diaries.* New York: Holt, Rinehart & Winston, 1974.
Phillips, Herbert L. *Big Wayward Girl: An Informal Political History of California.* Garden City, NY: Doubleday, 1968.
Pollack, Jack Harrison. *Earl Warren: The Judge Who Changed America.* Englewood Cliffs, NJ: Prentice-Hall, 1979.
Putnam, Jackson K. *Modern California Politics.* San Francisco: Boyd and Fraser, 1984.
Rapoport, Roger. *California Dreaming: The Political Odyssey of Pat and Jerry Brown.* Berkeley, CA: Nolo Press, 1982.
Rarick, Ethan. *California Rising: The Life and Times of Pat Brown.* Berkeley: University of California Press, 2005.
Rawls, James J., and Walton Bean. *California—An Interpretive History.* Boston: McGraw Hill, 1998.
Reichley, James. *States in Crisis: Politics in Ten American States, 1950–1962.* Chapel Hill: University of North Carolina Press, 1964.
Reinhard, David W. *The Republican Right Since 1945.* Lexington: University Press of Kentucky, 1983.
Schlesinger, Arthur. *Journals: 1952–2000.* New York: Penguin Press, 2007.
Schuparra, Kurt. *The Triumph of the Right: The Rise of the California Conservative Movement.* Armonk, NY: Sharpe, 1998.
Smith, Hedrick. *The Power Game: How Washington Works.* New York: Random House, 1988.
Starr, Kevin. *Embattled Dreams: California in War and Peace.* New York: Oxford University Press, 2002.
———. *Golden Dreams: California in an Age of Abundance, 1950–1963.* New York: Oxford University Press.
Thompson, Charles A. H., and Frances M. Shattuck. *The 1956 Presidential Campaign.* Washington, DC: Brookings Institution, 1960.
Volkan, Vamik, Norman Itzkowitz, and Andrew D. Dod. *Richard Nixon: A Psychobiography.* New York: Columbia University Press, 1997.
Warren, Earl. *The Memoirs of Earl Warren.* Garden City, NY: Doubleday, 1977.
Weaver, John. *Warren: The Man, The Court, The Era.* Boston: Little, Brown, 1967.
White, G. Edward. *Earl Warren: A Public Life.* New York: Oxford University Press, 1982.
White, Theodore H. *America In Search of Itself: The Making of the President, 1956–1980.* New York: Harper and Row, 1982.
Wills, Garry. *Nixon Agonistes: The Crisis of the Self-Made Man.* Boston: Houghton Mifflin, 1970.
Woodstone, Arthur. *Nixon's Head.* New York: St. Martin's Press, 1972.

## Articles

Alsop, Stuart. "The Great California Drama." *Saturday Evening Post*, October 18, 1958.
Anderson, Totten J. "The 1958 Election in California." *The Western Political Quarterly* (March 1959).
Brashear, Ernest. "Who Is Richard Nixon?" *The New Republic*, September 1, 1952.
"California, Here It Comes for Big Stakes." *Life*, September 30, 1957.
"California: Key to '56?" *U.S. News and World Report*, October 14, 1955.
Cater, Douglas. "Knowland: The Man Who Wants to Be Taft." *The Reporter*, March 8, 1956.
Champion, Hale. "California's Governor Knight: Balance of Republican Power?" *The Reporter*, February 23, 1956.
Clark, Albert. "Presidential Hopeful Gamble: That Nation is More Conservative than the 'New' GOP." *Wall Street Journal*, March 5, 1957.
"Don Juan in Heaven." *Time*, May 30, 1955.
Donovan, Richard. "Birth of a Salesman." *The Reporter*, October 14, 1952.
Dugger, Ronnie. "Mr. Knowland's Opponent." *The New Republic*, June 30, 1958.
———. "Politics in California." *The New Republic*, June 23, 1958.
Elstob, Carolyn. "All to the Good." *Game and Gossip.*
"'56 Nears, Nixon-Knowland Rivalry Grows." *U.S. News and World Report*, July 16, 1954.
"Four Men on a Dark Horse." *Fortnight*, December 1955.
Friedman, Ralph. "The Gay Beaver." *Frontier*, June 1958.
"Goodwin Knight: Will He Run?" *Fortnight*, January 1950.

Hall, Martin. "A House Divided: California's GOP." *Frontier*, October 1954.
Harrison, Gordon. "Warren of California." *Harper's Magazine*, June 1952.
Haveman, Ernest. "California's Excellency Excels at Jokes as Well as Politics." *Life*, March 29, 1954.
Healy, Paul. "The Grim Senator from California." *Saturday Evening Post*, April 25, 1953.
Hinderaker, Ivan. "The 1952 Elections in California." *Western Political Quarterly,* March 1953.
Isaacs, Stanley P. "Knight Over California." *The Nation*, May 29, 1954.
Keller, William J. "What Governor Knight Thinks of His Party." *Frontier*, September 1958.
Kenny, Robert. "The Crisis Nixon Forgot." *Frontier*, April 1962.
Kerby, Phil. "Richard Nixon Charts His Own Course." *Frontier*, June 1956.
Knebel, Fletcher. "Did Ike Really Want Nixon?" *Look*, October 30, 1956.
_____, and Dan Fowler. "He Would Rather Be Right and President." *Look*, April 5, 1955.
Kossen, Sydney. "Nixon Gives Goodie the Cold Shoulder." *San Francisco News*, October 15, 1958.
Kurland, Philip B. "Earl Warren: Master of the Revels." *Harvard Law Review* 96, no. 1 (1982).
Lubell, Samuel. "Who Will Take California?" *Saturday Evening Post*, October 20, 1956.
McWilliams, Carey. "Bungling in California." *The Nation*, November 4, 1950.
_____. "Government By Whitaker and Baxter." *The Nation*, April 14, 1951.
Miller, William Lee. "The Debating Career of Richard M. Nixon." *The Reporter*, April 19, 1956.
Moley, Raymond. "Knight's Predicament." *Newsweek*, September 9, 1957.
_____, "Knowland, Nixon and Knight." *Time*, October 10, 1958.
_____. "Nixon vs Douglas." *Newsweek*, August 28, 1950.
Morris, Joe Alex. "I Say He's a Wonderful Guy." *Saturday Evening Post*, October 6, 1952.
"Nixon: A Political Sinecure Becomes a Success Story." *Newsweek*, October 5, 1953.
"Nixon or Not: It's Up to Ike." *U.S. News and World Report*, March 16, 1956.
"Nixon — The Real Number Two Man." *U.S. News and World Report*, October 2, 1953.
"Only One More Place to Go." *Business Week*, October 8, 1955.
Pearson, Drew. "Nixon's Coup d'Etat in California." *San Francisco Chronicle*, November 7, 1957.
"Poor Richard Nixon." *The New Republic*, May 7, 1956.
Roper, William L. "The Man Who Might Be President." *Frontier*, September 1955.
Rovere, Richard H. "Nixon: Most Likely to Succeed." *Harper's Magazine*, September 1955.
Salzman, Ed. "A Personal Perspective." *The California Journal* 5, no. 4 (April 1974).
_____. "'Honest Bill'—He Liked Nixon Least." *Sacramento Bee*, April 14, 1974.
Scheussler, Raymond. "An Eagle to Watch." *Eagle*, June 1955.
Schuparra, Kurt. "Freedom vs Tyranny: The 1958 California Election and the Origins of the State's Conservative Movement." *Pacific Historical Review* (1994).
"70 Convention Votes — And a Feud with Nixon." *U.S. News and World Report*, October 28, 1955.
Steif, William. "Nixon's Uphill Campaign (The Republicans Are His First Problem)." *The New Republic*, February 26, 1962.
Synon, John. "Knowland at the Crossroads." *Human Events*, June 16, 1958.
Taylor, Frank J. "How to Run for Office." *Saturday Evening Post*, October 29, 1955.
Titus, Charles H., and Charles R. Nixon. "The 1948 Elections in California." *Western Political Quarterly* 2 (March 1949).
White, Theodore H. "The Gentlemen from California." *Collier's*, February 3, 1956.
White, William S. "What Bill Knowland Stands For." *The New Republic*, February 27, 1956.
"Why Do the Democrats Hate Nixon So Much?" *The Washington Post*, September 25, 1955.
Wick, James L. "Knowland ('Mr. Integrity') Enters the Race." *Human Events*, February 4, 1956.
Wilson, Richard L. "California: The Year's Most Important Election." *Look*, October 28, 1958.

## Newspapers

California Independent Review
Corona Daily Independent
Fresno Bee

Long Beach Press Telegram
Los Angeles Eagle
Los Angeles Examiner
Los Angeles Herald-Express
Los Angeles Sunday News
Los Angeles Times
New York Times

Sacramento Bee
San Francisco Call Bulletin
San Francisco Chronicle
San Francisco Examiner
Wall Street Journal
Washington Post

# Index

Numbers in ***bold italics*** refer to pages with illustrations.

Acheson, Dean 56, 71, 80, 127, 199
Adams, Earl 116
Adams, Sherman 104, 130, 146, 148–149, 162, 163
Ahmanson, Howard 143–144, 158
*Alhambra Legionnaire* 68
Alsop, Stuart 81, 128–129, 145, 177
American Bar Association 194
American Federation of Labor 137
American Medical Association 83, 84
Anderson, Totten J. 185
Arbuthnot, Roy 143–144, 174
Arlt, Paul 2
Arnold, William 48–49, 63, 71
Astor, Mary 36

Baker, Howard 121
Barrett, Douglas 138, 145, 163, 165, 169, 174, 178
Baxter, Leone 12, 177, 178
Behrens, Earl 19, 56, 58
Block, Herb (Herblock) 126
Boddy, Manchester 69, 71, 76
Brennan, Bernard 66, 72, 91, 96
Brown, Edmund G. (Pat) 11, 18, 19, 20, 29, 48, 69, 81, 84, 111, 145, 157, 170, 178, 179, 182–184, 186, 187, 191, 192, 194–195, 196, 197, 202
Brown, Jerry 111
Brownell, Herbert 75, 105–106
Bryan, William Jennings 33, 34
Buckley, William 160
Burton, Phillip 76

Caldecott, Tom 143–144, 157, 162
California: campaigning in 11–13; growth and development 8–10, 183; political trends 10, 168, 183
California Republican Assembly 12, 25
Case, Clifford 80
Champion, Hale 155, 157
Chandler, Dorothy (Buff) 42, 176–178
Chandler, Norman 11, 16, 21, 42, 43–44, 66–67, 73, 173, 176–177, 187, 188
Chiang Kai-shek 55, 79
China (Communist) 55, 71, 80, 122, 184
China (Nationalist) 55, 79
Chotiner, Murray 18, 30–31, 44–46, 70, 73, 82, 85, 91, 100, 102, 105–106, 139, 143–146, 161, 200–201
Christopher, George 41, 58, 138, 181–182
CIO Political Action Committee 45, 46
Clay, Lucius 118
*Collier's* 80, 148
Communism 16, 30, 45–46, 48, 55–56, 60–62, 68–71, 73, 86–87, 90, 127, 130–131
Congress of Industrial Organizations (CIO) 45
Coolidge, Calvin 24
Costello, William 159
Cray, Ed 118
Creel, George 19, 27
Cristina, Vernon 180
Cross-filing 10–11, 13, 30, 62, 82, 168

Dart, Justin 42
Davis, Paul 103–104
Day, Roy 43, 61, 63, 66–67, 70, 155
de Toledano, Ralph 74
Dewey, Thomas E. 6, 21, 27, 53, 54, 61–

229

62, 75, 76, 78, 79, 86, 91–92, 107, 109, 140
Dickson, Ann 193
Dinkelspiel, John 98
Dirksen, Everett 151
Douglas, Helen Gahagan 41, 65, 68–77, 85, 196
Douglas, Melvin 68
Downey, Sheridan 37, 63, 65, 68–69, 79
Drown, Jack 174
Dulles, John Foster 92, 109, 130, 149, 152, 153

Eisenhower, Dwight D. 7, 33, 38, 78, 84, 86–89, 91–102, *103*, 104–111, 114–122, 125–126, 129, 130, 134, 137, 139, 141, 142, 146–155, *151*, 158–167, 168, 178, 183, 185, 197, 199–200
Eisenhower, Milton 92
Engle, Claire 179, 182, 185–186

*Face the Nation* 159
"Fair Play" Amendment 100–102
Faries, McIntire (Mac) 79, 91, 94, 106, 108, 119
Finch, Robert 98, 173
Finks, Harry 180
*Fortnight* 30, 50, 60, 154
Franklins 40
*Frontier* 119

Gellman, Irwin 2
Goldwater, Barry 121, 192
Great Depression 1, 8, 9, 35, 40
Gunther, John 19

Halberstam, David 42, 175–176, 178
Harding, Warren 23
*Harper's* 128
Harriman, Averill 76, 157
Hearst, William Randolph 57, 70, 72, 186
Hill, Gladwin 184
Hillings, Pat 66, 70, 74, 93, 99, 102, 108, 143, 174
Hinshaw, Carl 154
Hiss, Alger 61–63, 68, 70–71, 74, 76, 200
Hoover, Herbert 24, 83
Hoover, J. Edgar 63, 75, 131
Hope, Bob 32
House Un-American Activities Committee 61, 69
Houser, Fred 17, 37
Hughes, Emmet John 128–129, 130, 149, 150, 166, 198–199
*Human Events* 158

Jewett, Emelyn Knowland 94–95, 124, 132, 161, 169, 172, 192
Johnson, Gardiner 19, 87
Johnson, Hiram 9–10, 28, 34, 35
Johnson, James W. 2
Johnson, Lyndon B. 76, 81, 121–122, 192
Jorgensen, Frank 64–67, 70, 97, 99, 109, 139–141, 143–145, 155, 164, 174, 182–183

Katcher, Leo 48, 114
Kennedy, John F. 38, 60, 61, 76, 110, 190, 192, 194, 195, 196, 202
Kenny, Robert 22, 187
Klein, Herb 71
Knight, Arvilla 136, 139
Knight, Goodwin 1, 2, 5, 8, 11, 18, 22, 31, *54*, 84, 112, *113*, *116*, *140*, *142*, *156*, *180*, *187*, 188; childhood and education 34; and Earl Warren 20, 50–59, 65–67, 83, 119, 136, 137, 202–203; early career 6, 35–37, 175; as governor 120, 136–138, 154, 172, 173, 203; health 33, 178, 191; as lieutenant governor 50–52, 55–58, 137; and 1946 campaign 37; and 1950 campaign 52, 57–59, 64–67, 175; and 1954 campaign 137–138, 145; and 1956 campaign 135, 138, 141–144, 146, 148, 150, 153–157, 159, 161–165, 173–174; and 1958 campaign 168–187; personality and style 6–7, 31, 32–37, 50, 52, 59, 66, 138, 139, 141, 143–144, 146, 155, 157, 168, 175, 178–181, 188, 197, 201; political views 35, 55–59, 137, 155, 157, 172, 203; and Richard Nixon 66–67, 139–148, 153–156, 159, 163–166, 173–174, 177–179, 181, 185, 189–191, 197, 202–203; and William Knowland 123, 143, 159, 164, 169–187, 189, 192, 202–203
Knight, Virginia Carlson 136, 143, 146, 156–157, 165, 166, 171–172, 174–176, 178, *180*, 181, 182, 191
Knowland, Eleanor 23
Knowland, Estelle 119, 167, 172, 184
Knowland, Helen Herrick 29, 81, 104–106, 111, 121–123, 133, 169–170, 179, 186, 193
Knowland, Joe (father of William) 6, 11, 17, 21–27, 64, 80, 94, 123, 131, 159, 160, 169, 192–193
Knowland, Joe (son of William) 123, 192
Knowland, Russ 23, 123, 192
Knowland, William 1, 2, 5, 8, 20, 21, 22, *26*, 85, *113*, *116*, *133*, 136, *140*, 146, 153, *156*, *187*, 188; appointment to U.S. Senate 28–30; childhood and education 23–24, 29; and Dwight Eisenhower 94, 101–102, 104, 106, 114–117, 119–122, 125,

134, 159–162, 185, 202; and Earl Warren 24–28, 53, 79, 90, 94, 100–102, 104–106, 108, 111–112, 119, 124–125, 131, 202; early career 6, 24–25, 27; and Goodwin Knight 120, 143–144, 158–160, 162–165, 169–187, 203; marriage, financial problems, and family 29, 82, 122–124, 169–170, 192–193; military service 27, 29, 80–81; and 1946 campaign 30–31, 37, 64; and 1948 campaign 53, 61, 79; and 1952 presidential campaign 78, 86, 88, 94–95, 100–102, 104–110, 112, 114–116, 131, 132, 159; and 1952 reelection campaign 81–82, 94, 120; and 1956 campaign 158–164, 173; and 1958 campaign 168–187; personality and style 7, 23–25, 28–30, 32, 42, 71–72, 79–82, 109, 117, 120–125, 131, 134, 158, 168, 170–171, 175, 179, 182–184, 188, 192, 197–198, 201; political views 23, 79–82, 120–122, 134, 158, 160, 172–173, 175–176, 183–184; and Richard Nixon 64–65, 67, 90, 95–96, 101, 104–106, 108, 110–111, 114–117, 123, 129–134, 143, 158–159, 161–164, 166, 170, 179, 185, 192, 197, 202; as senator 79–80, 158
Korean War 69, 79–82, 134
Kornitzer, Bela 42
Kuchel, Thomas 80, 114, 146, 162

Leary, Mary Ellen 28, 76
Lee, Russell Dr. 124
Lewis, Fulton, Jr. 48, 63, 87
Liebling, A.J. 62
Lincoln, Luther 138, 163–164
Lodge, Henry Cabot 92, 106, 109, 153
*Look* 132, 158, 196
*Los Angeles Examiner* 70, 147, 174
*Los Angeles Herald-Express* 57
*Los Angeles Times* 11–12, 16, 21, 30, 37, 43, 57, 64, 66–67, 70, 72, 80, 87, 96, 107, 115, 138, 146, 158, 161, 171, 172–173, 176–177, 179–180, 182–183, 186, 187
Loyalty oaths 16, 56, 90

MacArthur, Douglas 56, 80–81, 84, 89, 102
Manchester, William 125
Manolis, Paul 123, 179, 186, 187, 192, 198
Marcantonio, Vito 70
Marshall Plan 60–61, 70, 81
Mason, Paul 138, 180, 190–192
Mazo, Earl 69, 194, 201
McCall, Harrison 44
McCarthy, Joseph 123, 125
McCormac, Keith 73, 107

McGrory, Mary 195
McWilliams, Carey 22, 76
*Meet the Press* 153
Mellon, Thomas J. 96, 99
Menjou, Adolphe 87
Merriam, Frank 12, 35
Miller, William Lee 71, 128
*Minneapolis Tribune* 194
Moley, Raymond 19, 63, 149
Montgomery, Gail B. 2
Moody, Blair 29, 122, 123, 169
Moody, Ruth 122, 123, 169
Morris, Roger 2, 15, 89, 93, 100, 108, 109, 114
Mosher, Clint 177, 183, 190
Mundt, Karl 61
Murphy, Frank 118

*The Nation* 37, 79
National Labor Relations Act 61
*National Review* 160
New Deal 9, 35, 43, 45, 83, 200
*The New Republic* 150, 158
*New York Post* 114
*New York Times* 114, 120, 121, 147, 148, 158, 161, 169
*The New Yorker* 156
*Newsweek* 19, 60, 63, 68, 125, 127, 134, 182
Newton, Jim 17, 110
Neylan, John Francis 118
Nixon, Arthur 39
Nixon, Frank 39, 166
Nixon, Hannah 39, 112, **113**, 132, 165, 166
Nixon, Harold 40
Nixon, Pat 39, 41, 111–112, **113**, 126, 132, 133, 139, 157, 165, **187**, 189
Nixon, Richard 1, 2, 5, 6, 8, 12, 16, 20, 22, 75, **103**, **113**, **116**, **133**, 136, **140**, **142**, **156**, 158, **180**, **187**, 200; childhood and education 38–40, 42; as congressman 60–63; and Dwight Eisenhower 86–89, 91–111, 114–117, 120, 125–126, 129–130, 134, 138, 150, **151**, 152–153, 160, 162–165, 199–200, 202; and Earl Warren 47–49, 61, 62, 64–65, 68, 73–75, 85, 87–93, 95–112, 115, 119, 130, 151–152, 155, 193–195, 198, 201, 203; early career 7, 40–41; and fund crisis 112–117, 125–126, 128, 129, 199; and Goodwin Knight 63–68, 85, 120, 139–144, 146–148, 154–155, 161–162, 164–166, 173–179, 181, 185, 189–191, 198, 201, 203; military service 41; and 1946 campaign 7, 31, 37, 43–49; and 1948 campaign 61, 62; and 1950 campaign 63–77, 125, 199; and 1952

campaign 59, 67, 78, 86–117, 125, 199; and 1954 campaign 126, 127, 145, 150, 200; and 1956 campaign 135, 138, 141, 143, 144, 148, 150–153, 160–167, 173; and 1958 campaign 168, 173–179, 181, 184–185, 187, 202; personality and style 7, 32, 38–49, 60, 67, 71–73, 75, 77, 81, 95, 108–109, 117, 125–131, 150, 166–167, 196, 197, 198–201; political views 48, 61, 72, 126, 128, 184; as vice president 120, 125–126, 128–131, 133–134, 148–150, 152, 195–196; and William Knowland 63–65, 81, 88, 94–95, 104–112, 123–124, 130–134, 161–162, 166–167, 170, 173–176, 179, 182, 184–185, 198, 201, 203

*Oakland Tribune* 6, 11, 17, 23, 24, 26, 30, 64, 67, 123, 158, 169, 172, 175, 188, 192, 193
Office of Price Administration 41
Olson, Culbert 17, 20, 21, 25
Orthogonians 40

Palmer, Kyle 11–12, 16, 21, 37, 43–44, 49, 57–58, 64–67, 73, 85, 86, 87, 94, 96, 146, 161, 168–169, 171, 173, 176, 178, 182, 188
Partisan Republicans 72
Pearson, Drew 104, 105, 132, 134, 179
Perry, Herman 65, 87–88, 90, 110
Phillips, Herbert 24, 77, 138
Polland, Milton 33, 180–181, 191, 203
Powers, Harold (Butch) 97
Progressivism 9–10, 15, 28, 35

Rayburn, Sam 38, 76
Reagan, Ronald 191, 193
*The Reporter* 155, 157
Republican National Committee 25
Republican right wing (California): and Earl Warren 55, 58–59, 72, 83, 85, 87–88, 102; and Goodwin Knight 55–59, 72; and Richard Nixon 72, 85, 88–90, 92–93, 131, 174; and William Knowland 170
Reston, James 158
Reuther, Walter 186
Richards, Richard 137
Rogers, Will 195
Rogers, Will, Jr. 30
Rolph, James 1, 37
Roosevelt, Franklin D. 24, 27, 35, 44, 53, 61–62, 83, 200
Roosevelt, James 11, 58, 65, 73–74
Roosevelt, Theodore 34

Rovere, Richard 128–130, 134
Russell, Richard 80

*Sacramento Bee* 159
*San Francisco Chronicle* 11, 67, 164, 165, 179, 186
*San Francisco Examiner* 147, 177
*San Francisco News* 76
*Saturday Evening Post* 37, 143
Schlesinger, Arthur 196
School of Military Government 27
Sevareid, Eric 125
Sinclair, Upton 12, 35
*Six Crises* 196
Small, Merrell 19, 22, 48, 73, 110, 193, 194, 195
Southern Pacific Railroad 9, 16
Soviet Union 45, 55, 61–62, 68–69, 160, 168
Sparkman, John 147
Starr, Kevin 17–18, 47
Stassen, Harold 49, 53, 61, 62, 74, 114–115, 162–163, 165
Steinberg, Blema 41
Stevenson, Adlai 38, 84, 113, 122, 126–127, 151, 200

Taft, Robert 78, 84, 86–89, 92–97, 100–102, 104, 106–108, 110, 112, 118, 120, 122, 132, 158, 161
Taft, William Howard 34
Taft-Hartley Bill 61
*Time* 18, 28, 32, 79, 94, 145, 146, 149, 154, 172, 182
Truman, Harry S 22, 38, 53, 54, 56, 60, 62, 68–71, 73, 78, 80–81, 83–84, 86, 110, 118, 126, 179, 199

*U.S. News and World Report* 125, 130, 134, 148, 154, 155

Vinson, Carl 118
Voorhis, Jerry 7, 31, 43–49, 62, 71, 75

Warren, Earl 1, 2, 5, 8, 10, 11, 12, **26**, 30–31, 37, 41, 47, **54**, 82, **103**, **113**, **116**, 131, 136, **140**, **142**, 147, 148, 151, 154, 173, 175; childhood and education 16; early career 6, 9, 17, 21, 24–26, 30; father 16–17; and Goodwin Knight 50–53, 55–59, 136, 137, 193, 197, 202; as governor 15–16, 20–21, 27, 55, 85; health 83, 85; and 1948 campaign 53–55, 61, 79, 98; and 1950 campaign 58, 64–66, 73–74, 85; and 1952 campaign 59, 78, 82–84, 87–109, 115, 118, 119; and 1956 campaign 161,

166; personality and style 7, 15–20, 24, 47–49, 50–53, 57, 59, 65–66, 73–74, 82–84, 87–89, 98, 109, 119, 124, 138, 197, 201; political views 15–16, 20–21, 48, 55–56, 72, 79, 83–84, 89, 119, 121, 124; and Richard Nixon 47–49, 61, 62, 65, 72–75, 85, 89–91, 95–112, 114, 129, 130, 139, 147, 166, 189, 194–195, 197, 202; and Supreme Court 101–102, 111, 118–120, 130, 161, 193; and William Knowland 24–28, 53, 79, 84, 88, 94, 105, 112, 123, 124, 170, 193
Warren, Earl, Jr. 56, 73–74, 84, 111
Warren, Nina (Honey Bear) 83
*Washington Post* 126, 154
*Washington Star* 82
Watergate 38, 195

Webb, James 26
Weinberger, Caspar 41, 138
Werdel, Thomas 87–88, 90, 92, 93
Whitaker, Clem 12, 17–18, 156, 177, 178, 180, 181, 182, 184
Whitaker and Baxter 12, 17, 37, 156–157, 159, 177, 181
White, Theodore 13, 33, 148, 203
White, William S. 40, 82, 158
Wick, James 158
Wills, Garry 13, 39
Wilson, Woodrow 27, 34
Woods, Rose Marie 173
World Affairs Council 145

Yalta Conference 62

www.ingramcontent.com/pod-product-compliance
Ingram Content Group UK Ltd.
Pitfield, Milton Keynes, MK11 3LW, UK
UKHW041946140426
5217IPUK00014B/674